PISCINAE

STUDIES IN THE HISTORY OF GREECE AND ROME

P. J. Rhodes and Richard J. A. Talbert, editors

PISCINAE

ARTIFICIAL FISHPONDS IN ROMAN ITALY

James Higginbotham

The University of North Carolina Press

Chapel Hill and London

The paper in this book meets the guidelines for permanence
and durability of the Committee on Production Guidelines for
Book Longevity of the Council on Library Resources.

Library of Congress Cataloging-in-Publication Data

Higginbotham, James Arnold.

Piscinae: artificial fishponds in Roman Italy /

James Higginbotham.

p. cm. Includes bibliographical references (p.   ) and index.

ISBN 0-8078-2329-5 (cloth: alk. paper)

1. Italy — Antiquities, Roman.   2. Fish remains (Archaeology)
— Italy.   3. Fish ponds — Italy — History.   4. Fish trade — Italy
— History.   5. Fisheries — Italy — History.   I. Title.

DG105.H54   1997   937 — dc20

96-29229   CIP

01 00 99 98 97   5 4 3 2 1

TO MY FAMILY

Nam quid ea memorem, quae nisi iis qui videre
nemini credibilia sunt, a privatis compluribus
subvorsos montis, maria constrata esse?
— C. Sallustius Crispus, *Bellum Catilinae* 13.1

CONTENTS

FIGURES

FIGURES

xv

FIGURES

PREFACE

This book had its beginnings with my work as part of the excavations at Paestum (Italy) carried out by the Universities of Michigan and Perugia (Italy) under the direction of Professors John Griffiths Pedley and Mario Torelli. During four seasons of excavations between 1982 and 1985, I supervised the stratigraphic excavation of a small Roman fishpond which was part of the extramural sanctuary in the località Santa Venera. Study of this pond fostered my interest in Roman *piscinae* that culminated in this book. I owe a great deal to my colleagues Professor Pedley, Professor Torelli, Gail Hoffman, Concetta Masseria, Meg Morden, David Myers, and Giampiero Pianu for their learned input and encouragement. Special thanks go to my operai Carmine Federico, Cosimo Federico, Luigi Pinto, and Arturo La Corte who supplied the technical expertise that unearthed the *piscina* at Santa Venera and who bear some responsibility for sending me in pursuit of fishponds.

The research presented in this book was completed with the valued assistance of a number of individuals and institutions. The bulk of the field work for this project was carried out between 1988 and 1989 during my tenure as an Oscar Broneer Fellow in Classical Art and Archaeology at the American Academy in Rome and as a Fulbright-Hayes Scholar in

Italy. The generous support of the American Academy and the Fulbright Commission is greatly appreciated.

This project was facilitated by the cooperation of the Soprintendenze Archeologiche di Lazio, di Pompei, and delle provincie di Salerno, Avellino e Benevento, all of whom provided access to some of the monuments included in this study. To Dottoressa Giuliana Tocco, Soprintendente Archeologica delle provincie di Salerno, Avellino e Benevento, Dottoressa Marina Cipriani, Directore del Museo Nazionale di Paestum, and Giovanni Avagliano I wish to convey special thanks for assistance provided during my visits to Paestum.

My thanks go out to my colleagues at the American School in Athens and the American Academy in Rome who were always on the lookout for any scrap of evidence concerning fish and fishponds and who enthusiastically supplied much needed encouragement. I wish to express my gratitude to my colleagues and traveling companions at the American Academy in Rome, Professor Charles Babcock, Larry Ball, Linda Cook, Anna Moore, and Joanne Spurza, who gave generously of their time and were of immense help to many aspects of my research. I also wish to express my thanks to Karin Einaudi and Mary Jane Bright of the Fototeca Unione for their assistance in locating photographs of Italian fishponds.

I have been fortunate to benefit from the help of many friends and colleagues. John Pedley has been a constant source of encouragement and support. As we have worked together over the last several years I have gained much from his insight and direction. An advisor and friend, he has assisted at every stage and he has my deepest thanks. In Elaine Gazda I found one of the rare individuals who derived as much pleasure from fishponds as I. Professor Gazda's interest and the contribution of her expertise were indispensable to my research. This book owes much to her careful reading and informed guidance. I wish to convey my sincere gratitude to Professor Sharon Herbert for continual guidance and support. It was at her instigation and under her tutelage that I decided to pursue a career in classical archaeology.

Throughout the course of my work I profited greatly from discussions with a variety of scholars while in Greece, Italy, and in the United States, including Fred Albertson, Herbert Bloch, John Camp, Bruce Frier, Kim Hartwig, John Humphrey, George Huxley, Michael Jameson, Adriano La Regina, James Packer, David Ross, Russell Scott, Mario Torelli, and Paul Zanker.

A special debt of gratitude goes to my wife, Janice Jaffe, whose un-flagging support and encouragement were vital to the successful com-pletion of this book.

PISCINAE

INTRODUCTION

Both the archaeological remains and the ancient literary record reveal that during the later Roman Republic and the early Empire, the practice of raising fish, or pisciculture, reached an impressive level of complexity. The Roman artificial fishpond was a structure carefully crafted to provide a suitable environment for fish that were being kept for market, bred for future consumption, or confined for the sensory enjoyment of the owner. More than an enclosure, an artificial fishpond was designed to control the movement of fish, facilitate the flow of water, and, in some cases, regulate the degree of salinity within the pond. These structures ranged in size from elaborate sea-girt ponds covering acres to small freshwater ponds that decorated the peristyle gardens of urban villas.[1] Through the following comparative analysis of the physical remains of

Roman fishponds and ancient literature we can assess the reliability of the literary accounts and substantially increase our understanding of Roman pisciculture as it was practiced in Italy. In exploring the architectural, literary, and historical contexts of Roman fishponds, this study will touch on some of the broader issues that shed light on social, economic, and religious life in Italy during the late Roman Republic and early Empire.

MODERN SCHOLARSHIP

Interest in distinguishing and identifying different species of fish first drew modern scholars to the subject of ancient pisciculture. The taxonomic classifications of Carolus Linnaeus and the Comte de Buffon in the eighteenth century owe some of their terminology to the nomenclature gleaned from classical texts. It was in the early nineteenth century, concurrent with the beginnings of archaeology as a discipline, that some of the first tentative associations were made between architectural remains of fishponds and the ancient literary record. As early as 1828, Di Filippo Alessandro Sebastiani drew on the account of Columella to identify the function of the great freshwater tank at the so-called Villa of Quintilius Varus just outside Tivoli.[2] The design of this tank led Sebastiani to conclude that fish were raised at the villa.

Despite Sebastiani's observation, fishponds did not attract much interest until the early twentieth century. Raffaele Del Rosso published a study of fish and fishponds, both ancient and modern, in Etruria Maritima.[3] Del Rosso studied the long tradition of raising fish in this region and endeavored to connect ancient *piscinae* with known personages of Roman history. His publication was followed by important studies by Luigi Jacono on the seaside and offshore ruins of the area near Naples, including the Pontine island group.[4] Like Del Rosso, Jacono also sought to confirm the accounts in the ancient literary record and began to characterize the construction and function of Roman fishponds.

Since Jacono, the study of Roman pisciculture has progressed along several paths. The ancient fishing industry, involving the manufacture and trade of processed fish products such as *garum*, has received the lion's share of attention.[5] These studies have focused on tanks and complexes in Spain, southern France, and North Africa. Though *garum* production certainly took place in Italy, the bulk of this trade emanated from the western provinces.[6] The importance of the fishing industry to diet and the economy during the late Republic and early Empire was studied in the 1950s by Thomas Corcoran. Corcoran surveyed the gathering, processing, distribution, and consumption of fish and processed fish products as revealed primarily through the ancient literary sources. His study, however, pays little attention to the physical remains of fishponds.[7]

The Romans who indulged in the practice of raising fish and the building of *piscinae* form the focus of an important socioeconomic examination by John H. D'Arms.[8] Although it too offers limited discussion of the archaeological remains of fishponds, D'Arms's study provides a portrait of the life in and around the Bay of Naples, the *crater illum delicatum*, where the elite of Rome built their sumptuous *villae maritimae* and *urbanae*, often adding a fishpond to the architectural plan of the property.[9]

Building on the work of these scholars, the present comprehensive study of the physical remains of Roman fishponds offers new insights into Roman pisciculture. This book stresses the description and analysis of the architectural features to determine how *piscinae* were constructed, how these structures worked, and what their presence and function reveal about the social atmosphere of the time. The detailed presentation of the architectural remains is compared with the accounts presented in the ancient literary record in order to offer the most complete picture of Roman pisciculture and to assess the veracity of the literary accounts.

A HISTORICAL OVERVIEW OF FISHPONDS
BASED ON THE LITERARY EVIDENCE

The literary sources, from writers in both Greek and Latin, provide a plausible outline of the development of pisciculture in antiquity beginning well before the Roman era. Plato mentions that pisciculture ($i\chi\theta\acute{v}\omega\nu$ $\tau\iota\theta\alpha\sigma\epsilon\acute{\iota}\alpha$) was practiced along the banks of the Nile. The Egyptians built large enclosures or "lakes," which were often incorporated into religious complexes and royal palaces.[10] Among the Greeks, the raising of fish was often practiced in natural enclosures such as lakes. In Boeotia, eels raised in the Kopaic basin were prized as a food source.[11] The Greeks also used fountains or artificial ponds to keep fish sacred to various deities. These sites were most often located in the Greek East and kept fish that either were significant to the cult or supplemented the income of the temple properties.[12]

The western Greeks, however, seem also to have built fishponds. Diodorus mentions a large fishpond built by the citizens of Acragas in Sicily after the battle of Himera in the early fifth century B.C. He describes the pond, an ἰχθυοτροφεῖον, as being twenty feet deep and twenty stades, or about two and a quarter miles in circumference.[13]

ANCIENT LITERARY SOURCES
ABOUT ROMAN PISCICULTURE

Most of the ancient literary information about Roman pisciculture and associated structures comes from the late Republic and early Empire. The primary ancient sources for the history of pisciculture and the techniques associated with constructing fishponds are M. Terentius Varro, L. Iunius Columella, and the Elder Pliny. Other authors, including Cicero, Martial, Horace, and Macrobius, help supplement the information supplied by these three with additional anecdotes and commentary.[14] Together they contribute an important part of the historical context within which Roman pisciculture can be understood. They do not, however, provide a complete guide to the technical aspects of the practice.

Varro, writing in his eightieth year, around 37 B.C., presents the earliest detailed account of the Roman practice of raising fish.[15] While providing some technical information, he focuses primarily on anecdotes depicting the excesses and extravagances of fishpond owners, or *piscinarii*. Columella, writing almost a century after Varro, describes the situation of fish-raising in the later first century A.D. Building on Varro's work, he attempts to place Roman pisciculture in a historical framework, from the humble beginnings of Rome's early history, to the extravagances of the wealthy *piscinarii* of the Republic, to the "honest and laudable" practice of his own day. Fish raising during Columella's lifetime spread to less affluent sectors of Roman society and ceased to be solely an occupation of the wealthy. To meet the need for a practical manual about raising fish, Columella wrote a far more technical account than Varro.

According to the literary accounts, the raising of fish also has a long tradition on the Italian peninsula. Both Varro and Columella place the beginnings of Roman pisciculture in the freshwater lakes and streams of Italy. Columella records that, in Rome's distant past, bodies of fresh water had been stocked with spawn (*seminii*) brought from the ocean. The inland bodies of water mentioned by Columella were all in territory once controlled by the Etruscans.[16] Both Plautus and Scipio Aemilianus attest to the presence of fishponds (*piscinae*) in the vicinity of Rome by the late third or early second century B.C.[17] It is tempting to conclude from the literary evidence, therefore, that the Romans adopted the practice of constructing fishponds from their neighbors to the north, but the Greeks in southern Italy could also have played a role in the development of Roman pisciculture.[18]

The Elder Pliny, while relating the same anecdotal information about Roman pisciculture as do Varro and Columella, incorporates few architectural or technical details in his work. His *Historia Naturalis*, though often relying on hearsay and tall tales, nevertheless provides the greatest amount of information about the fish that inhabited Roman fishponds. Pliny assigns the development of artificial enclosures for the raising of oysters and fish to the years before the Marsic War, prior to 91 B.C. He attributes the "invention" of the fishpond to L. Licinius Murena early in the first century B.C.[19] The *cognomen* Murena, which means eel, is said by Varro to have been given on account of his close association with this fish.[20] The Elder Pliny, however, credits C. Hirrius with the adaptation of the fishpond solely for the raising of *murenae* or eels. The introduction of seaside fishponds (*piscinae salsae* or *amarae*), at the beginning of the first century B.C., indicates a change in taste — a preference for the fish caught in the sea to those from bodies of fresh water. The elaborate seaside fishpond evidently stimulated the ingenuity of Rome's gastronomes, who always strove to procure greater delicacies for the palate.[21] During the first century B.C., freshwater fish were considered suitable for the table of the poor, while saltwater catch was more prized and often part of the cuisine of the elite.[22] This change in taste would seem to reflect the increased desire of the Romans for *luxuria*, prompted by their exposure to the riches and culture of the Greek East during the conquest of the eastern Mediterranean in the last two centuries B.C.[23] Still, when viewed in relation to the archaeological remains, these accounts would appear to present only a set of ideal norms that were rarely emulated in reality.

STUDY OF THE ARCHITECTURAL REMAINS

The available archaeological evidence somewhat alters and certainly adds much more detailed information to the outline provided by literary accounts of the Roman practice of raising fish. Archaeological surveys and excavations have identified and examined fishponds scattered throughout the Mediterranean. Study of these physical remains, however, presents some formidable difficulties. Access to seaside ponds is sometimes impossible because of the general rise in the sea level along the coasts of Italy since the first century B.C.[24] Thus, many Roman fishponds are now inundated. Inundation has not only obscured many fishponds but has also hastened their deterioration. The action of water of any kind can be damaging to architecture; even fishponds fed by fresh water suffer.[25] Another problem is that many *piscinae* have been buried or obscured by silt carried by the very water sources they employed, a process that occurred even in antiquity.

The variety of architectural forms that *piscinae* represent poses a fourth difficulty because they resist easy identification or classification. As a result, scholarship about fishponds has tended to focus on solitary units or small numbers of ponds.[26]

Despite these hindrances, however, an analysis of the archaeological remains reveals important physical features absent in the ancient literary accounts. While the ancient literary record provides an anecdotal history and some technical information, the archaeological evidence presents a more realistic picture of this ancient practice.

A gazetteer of Italian *piscinae*, appended to this book, describes the archaeological remains and documents the details and varieties of design. It includes the remains of most of the fishponds in Italy that could be identified with certainty.[27] To this end I catalog and describe the significance of architecture designed or adapted for the purpose of raising fish. Where systematic excavation was not possible, visual and graphic analyses were employed to render the most accurate and complete descriptions of the fishponds included here.

Italy is the focus of this study because of the abundance of literary references to Italian fishponds. Moreover, Italy possesses the greatest number of surviving *piscinae* and is, by all ancient accounts, the site of the earliest and greatest interest in constructing large enclosures for the raising of fish. This study includes both the seaside enclosures referred to by ancient authors and the inland fishponds that are overlooked by the literary accounts.

Toward a more complete understanding of Roman pisciculture, the first chapter of this book discusses the technical aspects of fishpond design, construction, and operation. Chapter 2 examines the species of fish most closely associated with the Roman practice of raising fish. Chapter 3 explores the social implication of owning a fishpond and how the *piscina* can be used as an indicator of social and political change. Descriptions of each of the extant Roman fishponds in Italy included in this study, supplemented by plans and illustrations, are collected in a gazetteer at the end of the text. The comparative treatment of both literary and archaeological sources offered in this book provides a foundation for understanding the role fishponds played in the social and economic fabric of ancient Rome.

Detailed study of each of these ponds in their surroundings, including their ownership and operation, broadens our understanding of Roman social life. In order to develop fully such a portrait, this book explores who owned fishponds and how the social status of the owners changed over time; whether *piscinae* were constructed to provide income for the owner or just as a source of pleasure; and what accounts for the drop in popularity of raising fish during the Empire. By exploring a neglected but revealing category of architecture, this study contributes the foundational information for understanding the role of fish and fishponds in the material and social fabric of Roman Italy.

ADDENDUM: A NOTE ON TERMINOLOGY

The Latin language possesses four terms that were most often used to denote an artificial enclosure for the keeping, breeding, or raising of fish: *piscina, vivarium, stagnum*, and *cetaria* or *cetarium*. *Piscina* was a common generic term used to describe any artificial body of water, whether for swimming, drinking, or raising fish.[28] *Vivarium* referred to any structure given over to the keeping of animals and commonly meant a body of water in which fish were kept.[29] *Vivarium*, used in its adjectival form, *vivarius*, was joined with *navis* to indicate a boat with live tanks for fish. *Stagnum* referred to a standing body of water, natural or artificial, where fish could be kept. *Stagnum* conveyed the sense of stagnant water and was used, along with *lacuna*, to denote a brackish lagoon or tidal basin where it was possible to keep fish. Though often misinterpreted as a fishpond, *cetaria* (or *cetarium*) refers to a tank for salting fish and is most often associated with Spanish fisheries.[30] These terms were not used consistently nor with precision; their application seems contingent on their significance to the writer.[31] For the sake of clarity in this study, fishpond, or the Latin *piscina*, is the sole term used to describe an artificial enclosure built for the raising of fish.[32]

FISHPOND CONSTRUCTION AND OPERATION

The construction and operation of ancient *piscinae* required the combination of technical expertise from the fields of biology, hydraulics, and architecture. Crucial to the operation of a fishpond was a design that would create a hearty environment for the fish the owner intended to cultivate. This entailed paying close attention to the habits of the fish and to designs that would allow the fish to thrive. The ancient understanding of fish habits was such that Columella could outline the gross criteria that would create the appropriate environments for the most common varieties of fish raised in fishponds.[1] His criteria included the selection of an appropriate site and water source, the creation of a system for the conveyance of water, and the design of details that would facilitate the confinement, vitality, and harvesting of the fish, as well as the overall enjoyment of the pond by its owner and his guests.

Columella's treatise supplies the most detailed account of Roman pisciculture preserved in the ancient record. Yet, he presents only a broad outline of the Roman practice of raising fish. The literary sources supply a unique insight into Roman pisciculture. Their descriptions, at times, help identify otherwise enigmatic features in fishpond design (such as the function of protective recesses in the sides of fishponds) but their accounts do not constitute a comprehensive guide to fishpond design and operation. The fishponds described in the ancient literary record appear as hypothetical or perhaps ideal archetypes and do not adequately characterize the variety of designs and systems used by the Romans.

The study of the archaeological remains substantially increases our knowledge of Roman pisciculture and the structures associated with this practice. None of the ancient literary accounts mention important features revealed through the examination of the ruins, such as viewing platforms, dining rooms, fish traps, fishing towers, ceramic eel pots, the popularity of inland ponds supplied by fresh water, and the use of fresh water in sea-fed ponds.

This chapter explores the technical concerns related to the construction, operation, and chronology of Roman fishponds. The examination focuses on the topics of site selection, water circulation, regulation of salinity, construction, and design. The following discussion recounts the pertinent ancient testimonia and then adds the archaeological evidence in order to create the fullest account of Roman pisciculture as it was practiced in Italy.

SITE SELECTION

Both the literary and archaeological evidence contribute to our understanding of locations where the Romans placed their fishponds. The siting of a Roman artificial fishpond depended on a number of factors. The most important included the nature of the terrain where the pond was to be built, the proximity to sources of water, and the aesthetic appeal of the site. The construction of artificial enclosures on natural rock shelves or outcroppings that project into the sea is a common design feature of seaside *piscinae*. The fishponds at Pianosa (Fig. 8), Santa Liberata (Fig. 9), Giglio (Fig. 13), Torre Valdaliga (Figs. 16, 17), La Mattonara (Figs. 18, 19), Punta San Paolo (Fig. 20), Punta della Vipera (Figs. 21, 22), Grottacce

(Fig. 26), Palo (Fig. 30), Nettuno (Figs. 50, 51), Astura (Figs. 52 – 54), Formia (Figs. 71, 72), Scauri, Ponza (Figs. 73 – 78), Ventotene (Figs. 79 – 81), and Sorrento (Figs. 101 – 3) made use of the coastal rock formations. This type of geological formation supplied natural material from which an enclosure could be cut and provided a stable platform for the foundations of concrete walls.

The choice of rocky topography was influenced by the existence of natural coves and inlets, which provided ready-made enclosures where fish could be confined. Sheltered from the force of the sea and possessed of rocky hiding places, these natural enclosures were sites where fish were known to congregate. Fishponds located at Pianosa, Giglio, Torre Valdaliga, La Mattonara, Palo, Sperlonga, Ponza, Ventotene, and Scauri made use of preexisting inlets, coves, and grottoes.

Like rocky inlets and coves, coastal lagoons also presented sheltered areas, which provided the brackish environment desired for the raising of fish. Concrete walls in the lagoons of Orbetello and Cosa attest to the modification of these inland bodies of water for the purpose of raising fish. Although fish were probably cultivated in other lagoons on both coasts of Italy, the physical evidence is scarce.[2] The physical characteristics outlined here explain, in part, the density of seaside *piscinae* along the Etruscan coast, where the terrain and the natural hydraulic environment were most conducive to fishpond construction.

The placement of fishponds was determined to a large extent by the need to have access to both salt and fresh water in sufficient quantities to insure adequate circulation and the appropriate degree of salinity. Originally restricted to sites where natural conditions could provide both sources, the use of aqueducts and cisterns gave owners greater latitude in choosing the location of their fishponds. The choice of water source constituted an important typological distinction for Varro. However, he ignores the combined role of fresh and salt water and suggests an oversimplified division. Writing around 37 B.C., Varro states unequivocally that there are two types of fishponds: those fed by salt water and those supplied by fresh water.[3] Varro's distinction between *piscinae salsae* and *dulces* probably denotes the primary and not the exclusive water source used. After recounting the excesses of owning a fishpond fed by the sea, Varro describes the freshwater fishpond as a *piscina mediterranea*, or an inland pond.[4] Many of Varro's *piscinae salsae*, while relying principally on the sea, were often supplied by fresh water as well, which created a brackish environment. Thus, it is perhaps better to think of Varro's two

11

types of *piscinae* as enclosures located near the sea and those located inland.

According to Columella, the earliest enclosures built in Italy for the raising of fish were fed by fresh water.[5] Later, in the last century of the Republic, the Romans began to build fishponds which made use of the sea as their principal water source. These seaside enclosures were more elaborate and costly than their inland forebears. Varro asserts that "in the first place they were constructed at great cost, second they were stocked at great cost, and third they were maintained at great cost."[6] In consequence, seaside *piscinae* were generally held to be the province of the rich while ponds fed by fresh water became associated with poorer individuals.

SEAWATER HYDRAULICS

Fishponds located at coastal sites could take advantage of the natural forces of the sea to circulate seawater within the enclosures. Fishponds fed by salt water were always located near the sea.[7] Seawater was moved by the force of tides and waves and thus was not circulated far from its source. According to Columella, saltwater fishponds should be designed so that incoming waves could move the water "and not allow the stagnant water to remain inside the enclosure."[8] "For a fishpond is most like the open sea in that the agitated water is circulated continually by the winds and cannot become warm because the wave churns cold water from the depths to its crest."[9]

Columella presents more detailed instructions on the subject of seawater circulation than does Varro, but both insist that adequate circulation is vital for the successful functioning of a seaside fishpond. Circulation aerated the water, maintained cool temperatures, and helped regulate the salinity of the water inside the fishpond. Hortensius, as Varro relates, is critical of the carelessness of Marcus Lucullus because he did not provide his *piscinae* with adequate channels (*aestuaria*) to the sea and, as a consequence, Lucullus's fish lived "in unhealthy confines." Varro goes on to repeat Hortensius's praise for the efforts of the brother of Marcus, Lucius Lucullus, who excavated a channel from the sea to his fishponds so that waters "flowed back and forth" (*reciproce fluerent*).[10]

Columella pays considerable attention to the hydraulic systems of seaside fishponds.[11] He states that *piscinae*, "whether excavated from the rocky shore or constructed with hydraulic concrete," should be designed with channels (*itinera* or *aestuaria*) that would allow the seawater to penetrate inside the enclosures.[12] Smaller channels (*cuniculi*) would distribute the water and further insure adequate circulation inside the fishpond. Columella suggests that *itinera* be positioned on every side of the fishpond low on the wall of the enclosure so that the water forced through these openings would originate from the cooler depths of the sea.

All openings into the fishpond were to be covered with grates (*cancelli*) to prevent the fish from escaping (for an example at Astura, see Fig. 59). Columella suggests the use of bronze *cancelli* pierced by small holes, which would prevent the fish from escaping while not interfering with circulation.[13] He recommends that, when constructing an enclosure in the ocean, the level of the sea be seven Roman feet (2.06 meters) above the bottom of the pond. Fishponds constructed on rock or on ground that was just above the level of the sea should be excavated to a depth of nine feet (2.65 meters) and provided with *cuniculi* which would enter the enclosures two feet (59 centimeters) down from their tops. This would leave two feet (1.18 meters) of freeboard between the top of the pond and the water level.

Fishponds built on rocky shelves that were close to the level of the sea required rock-cut channels to facilitate circulation. The *piscina* at Punta della Vipera (Figs. 21–23), on the Etruscan coast, is close to the specifications outlined by Columella for a pond that "was excavated in the living rock" (*exciditur in petra*). The *piscina* was designed with three rock-cut channels (*cuniculi*) that funneled seawater into the fishpond. The rectangular perimeter that protected the enclosure was built of hydraulic concrete and provided with openings that were aligned with the rock-cut channels. The arched openings pierce the mole nearly two Roman feet below the top of the tank. This arched configuration is just as Columella recommended but stands out as unusual among the extant examples of *piscinae* in Italy. Eight additional *itinera* complete the connection to the sea.

FRESHWATER HYDRAULICS

The rules of hydraulic circulation, related by Varro and Columella, apply only to those *piscinae* supplied by the sea, but those rules embody principles applicable to freshwater structures as well. Provisions for ample and vigorous circulation were of utmost importance for the design of inland *piscinae*. Despite the lack of technical descriptions of freshwater ponds in the ancient literary record, fresh water was an easier supply to control. Fresh water can be piped to locations far removed from natural sources by means of aqueducts and conduits. Simple gravity flow can maintain a freshwater hydraulic system many miles in length. The magnitude of the drop in altitude from the freshwater source to the fishpond would be in direct proportion to the pressure and rate of flow of the water entering the enclosure and thus would provide a vigorous flow adequate for the needs of circulation.[14] This hydraulic technology would have permitted greater latitude in selecting a site for constructing a fishpond.

The conveyance of fresh water, ignored by Varro and Columella, involved technology described in detail by Vitruvius and Frontinus, though neither of these authors writes about *piscinae*. Vitruvius supplies much information on fresh water from a builder's point of view. He details its properties, where and how to find it, and how it is moved. Frontinus provides details of the measurement, procurement, and distribution of Rome's water supply. The manipulation of fresh water was probably not so novel as to warrant the attention of Varro or Columella who found the harnessing of the sea more compelling.[15]

Information about the mechanics of freshwater circulation, as it pertains to the hydraulics of *piscinae*, comes primarily from the physical remains. The fishpond located in the extramural sanctuary of Santa Venera at Paestum (Fig. 104) was equipped with a simple freshwater circulating system, the details of which are described by Vitruvius.[16] Water from the nearby Capo di Fiume was conveyed to the fishpond by means of a canal built of brick and mortar (*canalis structilis*). The water emptied into a catch basin (*castellum*) where sediment could settle as clean water cascaded from the basin into the pond. Overflow from the pond was carried away by clay collared pipes (*tubuli fictiles*) and discarded in a nearby drain.

At Pompeii, lead pipes (*fistulae plumbeae*) were used to supply fresh water to the villas and houses in the city and to the small *piscinae* which decorate their peristyle gardens. In the Praedia Iuliae Felicis, fresh water was collected in a vaulted cistern attached to the house. From this reservoir a small lead pipe carried the water to the short end of the long *euripus*, where it emptied into the top of the tank. In addition, water from the *triclinium* fountain contributed to the pond's circulation. Overflow was discharged through three clay pipes positioned below the top of the pond. The location of these outlet pipes kept the level of the water well below the ornamental marble border at the top of the pond and permitted the excess water to irrigate the surrounding garden. At the bottom of the tank, opposite the end where water fed into the *euripus*, a small aperture opened into a sewer line. This drain was used to clean the fishpond of accumulated sediment and detritus. The hole was covered with a lead access panel fashioned with small protruding bosses to ease removal and repositioning. Similar arrangements for cleanouts are preserved in the *piscinae* on the Palatine, at the so-called Villa of Horace near Licenza, and north of Rome along the Via Flaminia at Grottarossa, where the remains of a lead access panel can be seen. The ability to easily drain the pond was an attractive feature of freshwater fishponds. *Piscinae* fed by fresh water supplied by artificial conduits could be emptied for maintenance and cleaning, a feature difficult to duplicate in those enclosures associated with the sea.

Freshwater hydraulics were employed at most seaside *piscinae* to supply the water necessary to control the salinity and temperature of the ponds. At the large rectangular pond at Torre Astura, a concrete and masonry bridge, which was more than 120 meters long, connected the enclosure to the villa on the shore (Fig. 60, top). Fresh water was carried across this bridge by a covered aqueduct and distributed through channels to the pond.

The absence of a natural spring caused the builders of the villa at Santa Liberata near Porto Santo Stefano on the Etruscan coast to resort to the use of cisterns for storing the fresh water needed for the nearby fishpond (Fig. 9:C). The fresh water was distributed within the pond through a system of smaller cisterns and channels. This arrangement was also used by the builders of the coastal villa at Grottacce near Santa Marinella on the same coast. A total of fourteen cisterns, some placed outside and some built into the villa itself, stored fresh water for various uses which included supplying the fishpond below (Fig. 26:C).

BRACKISH CONDITIONS

Brackish water zones occur as a transition from salt to fresh water and so vary considerably between ebb and flood tide.[17] These transitional zones occur naturally in coastal lagoons and where fresh water empties into the sea. Slight variations in the salinity of the water attract many kinds of fish and may be responsible for the initiation of reproductive migrations with some species.[18] Brackish water lagoons and estuaries are nutrient-rich and consequently support a high density of aquatic life. The addition of fresh water to seaside *piscinae* also helped to regulate the temperature.[19]

Seaside fishponds were often located where convenient freshwater sources could be used to create brackish conditions within the enclosures. It is suggestive that the Romans were aware of a positive relationship between brackish conditions and fish. Ancient anecdotal evidence indicates that the Romans knew such conditions could attract fish. Cicero relates an instance of fraud where a Roman is enticed by an unscrupulous Siracusan banker to purchase a Sicilian villa on account of its proximity to waters teeming with fish.[20] The fraud was perpetrated with the help of many fishermen from more fertile waters who were hired to be present with their catch when the prospective buyer was being shown the property. Interesting for our purposes was the explanation provided by the banker to account for so many fish in these particular waters — the presence of a freshwater spring (*aquatio*) that emptied into the sea. This explanation and the many fishermen in the waters nearby lent credence to the banker's claim and the Roman immediately bought the villa.

The archaeological evidence is decisive in showing that the Romans preferred brackish conditions for their seaside *piscinae*. Where springwater was unavailable, fresh water was secured by special arrangements, which included cisterns and aqueducts. Arrangements for mixing salt water and fresh water to create a brackish environment were common features in Roman fishponds and are well represented in the archaeological record from both the late Republic and early Empire.

The fishpond built into the Grotto at Sperlonga relied on springs that issued from fissures in the cave. These springs still pour fresh water into the confines of the cave today. Augmenting this water source was a channel that connected the fishpond to the sea. There is some literary evidence for the practice of bringing seawater into freshwater ponds. By connecting his inland ponds to the sea, L. Lucullus earned the appellation of *Xerxes togatus* from a chiding Pompey who was likening the channels of Lucullus to those the Persian king had built through the isthmus at Mount Athos.[21] Though not specifically outlined in the ancient literary record, the mixture of salt and fresh water appears to have been the preferred environment for seaside fishponds.[22]

Artificial enclosures or fishponds, in many cases, are architectural attempts at formalizing and controlling natural fishing grounds. The earliest attempts at organized fish-raising probably began at spots where fish were known to congregate. Sheltered zones where fresh water emptied into the sea would have been ideal sites to catch fish or to confine them until they were to be consumed. The harbor and fishery at Cosa were constructed so as to be able to exploit a naturally brackish lagoon (Fig. 12). Fish making for the waters of the lagoon had to pass through the narrows of the "Tagliata"—a rock-cut channel that followed a natural fissure in the promontory. Here they could be trapped and held until harvested or directed into tanks positioned in the lagoon.[23]

Many seaside fishponds were constructed on terrain that naturally possessed features conducive to the raising of fish. Architecture was employed to insure that fish did not escape and to help regulate the circulation of water in the enclosure. Typical of this evolution from natural fishing ground to artificial pond is the *piscina* at Torre Valdaliga (Figs. 16, 17). Located on the Tyrrhenian coast in Etruria, the site of Torre Valdaliga is most illustrative of the exploitation of the geological formations. Here, the natural topography was gradually altered to facilitate the raising of fish. The villa and fishpond were sited on a rocky shelf, which projected out into the sea. The volcanic rock of this shelf contained many natural inlets and tidal basins. During the first phase of the villa, in the early first century B.C., a single small inlet with a narrowed entrance was provided with a long rock-cut channel to help funnel seawater into the enclosure. During the winter, this inlet received fresh water through rivulets caused by rainfall, which changed the salinity and temperature of the seawater in the inlet. The addition of fresh water helped keep the water inside the enclosure from becoming stagnant and unhealthy for the fish. The rock-cut channel also served to advertise the brackish conditions inside the enclosure and thus lure fish into the inlet. The dependence on the cyclical supply of fresh water suggests that this enclosure was used seasonally.

The arrangement was amplified at Torre Valdaliga in the third quarter of the first century B.C. when a much larger cove, adjacent to the inlet just mentioned, was adapted architecturally for the raising of fish. Three long channels were cut into the rocky shelf to facilitate saltwater circulation and to entice fish into the confines of the fishpond. The interior of the cove was regularized by the addition of hydraulic concrete faced in *opus reticulatum*. Conduits, formed by parallel walls, distributed fresh water throughout the pond. Fresh water could be stored in cisterns, in the nearby villa, to supply the pond during seasonal dry spells. In both instances, the rock-cut channels performed the double purpose of circulating water and luring fish by allowing salt water in and brackish water out. The provision for a continuous freshwater supply in the second phase permitted year-round use.

CONSTRUCTION OF SEASIDE FISHPONDS

Two types of seaside fishponds are recorded by Columella: those which were excavated in rock and those constructed in concrete.[24] This ancient distinction provides a convenient basis for broad typological categories but must be qualified. Columella states that ponds cut entirely from the rock were most rare and this is substantiated by the archaeological record. The technique of construction was largely determined by the geomorphology of the coast chosen for the site of the fishpond. The rocky coast, in fact, is often too sparse or too precipitous to permit excavation of complete enclosures suitable for confining fish. Still, at times, the excavation and cutting of living rock was employed to fashion complete enclosures or to level the rocky seabed for the foundation of a concrete fishpond. Where suitable rock formations were available, they were utilized, but the rock was almost always inadequate to fashion a complete enclosure.[25] In these cases concrete was frequently used to complete enclosures partially formed by the cutting of the rocky terrain. The rock was often cut just enough to provide a suitable base upon which the pond could be constructed using more conventional means.

Hydraulic concrete, which could set in standing water, was perfectly suited for the construction of offshore installations such as seaside *piscinae*. Using either proper forms or cofferdams, virtually any shape and size could be fashioned in standing water from hydraulic concrete. Composed of pozzolana, lime, and aggregate, this type of concrete did not "dry," in the conventional sense, but hardened from a chemical reaction when mixed with water.[26] The volcanic ash, or pozzolana, was the critical ingredient. The sites of the fishponds in Italy were located in easy reach of pozzolana, or "Puteolan dust" (*pulvis Puteolanus*), mined around the Bay of Naples.[27]

The use of concrete allowed the architects and the owners a great deal of latitude in choosing the sites for their fishponds and the ultimate shapes of the enclosures. Walls of this type of concrete were built by placing wet mortar and aggregate between temporary wooden forms or shuttering.[28] The concrete having set, the forms could be removed or allowed to decay over time. The absence of masonry facing on most of these walls suggests that wooden forms and cofferdams (*arcae*) were employed to form many of the offshore fishponds. Vitruvius outlines possible methods for building concrete structures underwater.[29] Of these, one involved the arrangement of prefabricated forms or cofferdams that were made of wooden uprights held together by horizontal beams. The single-walled boxes were anchored on the leveled sea bottom and hydraulic concrete was placed into the forms.[30] This method appears to have been favored in the construction of seaside *piscinae*.[31] Most of the concrete walls and, in particular, the perimeter moles appear to have been constructed as single masses whose width and course were determined by the placement of the wooden forms. The facility conferred by concrete construction permitted thick protective moles to be positioned to define the perimeter of the fishpond.[32] Where natural formations were included in the pond architecture, the irregular contours of natural inlets and rock-cut enclosures could be straightened by the addition of a concrete lining, which would be formed between the rock and a single line of wooden shuttering.[33]

In a manner similar to harbor design, moles were laid out to protect an area within which a fishpond could be constructed. Breakwaters such as these were prescribed by Columella, who also suggests that these barriers be designed with openings that could permit the free circulation of seawater within.[34] These perimeter moles had the function of protecting the ponds from the violence of the sea and of creating peaceful conditions for raising fish.[35] It is not surprising that this impressive form of architecture was considered a manifestation of unbridled luxury.[36]

The plastic qualities of concrete allowed walls to be constructed with curvilinear lines. This configuration, when used in the design of the mole, was more effective at breaking the force of the waves than a rectilinear mole. In addition, the curvilinear plan reduced the number of corners where circulation would be difficult and sediment could accumulate. Arching walls appear more decorative and, when positioned offshore, they emphasized the sweep of the panorama.[37]

When conditions allowed, the concrete walls of some fishponds were constructed in dry conditions — protected by waterproof barriers or moles — and then flooded when the concrete had set. These walls could be built with a facing that was difficult to construct in standing water.

Walls faced with irregular stones, reticulate pyramids, and fired bricks were used to fashion structures within the perimeter of the fishpond. On Ventotene the grottoes and main tanks of the fishpond were excavated from a rocky shelf that emerged slightly from the level of the sea. The excavation of the rock was completed and concrete walls added prior to connecting the enclosure to the sea.[38]

CONSTRUCTION OF INLAND FISHPONDS

Inland ponds are usually smaller in size and rely exclusively on freshwater sources for circulation. The exclusive use of fresh water, while poorly represented in the archaeological record during the Roman Republic, is represented by many examples from the time of Augustus to the later first century A.D. A late Republican freshwater fishpond located at the so-called Villa of Quintilius Varus at Tivoli stands alone in this class of architecture. The pond occupies a large terrace of a multilevel villa beside the Anio. Built of concrete faced in *opus incertum*, the fishpond was fed by an aqueduct, which carried fresh water from the upper course of the Anio. Ponds fed solely by fresh water were apparently held in low esteem by the Romans of the late Republic. As I have already noted, Varro associated the possession of a freshwater pond with a lower socioeconomic status and indicated that there was a decided preference for saltwater species of fish.[39] The scarcity of freshwater fishponds in the archaeological record during the Republic tends to confirm their secondary importance.

This picture changed considerably during the early Empire. The reorganization of water systems under Augustus ushered in an era in which fresh water became accessible for many uses beyond the purely alimentary. Three new aqueducts were brought into Rome; one of them, the Aqua Alsietina, was built for the purpose of supplying the Naumachia Augusti and private gardens.[40] In Campania, at the same time, the Serino aqueduct was constructed to supply water to the cities around the Bay of Naples. Aqueducts such as these provided more fresh water for private use, for gardens, nymphaea, and fishponds. There were other reasons why freshwater *piscinae* became more common. Not only were they easier to locate, they were simpler to construct than their more elaborate seaside counterparts. The construction of inland ponds did not involve the inherent difficulties of fashioning concrete structures in the ocean or sculpting the rocky seascape to create elaborate *piscinae*.

Freshwater ponds, in most cases, could be constructed under dry conditions, waterproofed, and then filled with water when the enclosure was completed. Likewise, the ponds could be emptied for easy maintenance and cleaning. These *piscinae* were usually built of concrete walls with masonry facings.[41] Waterproofing mortar and even colored plaster lined the ponds that decorated the peristyle gardens of urban villas. Facility with concrete permitted the builder of the ponds in the Praedia Iuliae Felicis, the Casa di Meleagro, and the Villa di Diomede in Pompeii to fashion recesses by altering the contour of the walls.[42] The resultant niches increased the shady areas of the pond, which were critical for the survival of the fish.

Enclosures built inshore could not rely upon the force of the water outside the pond to offset the weight of water inside (hydrostasis). Inland ponds were built below the ground level so the weight of the earth could serve to buttress the sides of the enclosure. Special provision was made to stabilize the marshy ground around the concrete ponds inside the lagoon at Cosa. Successive layers of crushed rock, wooden planks, and ceramic *amphorae* were laid outside the walls to inhibit the erosion of the ground needed to counteract the weight of the water inside the pond.[43] The large pool, which is located in the center of the lower peristyle of the so-called Villa of Horace near Licenza, was buttressed with concrete piers (Fig. 46:P), but in most cases, the fill of earth around the exterior of the fishponds was enough to offset the weight of water within the *piscina*.

The archaeological evidence demonstrates that freshwater or inland ponds, associated with Rome's distant past or lower classes in the ancient literary record, became by the first century A.D. a popular and less expensive alternative to the more ornate seaside *piscinae*.[44] The preoccupation of authors of the late Republic and early Empire with large seaside fishponds is understandable from a literary point of view. The dalliances of Rome's aristocracy were much more entertaining and noteworthy than the practical details about the kinds of enclosures built for keeping and raising of fish. Moreover, freshwater ponds were not as exciting or prestigious as the saltwater variety. The spread of freshwater fishponds to owners of less pretense is reflected, perhaps, in the contrasting treatment recounted in our primary literary sources. What was for Varro a curious practice largely confined to Rome's elite and the source of many amusing anecdotes was for Columella, a full century later, a topic to be treated with some seriousness. This change in attitude suggests that the

FISHPOND CONSTRUCTION AND OPERATION

practice of raising fish in small freshwater ponds on a modest scale was more profitable and more commonplace.

Despite the lack of attention paid to freshwater ponds in the ancient literary sources, the archaeological remains illustrate that the smaller freshwater *piscina* was quite popular. Moreover, the accessibility of a constant freshwater source allowed for a wider distribution of inland ponds or *piscinae mediterraneae*. The sheer number of small inland ponds found during the first century A.D. at Italian sites, such as Pompeii, is evidence of the powerful allure of owning a *piscina*, a legacy passed down from the *piscinarii* of the previous century. Among inland ponds, circular and semicircular plans were common and are reminiscent of the forms used in many seaside *piscinae*. The phi-shaped *piscina* at Grottarossa, near Rome, with its central island compares favorably with coastal enclosures such as those on the island Pianosa or at Torre Flavia on the Etruscan coast. At Pompeii, small rectangular ponds with semicircular projections, such as those found in the gardens of the Casa di Paquius Proculus (I 7, 1) and the Casa del Centenario (IX 8, 3/6), recall the larger but similar plans at Grottacce on the Etruscan coast or at Nettuno (Fig. 50) and Astura – La Saracca in Latium (Figs. 52, 53).

DESIGN DETAILS

In general terms, Columella's requirements for saltwater fishpond design compare favorably with the archaeological remains. However, the specific details of Columella's designs represent ideals (as is also true of Vitruvius's architectural types), which are not embodied in any single structure. Virtually any deep pond with adequate circulation could maintain schools of fish. Many such structures are attested in Italy. At Pompeii and Herculaneum alone nearly eighty enclosures have been unearthed that could have served as fishponds.[45] While Columella recommends a depth of seven feet (2.14 meters), the physical remains indicate a range from less than one meter to over three meters.[46]

Certain architectural details were incorporated into the fishpond plan to help confine and maintain the fish and thereby facilitate their exploitation. For example, many fishponds were divided into smaller tanks permitting the owner to segregate his fish by species or age. Varro likens some ponds in his day to the boxes (*arculae loculatae*) used by painters to hold their pigments and verifies that these *piscinae loculatae* were built to keep various types of fish separate.[47] Vertical slots would have secured movable grates (*cancelli*).[48] These barriers could be slid up and down to allow fish to transit the connecting channel or opening.

According to the Elder Pliny certain species did not get along well together. The animosity that existed between the gray mullet (*mugil*) and the bass (*lupus*), and between the conger and *murena* usually resulted in tails being chewed.[49] The *murena* is singled out by the Elder Pliny as a fish that was easily irritated (the violent disposition of Pollio's *murenae* is well known) and Columella adjures that the eel should not be mixed with other species of fish.[50] Care had to be taken even when confining members of the same species of fish. The young of many varieties of fish are often the prey of their adult kin. The eel's ferocity is often aimed at its own kind. In the modern lagoonal fisheries near Orbetello small eels or elvers are segregated from predacious adults. Here in separate enclosures, small elvers are isolated from larger elvers and both are kept apart from adults.[51] Segregation of this sort aided the raising of fish by lowering the chances of predation, which could cut into the potential yield of the pond and destroy valuable fish.

Aside from affording protection, separate ponds could serve to sort fish for selected purposes. They might hold fish being gathered for market, chosen for immediate consumption, kept for breeding stock, displayed as curios, or kept as pets. In this way, internal subdivisions allowed for the more efficient use of the fishpond and facilitated the harvesting of fish. *Piscinae loculatae*, or compartmental ponds, are well attested in the archaeological record and prevalent in seaside locales. Most of the seaside fishponds included in this study are composed of two or more tanks.[52]

The walls that enclosed fishponds were designed principally to prevent the fish's escape. Certain species of fish require higher walls due to their ability to jump. Many fast swimming varieties of fish will jump when agitated or when confined in crowded conditions. The gray mullet (*mugil*), for instance, is renowned for its leaping and requires high walls relative to the level of the water.[53] Some walls unearthed during the excavation of the lagoonal fishery at Cosa exhibit substantial differences in height, which, according to the investigators, may indicate that the enclosures were built for different species of fish.[54]

The precise heights of fishpond walls relative to the ancient sea level are difficult to determine and would have varied with the range of the

23

ocean's tides. For inland ponds, the position of conduits can be used to determine the height of the water and the amount of freeboard. At Paestum, the *piscina* in the sanctuary at Santa Venera has an outlet located at the top of its wall, which would have permitted little freeboard. During operation, the level of the water would be within ten centimeters of the top of the pond. This configuration would suggest that the pond's designer was not aware of or concerned about the leaping ability of the fish to be confined at Santa Venera.

At Pompeii, the *piscinae* located in the Praedia Iuliae Felicis, the Villa di Diomede, and the Casa di Meleagro were designed so that the water levels would be maintained well below the tops of the ponds. The outlets, which regulate the level of the water inside the tank, are positioned nearly sixty centimeters (two Roman feet) below the edge of the *piscinae*. This arrangement would provide an ample barrier that would prevent leaping fish from escaping and would deflect them back into the water.

Other design features that may have prevented the loss of leaping fish are the platforms or steps that lined the interior of the pond. These plat-

forms functioned principally as walkways for those who maintained the fishpond. Either cut in rock or fashioned from concrete, such walkways lined the walls of many fishponds.[55] They were designed to emerge above the level of the water or to be slightly awash so that movement, by those using and servicing the ponds, would be unhindered. In addition, they would have prevented fish from reaching sufficient depth near the wall to be able to accelerate up and out of the enclosure. The ability to regulate better the level of fresh water coupled with the smaller scale of inland structures made platforms superfluous as walkways or jump inhibitors.[56]

The internal divisions of these *piscinae loculatae* could take on shapes that were pleasing to the eye as well as functional. This could be said of the circular tanks in the ponds at Punta della Vipera, Torre Flavia, Nettuno (Villino Nesi), Ventotene, and Torre del Fico (Circeo). Each could be viewed from attached platforms or from their associated villas. Moreover, the curvilinear design could withstand the force of surf using less construction materials than a straight wall.

The most unusual form of decorative tank is the diamond- or lozenge-shaped enclosures found in *piscinae* at Torre Astura, Formia (Giardino Publico and Via Vitruvio), and Ponza.[57] Inscribed within a rectangular enclosure, each lozenge defined five separate tanks: the large central lozenge and four smaller triangular tanks. This distinctive design may well have been the brainchild of a single builder operating in the late first century B.C. or early first century A.D.

Frequently, inland freshwater ponds were designed with plans that recall the influential forms of their seaside cousins. At Pompeii, while rectangular plans predominate, at least eight ponds were laid out with circular, or semicircular perimeters. Fifteen more incorporated semicircular alcoves and rounded walls into their designs. Internal divisions, as can be seen in the *euripi* of the House of Octavius Quartio, echo the *piscinae loculatae* found along the seacoast.

After building the enclosure and securing a vigorous water source, Columella suggests that some fishponds should have recesses (*specus*) built into the walls.[58] The designer's intention was to provide areas where fish could find shade and a respite from the heat of the day. Some of these *specus* were to be simple and straight where fish could retire, while others were to be twisted and constricted where *murenae* could hide.[59] Columella relates that many in his day thought that the recesses should be deep and winding.[60] He warns of the danger of stagnation in these deep recesses and preaches moderation. Similar recesses (*similes cellae*) should be incorporated into the sides of the fishpond deep enough to offer shade but sufficiently open to allow adequate circulation.[61]

The ambient temperature of water inside artificial enclosures was of paramount concern to the fishpond builder. Adequate circulation went a long way to insure cool temperatures and well-aerated water. Provisions for shade were also important for keeping ponds cool. Fishponds constructed in grottoes or excavated in the form of a cave offer the most obvious examples. The *piscinae* on the islands of Ponza (Figs. 74–76) and Ventotene are the best-preserved examples.[62] These islands are honeycombed with sea caves which are known today as fertile fishing grounds for eels (congers and *anguillae*). These fish seek shade in the wild just as they would in artificial enclosures. It would take only a small technical step to control these natural fishing grounds and enhance their ability to maintain large schools of fish.[63]

Most *piscinae*, however, were open to the air, and shade, where needed, had to be incorporated into the plan on a much smaller scale than in the examples on the Pontine Islands. The solutions to this problem found in the archaeological record generally correspond to those suggested by Columella.

Structures attached to the sides of fishponds so that they project out into and cover part of the enclosure can be seen in the *piscinae* at the so-called Villa of Quintilius Varus near Tivoli, the Piscina di Lucullo near Circeo, and the pond located in the domestic quarter at Paestum. At Tivoli and Circeo platforms are supported by small concrete barrel vaults, which project out toward the center of the enclosure (Figs. 43, 63).[64] The submerged tunnels, created by the vaults, provided shade for the fish as well as supporting a platform for viewing the pond and its inhabitants. The fishpond inside the city of Paestum has a slightly different structure that serves the same function (Figs. 108, 109). Post-and-lintel construction supports a platform that spans one end of the pond. It appears less a separate projecting structure than a support for the surrounding promenade over the fishpond. Thus, the platform shields the shallowest and potentially the warmest end of the *piscina* from the sun's rays. Here too, the structure serves the dual purpose of providing shade while allowing easy viewing of the pond. This design, which was employed at Tivoli, Circeo, and Paestum, appears to match best with Columella's *specus simplices et recti*.[65] These *specus* could be used for any of the species of fish commonly raised by the Romans.

26   Another, perhaps more artistic, solution to the problem of creating shade in the confines of a fishpond can be seen at Pompeii and on the Palatine in Rome. The garden *piscinae* located in the Casa di Meleagro, the Villa di Diomede, and the Praedia Iuliae Felicis at Pompeii were designed with walls that have rectilinear or semicircular recesses.[66] Laid out uniformly and arranged symmetrically, these niches probably best exemplify Columella's *cellae similes*. These cells are much more open than the vaults of the projecting platforms and would hinder circulation less. The many curves and angles insure that there will be shade somewhere in the pond through all of the daylight hours. The open areas of this system do not provide the same degree of protection from predators as do the projecting platforms, but fish have notoriously bad sight and any visual block probably helped shield the prey.

The *euripus* located in the peristyle garden of the Praedia Iuliae Felicis is a long and narrow fishpond crossed by three small arched bridges, which supply shade for the fish. The bridges divide the pond into four parts and each segment has two open recesses that alternate between rectangular and semicircular. Each recess is bisected by a horizontal tile, which provides a more constricted retreat at the bottom of the tank. This one pond combines both an open *cella* and a more restricted *specus* of the type mentioned by Columella.[67]

Ceramic vessels of diverse shape and size were used to form the most recognizable version of the constricted *specus*. Though not quite as twisted (*retortos*) as Columella describes, ceramic *amphorae* and other assorted shapes (jars, *dolia*, and cook pots) were probably the shapes the author had in mind.[68] This type of *specus* is well attested in the archaeological record in Italy, but rare in other parts of the Mediterranean (Figs. 1, 2).[69] They range from 119 *amphorae* in the Piscina di Lucullo near Circeo to a single *amphora* used in the pond belonging to the House of the Colored Capitals at Pompeii.

Most of the ponds employing the constricted *specus* are fed by fresh water and the two that lie near the sea, at Sperlonga and on Circeo, relied on freshwater springs as their principal water source. According to Columella, the small *specus* was particularly well suited for the *murena* and the eel is quite at home in fresh or brackish waters. It is, therefore, easy to suggest that those ponds equipped with *amphorae* and designed with little freeboard (*murenae* are not known as jumpers) were probably designed for the raising of eels (Fig. 3). The constricted *specus* design represents the most recognizable grouping that can be gleaned from the archaeological record. It is hardly surprising that these ponds, specifically developed for *murenae* by Gaius Hirrius, should receive special mention by the Elder Pliny.[70] Aside from the *murena* no specific correlation can be made between fishpond design and a particular species of fish, and the association between eels and fixed *amphorae* is not absolute. Other species of fish could take advantage of the constricted *specus* for protection and eels could live in ponds without them. With little doubt the *piscinae* at Sperlonga and Circeo, which were designed with low freeboard, loculate tanks, and many *amphorae*, are ponds for the raising of eels.[71]

Supplemental architecture was employed in many cases to shade exposed *piscinae*. This was particularly convenient near porticoes or within peristyle gardens. Varro mentions two oblong *piscinae* at his villa near Casinum that "faced the colonnade" (*ad porticus versus*).[72] A pond recently unearthed in a villa at the Mola di Monte Gelato was built in the shade of a preexisting portico echoing the description offer by Varro.[73] *Pergulae*, or vine arbors, were employed not only to shade adjacent dining areas (*triclinia*) but the ponds as well. The upper terrace in the House of Octavius Quartio at Pompeii was shaded by a long vine canopy, which shaded the small *euripus* as well as the *biclinium* nearby. In the lower

FIGURE 1. Luxor, Temple of Amun (al-Karnak)—fishpond at end of the Avenue of Ram-headed Sphinxes. (Photo by J. Higginbotham)

FIGURE 2. Luxor, Temple of Amun (al-Karnak)—fishpond at end of the Avenue of Ram-headed Sphinxes, with ceramic vessels incorporated into the fabric of the walls. (Photo by J. Higginbotham)

FIGURE 3. Eels in a fishpond equipped with wall recesses made from ceramic vessels. (Drawing by Joan Christoff)

garden, *pergulae* cover two selected tanks along the long *euripus*, offering a natural punctuation to the long watercourse.[74]

INTERIOR ARRANGEMENTS

Columella discusses the importance of creating the impression of a "natural" environment inside a fishpond. Besides the vital role of water, he mentions specific interior terrains that could be tailored to the needs of particular types of fish.[75] He recommends that the placement of the fishpond should take into account the nature of the surrounding terrain so the desired environment could be enclosed; every kind of fish cannot be kept in all waters.[76] A muddy stretch of shore (*limosa regio*) was considered to be ideal for raising flatfish (*pisces plani*) such as the sole (*solea*) and the turbot (*rhombus*). These conditions were also seen as suitable for raising various types of shellfish (*conchylii*).[77] Sandy beds with swirling waters (*arenosi gurgites*) were thought to be adequate for flatfish, but better for giltheads (*auratae*), dentex (*dentices*), the related umbrina (*umbrae*), and the red fish (*punicae*).[78] These sandy beds were believed by Columella to be less suitable for shellfish. Rocky seas (*saxo-*

sum mare) supplied an abundance of food for fish. *Merulae, turdi,* and *melanuri* were known as "rock fish" because of their affinity for rocky beds.[79] The internal conditions of Roman seaside fishponds are virtually impossible to verify from the archaeological record. The ponds have suffered much over the centuries and the terrain they enclose has changed in many cases. However, there is enough mud, sand, and rock in and around the ruins of these *piscinae* to suggest that the ancient terrain types, outlined by Columella, could have been created easily.[80]

In the cases of many of the fishponds fed by fresh water, the interior arrangements were meant to appeal to the eye of the owner as well as the needs of the fish. The interiors of many ponds decorating the gardens in Pompeii were coated with blue stucco, perhaps to approximate the color of the waters in their more illustrious and deeper seaside cousins. In these small *piscinae,* the addition of sands, rock, and clay vessels may have made the ponds more hospitable for the fish. However, no evidence for this type of interior treatment can be gleaned from the physical remains. In addition, there appears to have been no attempt to recreate artificial terrains inside ponds using frescoes or mosaics.

Other design features such as water source, interior terrain, and wall height are less specific in their association with fish species. The interior terrains, outlined by Columella, are difficult to reconstruct from the present state of the fishponds. The deposition of sediment and debris makes precise observations about the interior environments impossible. It is possible that different types of fish were kept in the same enclosure; such an arrangement would echo the aquatic collages seen in many mosaics and paintings of the era. Furthermore, the prohibitions against mixing various species could only have been learned through the experience gained from observing such interactions in an artificial environment where the culprits could be easily identified.

ARCHITECTURAL SETTING OF *PISCINAE*

Understanding the architectural setting for a fishpond and its relationship to other structures can clarify how a fishpond was maintained, why designs vary, and how the *piscina* could be enjoyed. The archaeological evidence shows that most fishponds were constructed on land or along the shorefront, juxtaposed to Roman villas. Of the fifty-six sites with *piscinae* considered in this study, forty-seven are associated with some certainty with villas or other private dwellings.[81] The location of these residences were often chosen to exploit the panoramic vistas or to take advantage of the natural coves and inlets along the shore. The artificial fishpond, with its perimeter moles reaching out and enclosing large areas of seascape, reflects the desire to control nature and to include plants, animals, and fish within the confines of the villa property.[82]

The vaulted structures near some fishponds probably served as storerooms for the tackle and other supplies needed during routine operation while supporting adjacent platforms. The resultant terraces supported by these vaults provided places from which to view the ponds and created decorative backdrops for the *piscinae*. In many cases these terraces supported walkways and platforms from which the pond and panorama could be enjoyed. At Torre Astura, a long bridge (Fig. 60 top) provided access to the insular fishpond and allowed visitors to experience the sights and sounds of the sea from sheltered pavilions in the midst of the *piscina* (Fig. 57: terrace for pavilions). Closely placed parallel walls in the fishponds at Torre Valdaliga and La Mattonara may have supported platforms that stood over portions of the ponds. These broad platforms could have afforded better views of the ponds while providing shade for fish confined in the enclosure.

On a smaller scale, the ponds at the so-called Villa of Horace near Licenza (Fig. 46:F), the Villa of Quintilius Varus at Tivoli (Fig. 43), and the Piscina di Lucullo (Fig. 62:P) were equipped with small platforms that projected toward the middle of the enclosures. From these platforms, visitors could enjoy the view from a slightly better point of vantage.[83] While providing similar protection to the fish these features also serve to emulate the larger and more prestigious seaside *piscinae*.

Many coastal *piscinae* were built in conjunction with dining facilities.[84] The ponds at Torre Valdaliga (Fig. 17), Torre Astura (Fig. 57), Circeo (Fig. 62), and Sperlonga (Fig. 68) were designed with platforms or islands that allowed diners and visitors to enjoy the ambience in close proximity to the water. One of the most elaborate examples of a fishpond/dining facility was built inside and in front of the grotto at Sperlonga. Here, the *triclinium* took the form of an artificial island surrounded by the fishpond offering an unobstructed view of the sculptural decorations in the grotto (Figs. 67, 68:P). A second outdoor dining pavilion was built opposite the entrance to the cave.[85] Landscape and

FISHPOND CONSTRUCTION AND OPERATION

topography augmented by architecture were fundamental to villa design. *Piscinae* helped broaden the definition of landscape to include not only the seashore but also the sea itself.

In an urban setting and away from the natural topography of the coast much more emphasis was placed on architecture to create the sense of landscape. Gardens constructed within the Roman house include many elements that recall the natural settings of coastal villas. Plantings of flowers, shrubs, and trees in landscaped or terraced settings were planned in imitation of natural topography. The sights and sounds of running water were important features of ancient pleasure gardens and *piscinae* figure prominently in the design of many Pompeian examples.[86] Pompeii supplies the most accessible and best-documented group of *piscinae* built within an urban and, specifically, a domestic setting.

The fishpond complemented the ensemble of elements that embellished Pompeian gardens.[87] In many examples, porticoes were employed to define the space in which the fishpond was set.[88] The colonnades presented an architectural backdrop for the pond while supplying a comfortable point of vantage for those visiting the garden. Within this architectural setting, urban fishponds emulated the juxtaposition of seaside *piscinae* with their villas.

Additional elements added to the "natural feel" of the garden and served to focus the attention of the viewer. *Pergulae*, or vine arbors, while providing a natural cover for the ponds and visitors, also functioned to highlight the location of the *piscinae* within the gardens. The movement and sound of running water produced by fountains, *nymphaea*, and cascades, drew attention to the ponds and their special features. Statuary could be added to the decorative scheme in the form of fountains or as ornamental embellishments.

Many of these characteristics were combined in the Casa di D. Octavius Quartio at Pompeii.[89] Here, two long, interconnected ponds, or *euripi*, were constructed on different levels within a large garden. A colonnade supporting a vine arbor shaded the upper *euripus* while parallel examples followed the course of the larger pond in the lower garden. Fountains helped maintain circulation and punctuated notable features along the ponds' course. An *aedicula* fountain formed the centerpiece of small dining *biclinium* which straddled one end of the upper pond. From here, water fell from the upper to lower pond by means of a two-story fountain house with a stepped cascade. The large *euripus* in the lower garden was designed with water jets including an elaborate fountain in the form of a pyramidal cascade.

The garden pond could be enjoyed and appreciated from different points of vantage, both public and private. The locations of many ponds within Pompeian houses permit the general or remote glimpse suitable for the casual acquaintance or client. Apertures or windows in the *atrium* and, specifically, in the *tablinum* allowed a more public audience to see the pond. This configuration accounts for nearly forty examples from Pompeii alone.[90]

Many of these same *piscinae* and others could be enjoyed from much more intimate surroundings. The location of dining areas and reception rooms around the garden often took into account the location of the fishpond. *Triclinia* set within rooms or shaded by *pergulae* afforded selected visitors or guests front-row seats to the splendors of the gardens and their ponds. At Pompeii, over twenty examples of *piscinae* are situated in close proximity to dining facilities with approximately an equal number located where they can be seen easily from reception rooms, or *oeci*, and garden *exedrae*.[91] The connection between ponds and dining areas is not solely aesthetic but has a gastronomic component as well. Fish or eels fresh from the *piscina* would make an impressive addition to private meals among friends and honored guests.

The large ornate *piscina* situated in the Casa di Meleagro (Figs. 94, 95) was designed to serve both the public and private needs of its owner.[92] Upon entering the Tuscanic *atrium* and awaiting a meeting with the owner, the visitor could catch an enticing glimpse of the pond in its spacious peristyle through a wide door to the left. By moving about the atrium it would be possible to see the interior of the peristyle with its *piscina* and fountains without entering the garden. Those invited into the more private preserve of the garden could view the pond from the shade of the peristyle where details of the *piscina*'s plan and decoration could be clearly seen. Venturing into the garden itself the guest could marvel at the deep blue (painted) water and the fish, which might be the featured course at dinnertime. In yet more private settings select guests could mingle in a large *exedra* or dine in the columned Corinthian *oecus* with a direct view of the pond with its fountains and cascade.

It is in their close association with dining and display that inland fishponds most resemble and imitate the larger seaside *piscinae*. The public and private vantage in both settings served to emphasize the social station of the fishpond owner.

FISHPOND CONSTRUCTION AND OPERATION

"After having arranged the folds by this method we shall introduce the aquatic flock."[93] With the facilities prepared fish were lured or brought into enclosures where they could be held until ready for harvesting. The construction of fishponds in well-known fishing grounds gave the owner ready access to a supply attracted by the natural features of the site. The lagoonal fishery at Cosa relied on the seasonal migrations of fish through passages created by the fissures in the promontory at the west end of the lagoon. These passages were modified to help trap fish going in and out. The lure presented by such brackish connections to the sea was used by the builders of other *piscinae* along the Etruscan coast at Torre Valdaliga, La Mattonara, and Punta della Vipera.

Without these natural aids, the fishpond owner had to rely on conventional methods of catching fish: nets, lines and hooks, and traps. According to Martial, Bassus employed a fisherman (*piscator*) to catch fish for his ponds.[94] In addition, more creative methods were employed to lure fish into prepared enclosures. In Phoenicia and Liguria, leader fish were used to lure their unsuspecting companions into ponds. Both the Elder Pliny and Oppian describe how a single fish was tethered through the gills, let out on a long line, and pulled back in leading others of his kind.[95]

34

Once caught, fish could be transported short distances in nets, trailing in the water, or in the boat.[96] For longer distances, and to insure the health of the fish, boats equipped with live tanks could be used.[97] Athenaeus describes a ship built by Archimedes, at the behest of tyrant Hiero II, which had a live tank built into the bow and was constructed of lead and wood. During the construction of the airport at Fiumicino in 1958–59 a boat with a live tank (*navis vivaria*) was unearthed near what was the entrance to the Claudian harbor (Fig. 4).[98] Vessels such as these could land on the protective moles of most seaside *piscinae* and simply transfer the catch to the pond. Piers and moles—such as those associated with the fishponds at Santa Liberata, Cosa, and Torre Astura—would have facilitated the transfer of fish into the enclosures as well as shipment to market.

Once in the fishpond the fish had to be fed.[99] Columella goes on at some length about the diets for various fish. Decaying fish parts, salted fish, assorted fruit, milk curds, dried figs, as well as small fish, are suggested as food for the confined fish.[100]

FIGURE 4. Fishing boat equipped with a live tank, uncovered during the excavation of the harbor of Claudius at Ostia. (From O. Testaguzza, *Portus* [Rome 1970] 143, boat 7)

No specific details are offered by the ancient literary sources as to how fish were harvested from fishponds. It is probable that these techniques were unremarkable from the point of view of these authors since the methods used deviated so little from conventional fishing methods. The difference, of course, was that fish confined in a pond were easier to catch. The advantages of fishing within a controlled environment, protected from the violence of the sea, and stocked with fish with nowhere to go and few places to hide, are obvious.[101]

The channels used by fish during their seasonal migrations were perfect spots to catch fish. Relatively constricted, the narrow defiles through which the sea communicated with the lagoon or fishpond could be easily shut off by means of sluice gates. Cuttings in the rock-cut channels at Cosa have led investigators to postulate the placement of gates or barriers designed to trap fish as they traveled through the connection between the lagoon and the sea.[102] In this manner, whole schools of migrating fish could be trapped and harvested.

The Elder Pliny refers to traps (*excipula*) being used to catch eels (*anguillae*) trying to leave Lacus Benacus (Lake Garda) by way of the Minicius (river Minicio). Pliny says that thousands are caught in each trap.[103]

FISHPOND CONSTRUCTION AND OPERATION

Excipula could function wherever fish are in great numbers, in migratory channels or in the fishpond itself. According to Oppian, some of these traps or weels are fashioned with funnel-shaped throats and wide bellies so that fish could easily enter but leave only with difficulty.[104] The author concludes by saying that the use of such a trap could allow the fisherman to sleep while working. In short, "great gain was made with little effort."[105]

The need for more efficient methods of trapping and harvesting fish is reflected in the architecture of many fishponds. Traps were designed into the *itinera* or openings of the concrete moles protecting some fishponds. The best-preserved examples of this feature can be observed in the *piscinae* at Astura–La Saracca and Formia (Giardino Publico, Fig. 71). The long concrete channel that projects seaward from the semicircular fishpond at Astura–La Saracca was fitted with movable gates so that fish entering or leaving the enclosure could be trapped. The interior of the semicircular enclosure is divided into rows of small tanks that follow the arc of the protective mole. The tank aligned with the long channel is five-sided with two of its walls forming a funnel into the long channel. Slotted runners for sliding gates line the openings that connect the pentagonal tank to the middle row of subtanks and to the seaward channel. This system appears to be configured principally for the entrapment of fish leaving the enclosure in response to the natural forces that compel migration. The pentagonal tank, acting as a funnel, would guide the escaping fish into the long channel where they would be trapped between the sliding gates.

The diamond- or lozenge-shaped tanks within the *piscinae* at Torre Astura, Formia (Giardino Publico and Via Vitruvio, Figs. 71, 72), and on the island of Ponza were used to segregate and harvest fish. This design subdivided a basic rectangular plan into five separate tanks. At Torre Astura, the apexes and sides of each lozenge were designed with openings with sliding gates which could allow fish to swim from this tank out into the large enclosure or into the small corner tanks. The lozenge-shaped tank provided four funnels that could guide fish through the openings at each apex. The same design was used in the construction of the *piscina* at Formia. Here, the funneled openings leading to the open sea are fitted with two sets of sliding gates for the purpose of trapping fish. The stone-cut lozenge tank on the island of Ponza does not appear to have openings at the apexes or in the sides. On Ponza, the lozenge is employed solely for the purpose of subdividing the pond and does not take advantage of the funnel configuration.

The most common method of mass fishing was netting. Writing in the second century B.C., Plautus describes a fisherman casting his net into a fishpond to get his catch.[106] The net would require much more effort than the weel but could be more efficient in its take. Oppian enumerates several types of nets, of which there were evidently three general kinds: casting nets, draw nets, and cover nets.[107] All three could be employed to retrieve fish from a pond. Fish watchers were often employed in fishing operations. According to the literary account, the watcher was often perched on a high mast or wooden platform[108] whence he watched for schools of fish and shouted orders to the fishermen below.[109] High platforms or towers are a common feature of fisheries in the Black Sea, Bosporus (Fig. 5), and Epirus. At Ioannina in Epirus the tower is placed at one corner of the enclosure. The net, anchored to one leg of the tower, is cast by fishermen under the direction of the watcher.[110] According to Aelian, the watcher directs netting like a general.[111] Many of the protective moles that surround the seaside fishponds in Italy could support temporary towers of this sort. The moles and their internal walkways would permit the fishermen handling the net to maneuver about the fishpond (Fig. 6). Elements that could have supported one of these corner watchtowers are noted at the *piscinae* of Santa Liberata near Porto Santo Stefano, San Paolo, and La Mattonara. Both San Paolo and La Mattonara have independent piers that stand near a single corner of the enclosures while the mole at the northwest corner of the pond at Santa Liberata is inexplicably enlarged and buttressed by an independent pier adjacent to the corner. Hardly necessary to break the surf, these concrete structures appear to have been designed to support a superstructure and allow the conjecture that a corner tower could have been set up here.

Other less efficient modes of harvesting could involve the use of hook and line, trident, spear, and even poison.[112] All of these methods could be implemented from the perimeter of the enclosure as well as from dividing walls, projecting platforms, and even boats launched inside the pond.[113] Poisons were in common use in Campania during the Elder Pliny's day.[114] The poison was often made by mixing the root of cyclamen with white clay. The drug would drive fish from their hiding places and into the nets.[115]

FISHPOND CONSTRUCTION AND OPERATION

FIGURE 5. Red mullet fisheries in the Bosporus. (Engraving entitled "Baluk Hana, les pêcherie du Bosphore," in T. Allom, *L'Empire ottoman illustre: Constantinople ancienne et moderne* [Paris 1838])

FIGURE 6. Method of netting fish, using walkways. (From T. Dollar, "Desert Paradox: Fish Farms on the Creosote Flats," *Arizona Highways* 66.5 [1990] 32)

The manner of concrete construction, used in the fashioning of artificial *piscinae* or the villas connected to these ponds, is in most cases the only key to the date of these structures. This, coupled with archaeological evidence gleaned from excavations, helps establish the chronology of fishpond construction. The earliest fishponds built with a datable building method employ concrete faced with *opus incertum*. This method was used in the pond at the so-called Villa of Quintilius Varus at Tivoli, the *piscina* at Monteverde in Rome, and the earliest phase of the so-called Piscina di Lucullo at Circeo.[116] The *opus incertum* used in these fishponds appears to date to the last years of the second century B.C. or, more probably, the early years of the first century B.C.

Study of the archaeological evidence shows that reticulate pyramids faced the greatest number of concrete walls used in the construction of Roman fishponds or the villas associated with them. Concrete faced in *opus quasi-reticulatum* was used in the fishponds at Sperlonga and the Villa of Agrippa Postumus at Sorrento.[117] More uniform *opus reticulatum* was employed in the construction of the fishponds at Torre Valdaliga, La Mattonara, Punta della Vipera, Fosso Guardiole, Fosso Sanguisuga, Grottarossa, Astura–La Saracca, Circeo (Piscina di Lucullo), Ventotene, Herculaneum (Palestra), and Pompeii (Villa di Diomede). Furthermore, concrete walls faced in *opus reticulatum* figure prominently in the structures of the villas on shore.[118] Where other evidence is lacking it is useful to hypothesize that the construction of a fishpond might coincide with a major building phase of its villa. Twenty-four of the sites included in this study can be linked to structures faced in *opus reticulatum*.

The use of *opus reticulatum* covers a broad period of time. The structures considered in this study range in date from the second quarter of the first century B.C. (the *opus quasi-reticulatum* at Sperlonga) to the third quarter of the first century A.D. (Grottacce and the Villa di Diomede at Pompeii). The majority of these cluster from circa 25 B.C. to circa A.D. 25 and roughly coincide with early Julio-Claudian era.

Fired clay bricks or tiles were used in the building of only a few *piscinae*. Those *piscinae* built entirely of brick are the circular fishpond at Torre Flavia, the oval ponds at the Villa of Horace near Licenza and the Domus Tiberiana on the Palatine in Rome, and in the large pool in the Domus Augustana on the Palatine. These ponds were built in the last

39

half of the first century A.D. Bricks were used in parts of the construction of the ponds the Villa di Diomede, Casa di Meleagro, and the Praedia Iuliae Felicis at Pompeii, all of which were built after the earthquake of A.D. 62 and before the eruption of Vesuvius in A.D. 79.[119]

The ancient literary sources present Roman pisciculture as a practice that enjoyed its greatest popularity from the last century of the Republic until the end of the first century A.D. The dates suggested by building techniques when combined with other archaeological evidence outline a chronological development that supports much of the literary testimonia. The earliest remains of fishponds in Italy date to the early years of the first century B.C. with the greatest number dating to the Augustan or early Julio-Claudian era. A few structures were constructed during the last half of the first century A.D., after which the physical remains of new large *piscinae* are difficult to identify.[120] These two centuries encompassed a time in Roman history when the open competition among the elite of the Republic led to civil wars and eventually gave way to the autocratic rule of the Empire. During these years the possession and operation of an artificial fishpond were indicative of great wealth and symbolic of almost royal status. The gradual decline in the popularity of the large seaside fishpond in the first century A.D. parallels the consolidation of power under the emperors, who discouraged the conspicuous display of wealth and status common in the Republic. Smaller freshwater ponds, which become common during the first century A.D., belong largely to those of lower station seeking to emulate the image of success created by the *piscinarii* of the late Republic.

40

2

FISH RAISED IN ROMAN *PISCINAE*

Many details of fishpond design discussed in the preceding chapter (salinity of the water, topography of the bottom of the pond, height of the walls and barriers, and circulation) were dependent on the species of fish cultivated. This chapter surveys the species of fish most closely associated with Roman pisciculture, focusing particularly on those most often named in the ancient literary accounts. Specific information on the habits and life cycles of fish mentioned in the ancient texts is often imprecise and has contributed to much confusion about the fish raised by the Romans and how ancient nomenclature relates to modern taxonomic classifications. Therefore, this chapter also draws together from diverse sources some of the pertinent biological information which would have influenced Roman fishpond design and operation. The resulting list represents the fish most commonly raised in Roman artificial enclosures and compares the ancient knowledge of these fish with the modern.

During the late Republic and early Empire when the popularity of fishponds was at its height, technical writers, poets, and satirists wrote of the fish popular among the Romans. The bulk of the literary information comes from nine treatises. Ovid's *Halieutica*, books 9 and 32 of the Elder Pliny's *Historia Naturalis*, Plutarch's *De Sollertia Animalium*, and Oppian's *Halieutica* deal specifically with fish. Pollux's *Onomasticon*, Aelian's *De Natura Animalium*, Athenaeus's *Deipnosophistae*, Varro's *De Re Rustica*, and Columella's *De Re Rustica*, which deal with the subject more tangentially, supply additional information about fish. Further evidence comes from a plethora of frescoes and mosaics that depict various types of marine life, often in aquatic settings. These ancient illustrations suggest an overwhelming preference for maritime fishes or those believed to have originated in the sea. The writers just listed confirm this impression by the attention they pay to maritime species as opposed to those coming from fresh water. This preference apparently continued throughout the Roman era, and is reflected in the relative prices of fish purchased in the Roman world. An edict of the emperor Diocletian, assigned to A.D. 301, provides that the best-quality sea fish could sell for nearly twice the price of the best-quality river fish.[1] These preferences must be considered as one attempts to determine which kinds of fish were most popular among the Romans and most likely to have been cultivated in artificial enclosures.

Authors of the late Republic and early Empire drew much of their information directly or indirectly from Aristotle's *Historia Animalium*.[2] Most of the fish described by Aristotle were native to the waters of Greece and western Asia Minor. Later treatises build on Aristotle's catalog by adding other species found in other parts of the Mediterranean world. To ascertain the relative popularity of different species as related in the literary sources, one may note how frequently they are mentioned and the opinions of the authors in question. Aristotle lists more than 110 varieties of fish, while the Elder Pliny describes 176 species or kinds. In total, there are some 260 species mentioned in all of Latin literature, while 400 varieties of fish are mentioned by Greek authors.[3] Of these fish, about 10 account for the vast majority of the citations dating to the time of the Roman Republic and Empire; thus these can be assumed to be the contemporary favorites.[4] The lack of taxonomical precision in the ancient literary record has contributed to some confusion today concerning the exact species that were raised in Roman *piscinae*. By comparing data from modern fisheries and ichthyological research with the ancient literary account, this chapter presents a selected discussion of the characteristics and habits of the fish most commonly named as being raised in fishponds, and endeavors to set straight the confusion surrounding the use of ancient and modern names for fish.[5]

The correlation of ancient ichthyology with modern requires some explanation. The varieties mentioned by classical authors do not always denote species as they are defined in a modern context. Ancient names for fish tend to be generic appellations that can apply to several species. This situation is generally the rule, but the reverse is also attested. The tunny — one of the most important food fish in the Mediterranean in all periods — is described by several names in the ancient literary record. The terms *thunnus* or *thynnus, pelamys, orcynus, cordyla, anthias, cetus,* and possibly *sarda* refer not only to different varieties of tunny but probably distinguish tunnies of different age, size, and sex.[6] In the face of these problems, the most probable specie or species are related to the ancient names by comparing ancient descriptions and depictions (from frescoes and mosaics) with modern taxonomy.

The selection of the ancient fish names to be considered here depends on a simple criterion: to describe only the fish mentioned by the ancient writers in conjunction with Italian fishponds. Working from this premise, seven varieties of fish form the core of this study: the *murena, mugil, lupus, aurata, mullus, rhombus,* and the *scarus.* The relative importance of these seven varieties of fish is difficult to assess. A higher monetary value usually reflected a scarcer commodity. Thus, using the price of fish or the most prevalent species as criteria can be misleading. The order in which the fish are presented in this study reflects the frequency of their mention in the ancient literary sources in connection with fishponds but is by no means a comment on their relative "value."

MURENAE

Eels, called *murenae* and less often *anguillae* and *congri,* are the fish most often mentioned in connection with fishponds (Fig. 3). There was no obvious distinction among these terms aside from the frequency of their use. *Murena* is used in the vast majority of instances where fishponds are discussed and probably was the most generic term. As such, the name *murena,* as with many ancient zoological appellations, refers to several species and probably denoted any eel-like creature. Under this ancient classification, common eels (*Anguilla*), congers (*Conger oceanicus*), morays (actually belonging to the family *Muraenidae*), and to a lesser extent lampreys (*Petromyzon marinus*) could be denoted by the term *murenae*.[7]

The eel is able to live in salt, brackish, or fresh water at a wide range of temperatures. The eel's adaptability is exemplified by its incredible life cycle. Adult eels, silver in color (*Anguillae argentatae*), leave coastal lagoons, lakes, and streams where they have lived for most of their lives to swim into the Atlantic Ocean. There, at a point near the Sargasso Sea, they spawn, with one female producing about ten to twenty million eggs. Then the adults die while their fertilized eggs develop into a larval stage (*Leptocephali*). These larvae drift, sometimes for several years, before transforming themselves into small eel-like fish called elvers. These elvers leave the Sargasso and trek back "home." European, or Mediterranean, eels travel some nearly five thousand kilometers before reaching the bodies of water that their parents left years earlier. Columella (*Rust.* 8.16.10), cognizant of the eel's migratory habits, postulated that the *murena* originated in the far-off Carpathian and Tartessian Seas. His hypothesis probably reflects an ancient attempt at explaining the migratory habits of the *murena*. The elvers grow into adults (*Anguillae giallae* because of their yellowish undersides) and continue to grow in the sheltered and nutrient-rich environment of the coastal bodies of fresh and brackish water until they leave, having changed to a silver color, to continue the cycle.[8] This pattern, of being able to live in a variety of environments, is common to all of the anguilliforms (common eels, congers, morays, and lampreys) discussed here.

All anguilliforms have long slender bodies with very small scales (over a hundred per square inch). The common eel, or *anguilla*, does have a jawed mouth and pectoral fins. Females usually reach one meter in length while males are seldom longer than fifty centimeters. If confined and not allowed leave to spawn (*anguillae* do not spawn in captivity), the common eel can live for decades (fifty years being the record). The conger is very similar to the common eel in appearance through most of its life. In old age, the adult conger exceeds the size of the *anguilla* and will reach over two meters in length and weigh over ten kilograms. The moray — definitely jawed and with lobed pectoral fins — can reach almost two meters in length and weigh twenty to thirty kilograms.

According to Plautus the eel was popular in Rome as early as the second century B.C.[9] But it was in the first century B.C. that the eel was first raised on a large scale. For the Roman fishpond owner, the popularity of the *murena* was based on its ability to thrive in strange waters and to command a high price.[10] Raising of this particular fish was so closely associated with L. Licinius, grandfather of the consul for 62 B.C., that he supposedly earned the cognomen *Murena*.[11] The yield of fishponds could reach staggering levels. It is recorded that G. Hirrius, who is credited with the invention of ponds solely for raising eels, supplied six thousand *murenae* for the triumphal banquets of Julius Caesar in 46 and 45 B.C.[12]

Widespread cultivation of this fish gave rise to many stories concerning the extravagant and ridiculous use of eels. The orator Quintus Hortensius and the triumvir Marcus Licinius Crassus were said to have kept eels as pets and to have wept when they died.[13] *Murenae* were also adorned with jewelry, earrings and neckbands, and were trained to come at the call of their names. A pet *murena*, kept in the ponds of Hortensius at Baculo, was decorated with jewelry by Antonia, wife of Drusus. The fame of this eel is said to have made people eager to visit Baculo in order to view the spectacle.[14] In a more horrific vein, Vedius Pollio punished the occasional disobedient and clumsy slave by throwing the offender into his *piscinae* where the unfortunate servant was eaten by his *murenae*. The cruelty of this particular fishpond owner is widely reported in the ancient literary record.[15]

Aside from these sensational incidents concerning *murenae*, the eel could represent a real financial asset to the fishpond owner. Pliny records that after the death of Lucullus the fish from his fishpond sold for four million sesterces. The *modica villa* of Gaius Hirrius sold for the same price on account of its fishponds.[16] These prices must in part reflect the value of the *murena*, on account of their versatility and the relative ease with which they could be cultivated in artificial enclosures.

In Italy today, the eel is an important commercial fish. Modern studies of the fish raised in lagoonal fisheries along the coasts of Italy, support the contention that the eel was a most important fish.[17] In the fisheries located in the lagoons near Orbetello, eels account for 50 percent of the fish harvested. The annual yield per thousand square meters of pond area is approximately four tons! Producing this volume requires stocking the lagoons with a mere ten kilograms of elvers.[18] These numbers indicate how the eel could be cultivated in densities not possible with any other species of fish.

Harvesting *murenae* was facilitated by the eel's migratory nature. The tendency of elvers to make for protected coastal waters and of adult eels to return to the open sea meant that at some point great quantities of fish could be trapped in constricted waters. Pliny mentions eel migrations in Lacus Benacus (Lake Garda), where these fish were confined by the thousands in traps constructed in the narrows of a tributary.[19] Harvesting in this manner was an important concern because eels could swim or eat their way through lines and nets and thus were notoriously difficult to catch.[20]

MUGILES

The *mugil* was both caught and cultivated in great numbers by the Romans. The ancient term *mugiles* is associated with several species of gray mullet.[21] This variety of fish is common throughout the Mediterranean and frequents warm shallow waters. The species most common in the Mediterranean are the *Mugil cephalus*, *Mugil chelo*, *Mugil capito*, and *Mugil auratus*.

Gray mullets are blunt-nosed and small-mouthed fish that swim in schools. They eat by picking up mud from the bottom and straining plant and animal material through sievelike gill rakers and pharyngeal teeth. As adults they seldom exceed fifty centimeters in length and weigh less than one kilogram. Though a sea fish, the gray mullet can adapt to brackish or freshwater environments.[22] *Mugiles* are known to migrate from the sea into brackish lagoons and river estuaries during the fall and winter months. Responding to changes in temperature and salinity, these fish find a richer supply of food in the sheltered waters of the lagoon. In the warmer months they return to the sea to spawn.[23] Gray mullet are known for their ability to jump, particularly when swimming in densely packed schools. This tendency would have made *mugiles* difficult to keep in artificial enclosures. Yet, in modern Italy, the gray mullet is a major commodity in the organized fish industry that exploits the country's coastal lagoons. Modern coastal fisheries in Italy are equipped with enclosures possessing walls that project high above the surface of the water in order to foil the escape of leaping gray mullets.[24]

The *mugil* is not specifically mentioned as a source of food by the Romans, but the Greek writers Hicesius, Dorion, and Polemon, all belonging to the time of the early Empire, praise certain varieties of gray mullet.[25] Columella highly recommends the *mugil* to the prospective fishpond owner as a hearty fish able to withstand the rigors of confinement.[26] On the lighter side, the Elder Pliny adds that the gray mullet was remarkable on account of its acute hearing, which enabled it to come when its name was called.[27] Although not included among the table delicacies mentioned in the ancient literary sources, the many references to the *mugil* attest to its importance as a food fish and favorite of fishpond owners.[28]

LUPI

The *lupus* mentioned in the ancient texts presents some difficulty when one tries to associate it with modern species. The descriptions of this fish are limited to comments on the color of its meat (white), the pattern of its skin, and its place of origin.[29] Though described as a sea fish, the *lupus* was frequently caught in rivers and streams. Perhaps the best clue to its identification lies in the name, *lupus*. Hicesius, quoted by Athenaeus, says that the fish is known for its voracious appetite and feisty behavior.[30] Isidorus, explaining that the names of some fish are based on characteristics of land animals, uses similar language to describe the *lupus*.[31] Considering these pieces of information, the most likely identification for the ancient *lupus* lies within the family *Labridae* (perhaps *Labrax lupus*, or *Labrax dicentrarchus*), commonly called the spigola, wrasse, or sea bass.

Labridae can be found in most temperate waters in the Mediterranean. With projecting teeth and mouth, these fish feed on mollusks, crustaceans, and other creatures that inhabit the rocky bottom.[32] They are fundamentally a sea fish but can often be found in rivers, streams, lakes, and lagoons that are linked to the ocean.

The *lupus* or λάβραξ, as it was known to the Greeks, is described by the ancient sources as a fish that frequented areas where seawater blends with fresh water.[33] Its habit of swimming far up rivers coupled with its ability to survive in shallows made the *lupus* particularly well suited for cultivation in fishponds.[34] Considered an intelligent fish by the ancients, the *lupus* was difficult to catch and adept at escaping the contrivances of *piscatores*.[35] The *lupus* was esteemed by the Romans from the late Republic until at least the fifth century A.D. According to Pliny and Macrobius, *lupi* caught in the Tiber at Rome *inter duos pontes* were preferred most, presumably, on account of their flavor.[36] Fish from other rivers were held in less regard. Varro tells a story, often repeated, in which Marcius Philippus communicates his scorn for a *lupus* he tasted during a visit to Casinum. Recognizing it to be a local fish, Philippus exclaimed, "May I perish if I did not think it was a fish!"[37] Another variety preferred by Romans was the "wooly-white" *lupus* mentioned by Pliny and Martial.[38] This variety was so named on account of its white meat and distinguished from the Tiber *lupus*, which was spotted.[39]

AURATAE

The *aurata* (*Sparus aurata*) or gilthead is identified with the Greek χρύσοφρυς and today is commonly called porgy, bream, dentice, umbrina, or dorade. The name, according to Ovid and Pliny, results from the fish's golden color.[40] The *aurata* is a member of the family *Sparidae*, which are flat-bodied, side to side, and broad through the body just in front of the dorsal fin.[41] This fish is very adaptable and can live in environments that vary greatly in temperature and salinity. *Sparidae* are found throughout the Mediterranean and favor reefs and bottoms both rocky and sandy. They have the ability to change color and blend in with their surroundings to avoid predators. *Auratae* swim in schools and are omnivorous. Adults can reach nearly forty centimeters in length and weigh one and a half kilograms.

The *aurata* was renowned in antiquity for its flavor and its ability to be bred and kept in artificial enclosures. According to Columella, the *aurata* was one of the first fish, along with the *lupus*, to be cultivated by the Romans, who were able to raise this sea fish in freshwater lakes.[42] *Auratae* raised in the Lucrine Lake were especially prized by the Romans and several recipes that use the fish are recorded by Apicius.[43] Although they are listed as sea fish by the Elder Pliny, Columella notes that *auratae* were raised in freshwater fishponds as well. Sergius Orata built fishponds specifically designed for the *aurata* and, like Licinius Murena, received his cognomen from his association with the raising of fish.[44]

MULLI

The *mullus*, called τρίγλη in Greek, is known today as either the red mullet or the surmullet. *Mulli* belong to the family *Mullidae* and are commonly called goatfish due to their long chin whiskers or barbels.· These "whiskers" are used by the fish to probe the bottom for food, which consists mainly of crustaceans and other invertebrates. Most of the species are pale pink to orange in color and can intensify in hue when excited.[45] Some *mulli* travel in schools whereas others are solitary. As a family (*mullidae*), these fish seldom exceed thirty centimeters in length and weigh less than one kilogram. The larger *mullus surmuletus* is found in warm waters of the Mediterranean and the coastal Atlantic and is most prized for its flavor. This larger species can reach forty centimeters in length and weigh more than one kilogram. Today the smaller species, *mullus barbatus,* is more common and hence less expensive.

Favored by the ancient Greeks, the mullet enjoyed its greatest popularity during the late Republic and early Empire.[46] Roman writers made little distinction between the larger *mullus surmuletus* and the smaller *mullus barbatus* and indeed these *mulli* are difficult to tell apart.[47] The ancient distinction was one based on the size of the fish and where it was caught. Larger *mulli* were most prized on account of their taste while smaller ones were less favored. Though based on taste, the preference for larger *mulli* over smaller probably reflects the modern zoological division between the surmullet and red mullet.[48] The *mullus* is usually mentioned by Latin authors as an example of extravagance. The expense and scarcity of the fish elicited the comments of satirists and moralists who saw in the *mullus* a symbol of unbridled decadence. Martial called the mullet *inmodicus*, or excessive, and pokes fun at Caecilianus who was tempted by an unattended morsel of mullet and stole the leftover by hiding it in a napkin.[49] Juvenal states that the *mullus* was beyond a moderate income and was too expensive for a married man.[50]

The competition to possess a large *mullus* (in excess of one kilogram) reached such a pitch that the emperor Tiberius proposed regulating the price for the fish.[51] It is apparent that the large *mullus* preferred by the Romans should be identified with the species *mullus surmuletus* or surmullet. The equation of the luxurious *mullus* and the surmullet is supported by Martial who states that for a *mullus* to be considered a luxury two pounds (a little less than one kilogram) was the smallest allowable weight. He goes on to say that these fish can only be found in deeper waters.[52] The difficulty of finding such a fish and transporting it to the market in Rome made it a most expensive commodity. Horace thought all of the expense to obtain a large *mullus* was silly because the fish had to be cut up anyway for eating.[53] Despite the cynicism of some Romans, *mulli*

49

continued to be bought and sold for excessive sums of money. Seneca tells of an auction where a large mullet, weighing over two kilograms, was sold for 5,000 sesterces.[54] It was upon learning that three such fish were sold for 30,000 sesterces that the emperor Tiberius proposed his price-controlling measures.[55] Nevertheless, prices continued to climb in the years after the reign of Tiberius.[56] The mind boggles at the thought of what the eighty-pound mullet caught by Licinius Mucianus, which Pliny records, could have fetched its owner.[57] By the fifth century A.D. the craze for mullet had subsided. Moreover, *mulli* in excess of one kilogram were common and did not command the prices of four centuries earlier.[58]

The potential for great profit would have made the *mullus* a likely fish to cultivate in artificial enclosures. In all probability, Columella's warning that *mulli* could not be raised in fishponds refers to the large *mulli surmuleti* which are accustomed to the open sea and to a more solitary life. Undoubtedly, many of these fish were kept in fishponds, as were many exotic and rare species of fish, but never in numbers that would affect the market and lower their cost. Contrary to the opinion of Columella, Pliny states that the *mullus* was a plentiful fish and does suggest that attempts were made to cultivate it.[59] According to modern investigators, the contradiction between Columella and Pliny can be explained by the existence of two distinct types of *mulli*, *surmuleti* and *barbarti*, which the ancient authors misunderstood as a single class of fish.[60] The mullet referred to by Pliny is probably the small *mullus barbatus*, which rarely exceeded the weight of one kilogram and could be raised in artificial enclosures.

RHOMBI

The ancient *rhombus* or flatfish (*piscis planus*) refers to the fish belonging to the order *Pleuronectiformes*, which includes both left- and right-eye flounders and sole.[61] This order is most notable for the dramatic transformation of the fish's body. At birth, flatfish possess a "conventional" appearance symmetrically arranged on either side of their bodies as defined by the line of the dorsal fin. Shortly after hatching, a *Pleuronectiform* changes from a normal looking fish to an ungainly flat fish with both eyes protruding from one of its sides. Once the transformation is complete, the fish drifts to the bottom where it spends the rest of its life. Flatfish like to hide in the sand or mud at the bottom. Some species can change color to become less conspicuous to predators. Of this order, right-eye flounders are not common in the Mediterranean, while the brill (*Scophthalamus rhombus*) and the turbot (*Scophthalamus maxima*) are the most common left-eye flounders in the sea. These flatfish can reach nearly a meter in length and weigh ten kilograms. The sole, or *Solea*, is common in the Mediterranean and around Italy. It has a more rounded body than the flounder but shares with its cousin the ability to thrive in waters of varying degrees of temperature and salinity. The European sole can reach a length of fifty centimeters and weigh one and a half kilograms. This species of flatfish is commonly raised in lagoonal fisheries in Italy today.

The Romans used the term *rhombus* to denote all flatfish. The Greeks possessed two words for this type of fish: ῥόμβος and ψῆττα. Their exact relationship to the Roman *rhombus* is debated,[62] but Diphilus of Siphnos, active in the early third century B.C., is quoted by Athenaeus as saying that the ῥόμβος and ψῆττα are alike.[63] One variety of *rhombus*, called *citharus* by the Elder Pliny, is said to have been the least esteemed of the *rhombi*.[64] Except for Pliny's distinction, the term *rhombus* was used generically whereas the terms *solea* and *piscis planus* are used infrequently.

Horace, who ridicules the extravagance of serving this fish, says that the *rhombus* was considered very fashionable in the Augustan age.[65] The great width of the *rhombus* won accolades for presentation when served at the tables of wealthy hosts.[66] Both Columella and Martial indicate that the *rhombus* was popular with fishpond owners.[67] Juvenal, in his fourth satire, recounts an amusing tale of a huge *rhombus* to illustrate the despotic nature of the emperor Domitian. The fish was so large that no platter could be found to hold it. The crisis over how to cook and serve this choice specimen prompted Domitian to summon his councilors to discuss the matter.

SCARI

The *scarus* was the most popular fish in the Elder Pliny's time and it is frequently mentioned in the ancient literary sources.[68] The term *scarus* was used to identify the parrot wrasse, but was used for other species as well. The family *Scaridae*, or parrot fish, is found throughout the Mediterranean in warm and temperate waters. The fish's modern name comes from the parrotlike beak, which is used to break the hard outer layers of shellfish, crustaceans, and corals. It has large scales and usually is brightly colored. *Scaridae* are observed in groups but are not a schooling fish.[69] The fish was valued by the Romans, as is attested by the comments of Horace, who says it was a costly fish in his day. Pliny adds that the *scarus* was "first-rate at this time" (*principalis hodie*), surpassing the *lupus* and others.[70] In the *Satyricon* (93.2), Petronius listed the *scarus* among the delicacies that were difficult to obtain.

According to Macrobius, the parrot wrasse was not native to Italian waters. Pliny and Columella place the original home of the fish in the eastern Mediterranean.[71] But during the reign of the emperor Claudius, a freedman of the emperor, named Optatus, collected great numbers of *scari* and transported them in tanks aboard ship to the waters off Latium and Campania. According to Pliny, the parrot wrasse became common after this forced introduction.[72] Petronius and Suetonius attest to the expense and rarity of the *scarus* and seem to contradict the assertion of Pliny.[73] This, taken with the statement of Columella that the parrot wrasse did not adapt well to being confined in fishponds, makes Pliny's claim less credible.[74] There is no doubt that attempts were made at keeping parrot wrasse in artificial enclosures, but it seems apparent that they were not cultivated with a high degree of success.

OTHER SPECIES

There must have been many other species of fish that were, at one time or another, kept in fishponds by the Romans. The frequency with which the *acipenser* and *helops* (both sturgeons), *asellus* (hake), *scomber* (mackerel), and the tunny are mentioned in the literary sources makes these fish likely candidates for organized fish farming. Yet no connection with fishponds is even alluded to by the classical authors.[75] The habit of keeping fish as pets or ornaments, which has been documented in the case of the *murena, mugil,* and the *mullus,* could be seen in the many exotic species kept in a fishpond for personal enjoyment and display. Martial names several species of aquatic life that he deemed as suitable gifts. It is interesting that most were creatures commonly raised in artificial enclosures by the Romans.[76]

Despite the preference for saltwater species, the Romans tended to exploit those species of fish which were known to congregate in coastal waters, often where salt and fresh water mixed. The ability to thrive in a wide range of salinity was crucial to the selection of fish to be cultivated in fishponds. With the exception of the *mullus* and possibly the *scarus*, all of the principal varieties of fish exploited by the Romans fit the definition of euryhaline fish, or species that can live in both salt and fresh water. Attracted to variations in salinity and temperature, euryhaline fish are drawn to river estuaries, coastal lagoons and lakes, and seaside springs.[77] The reliable supplies of food fish in these waters would have attracted fishermen and impressed upon them the importance of the special conditions they required. A logical next step would have been to improve the control and harvest of the fishing grounds, and thus embark upon a primitive form of pisciculture.

FISH RAISED IN ROMAN *PISCINAE*

3

ROMAN FISHPONDS AS EMBLEMS OF SOCIAL STATUS

The resources expended on the construction and operation of Italian *piscinae* were beyond the grasp of most individuals and, therefore, the possession of an artificial fishpond was a mark of singular status. Consequently, the *piscinarii* of the late Republic drew considerable interest and excited the contemporary imagination. Modern studies of the social and economic histories of the personalities who raised fish during the late Republic and early Empire have relied primarily on ancient literary and epigraphic data.[1] The addition of the archaeological data further expands our understanding of this tumultuous time and documents the extent to which the social movements affect the material culture. Tracing the history of this specialized architectural form over time reveals an interesting pattern that appears to be tied to the major social changes underway during the late Republic and early Empire. To understand this connection between social status and fishpond ownership, it is best to explore the motives or impulses that lay behind the construction and operation of a fishpond.

The inclusion of pisciculture in the agricultural manuals of both Varro and Columella indicates that the gentleman farmer often engaged in the practice of raising fish. Both writers include the cultivation of fish with the raising of birds, bees, and rabbits as a form of animal husbandry (*pastio villatica*) that could supplement the income of the villa owner, thus implying that access to a ready food source would be one obvious benefit of owning a fishpond.[2] The villa owner could make use of the stocks inside the ponds to augment the diet of his household or, if the pond were large enough, the Roman fishpond owner could even provide fresh fish to neighboring villas or communities from his pond's surplus. However, there are difficulties in accepting this scenario to explain the popularity of fishpond ownership. Varro, through the words of Axius, states that *piscinae salsae*, seaside fishponds, are more pleasing to the eye than the purse and serve to exhaust resources rather than to increase them; he avers that saltwater fishponds are constructed, stocked, and maintained at great cost.[3] This is especially true if one considers the possibility that fish were scarce in the Mediterranean in antiquity due to the age of the sea and excessive fishing. The lack of fish off the coasts of Italy during the second century A.D. is suggested by Juvenal, who laments that imports were needed to meet Italian needs.[4] In addition, it was most difficult and expensive, without refrigeration, to transport fresh fish great distances.[5]

There was, however, great profit in the production of preserved fish and processed fish products. According to the literary record, several sites in Italy were known for the production of *garum, liquamen, allec, muria,* and other processed fish products.[6] Beneventum, Pompeii, Velia, and Thurii are singled out as centers of fish sauce production by ancient authors,[7] although, despite the literary commentary, there is little physical evidence of the processing of fish products in Italy.[8] The salteries of the type unearthed at sites in Spain and North Africa cannot be identified with certainty anywhere in the Italian peninsula.[9] Because Italian ponds exhibiting a more utilitarian or "industrial" design are not readily apparent in the archaeological record, the existence of fishponds in Italy cannot therefore be explained by commercial reasons alone.

As suggested already, the lack of documented links between the large *piscinae* of Roman Italy and the production of fish sauces cast doubt on commercial profit as a major factor in pond construction. In Italy, the paucity of fish off the coasts coupled with successful imports from Africa, Gaul, and Spain made an already risky venture economically precarious. In addition to the economic factors social pressures also were at play. Because the sellers of fish products, though sometimes wealthy, were deemed of low social status, it is unlikely that the *piscinarii* of the late Republic would have indulged in such extravagant behavior solely for the "disreputable" profit.[10]

The possession of a fishpond represented control over a scarce and, hence, valued resource, which had to be carefully managed to meet personal needs as well as serving to further the competitive ambitions of the pond owners. Because fish, saltwater species in particular, figured prominently in the diet of the upper classes, the market value of fish was driven by the demand from banquets and club dinners.[11] As a consequence, self-sufficiency was an important component of Roman aristocratic *otium*, and if political or social profit could be gleaned from the surplus, so much the better.

Most of the fishponds in Italy appear to have been designed so that effective fish raising could be coupled with the pleasure of owning a private body of water replete with aquatic life. Aside from the alimentary uses for fish, the fishpond owner could keep exotic species for show or merely as pets.[12] *Piscinae* were also built in public and even religious contexts, as is evidenced by the ponds in the Palestra at Herculaneum and the sanctuary at Santa Venera outside Paestum. Here, as in the context of a private garden, the fishpond functioned primarily as a decorative element. But in a cultic or religious setting the fish could have served an additional function pertinent to the rites of the cult, serving as cultic symbols or as conveyors of divine prediction.[13]

Monetary gain was not completely divorced from this practice. In the competitive climate of the late Republic, where an expensive and rare commodity carried such potent symbolic value, fish could and were vended not as regular trade but to feed the appetite of those wanting to impress rivals and peers. Thus ponds could be of economic value, but only if someone were willing to pay the steep prices recounted in the ancient testimonia. These same sources, however, stress the importance of possession over the sale or even the consumption of their fish.[14]

FISHPONDS AS EMBLEMS OF SOCIAL STATUS

A key to understanding the motivation for building *piscinae* in Italy lies in their rise and fall in popularity. The dates of surviving fishponds in Italy echo the attention paid by the authors of the late Republic and early Empire. The earliest remains of *piscinae* date from the beginning of the first century B.C., and most were built between the mid first century B.C. and the first quarter of the first century A.D. After the end of the first century A.D. the archaeological remains record the restoration of preexisting fishponds but little new construction. The physical remains alone present a rather complex picture that does not lend itself to easy interpretation, and the line between commercial viability and sheer pleasure is a blurred one. Nonetheless, examination of the architectural remains of fishponds in Italy tends to confirm the image communicated in the ancient literary record, suggesting that pleasure overshadowed profit as a principal motive for owning a fishpond.

Most ruins identified as Roman fishponds are found on islands and along the coast of western Italy between the island of Pianosa to the north and the Bay of Naples to the south. Almost all of the *piscinae* considered in this study are associated with some certainty with villas or other private dwellings.[15] The locations of these residences were chosen often to exploit the panoramic vistas of the seashore and were located on some of the choicest pieces of real estate in Italy. It is clear that the possession of these sites required considerable resources and the owners must have been from the elite of Roman society.[16] To judge from the ancient literary commentary of the time, owning a fishpond was a mark of distinction associated with celebrity. Those Romans singled out by Varro, Columella, the Elder Pliny, and others as possessing *piscinae* come from the upper strata of Roman society. This ancient literary tradition records that these seaside fishponds could be economic liabilities and considers this "fad" a form of aristocratic hobby. This is a central theme in numerous anecdotes preserved in the literary record; they describe the extravagances and excesses associated with fishpond ownership. Among the most notable were the fishponds of Q. Hortensius in his villa at Bauli,[17] those belonging to L. Licinius Lucullus in his villas at Misenum and Neapolis,[18] those of C. Hirrius near Baia,[19] those of Servilius Vatia at his villa on an effluence of Lago del Fusaro,[20] and those of L. Marcius Philippus.[21] Q. Hortensius, as is recounted by Varro, did not eat the fish of his own ponds but sent to Pozzuoli for fish to supply his table, and employed many fishermen just to supply fry for his private preserve of fish.[22] Varro reports that, in order to feed the fish in his ponds, C. Hirrius required all of the revenue produced by the buildings surrounding his *piscinae*, some twelve thousand sesterces.[23]

The wealthy of the late Republic eagerly sought an escape from political duty (*negotium*) in Rome, and the construction and operation of fishponds were tied to the competition among this ruling elite.[24] Their elaborate villas, many with attendant *piscinae*, communicating the image of wealth and higher status, were emblematic of the opulence of this age. Most of the Roman fishponds in Italy that survive in the archaeological record were constructed in beautiful settings and designed to be attractive in their own right. In spite of the elaborate efforts to build and maintain impressive fishponds, some have seen them as examples of a pathological need for excessive luxury and extravagant displays.[25] Although the ponds of L. Lucullus succeeded in impressing Pompey, the latter hung the somewhat pejorative epithet of *Xerxes togatus* on his rival.[26]

Although Varro's account provides some technical information, he devotes most of his attention to anecdotes describing the excesses and extravagances of fishpond owners, or *piscinarii*. Nor is his attitude surprising in light of the physical remains. The larger *piscinae* with their elaborate tanks, walkways, gates, and nearby ports were clearly equipped with more features than were needed for purely personal use. Even the largest ponds were built with elements designed to facilitate the enjoyment of the fishpond. The desire for *otium* and *luxuria*, which centered around the fishpond, included dining, leisure fishing, and general sightseeing, activities that can be imagined as taking place at large and small *piscinae* alike.[27]

The enclosure of offshore property could convert public domains (*res publicae*) to private (*res privatae*). Any physical structures placed in the water belonged to the owner and these gave him preferential access to the adjacent waters.[28] Fishpond construction allowed Roman aristocrats of the Republic to extend the domain in which they lived and where they could enjoy their leisure time. Villa architecture enabled the owner to possess and even control elements of his natural environment.[29] In an aesthetic vein, *piscinae* were included among the varied *topiaria opera* (landscape gardening), which united elements of nature with the artistic and architectural aspects of villa design, and the ability to expend resources on such projects was a mark of singular status.[30]

The addition of fishponds to private villa architecture added the potential piscine resources of the sea to the traditional animal and plant products of the common farmstead. This also allowed the villa to be more self-sufficient and perhaps realize some financial return from any surplus.[31] The self-contained and self-sufficient villa offered leisure activity or *otium*, which was a welcome respite from the more onerous and restrictive environment in Rome.

Social status of individuals during the Roman Republic depended on a number of factors: birth, political aptitude, ownership of property, money, ambition. All of these were enhanced by the ability to exploit the economic boom of the late Republic and to avoid the political intrigues of this chaotic time.[32]

The possession of an artificial fishpond fulfilled many of these criteria for elevated status during the late Republic. *Piscinae*, like the villas they are often associated with, were frequently decorated so as to appeal to the viewer and involved sizable expenditures that were plainly visible. The fishpond itself was an unusual form of architecture, requiring sophisticated and expensive technology to construct and operate. The distinctive characteristics of *piscinae* and their fish made the possession more unique and valued during such keen competition. It is also apparent that these conspicuous displays of wealth by the *piscinarii* appealed to public fascination. Their behavior became the basis of tales that spread the reputation and reinforced social status to those who could not have been eyewitnesses to these unusual structures.

This practice of unbridled luxury incurred the wrath of the orator Cicero, who railed against the fishpond owners for being so preoccupied with their fish that they were neglecting the affairs of the Republic.[33] Although this sentiment was confined to the private correspondence of the orator and not part of any public outrage, it is implicit in the evidence for the extravagant activities of the republican elite that much time and resources were spent away from Rome and the traditional avenues of aristocratic power.

The abandonment of the "traditional" roles for the elite reflected in the time and resources spent on large *piscinae* paved the way for the autocratic control under the Empire. The decline in interest in large *piscinae* during the first century A.D. is reflected both in the literary accounts and the archaeological record. The mention of fishponds by ancient authors after the end of the first century A.D. is scarce and often nostalgic.[34] Surveys of the archaeological remains indicate that with the coming of the imperial age new construction of seaside fishponds became increasingly rare. The fishpond had become an option for the owners of small villas and houses and could be used to decorate public and sacred areas, as the advances in concrete and hydraulic technologies made the fishpond less difficult to construct and consequently less exclusive to own. New construction of fishponds was typified by smaller structures, usually built at inland sites, and fed by fresh water from the water systems built during the reign of Augustus and later. Not mentioned in the literary sources, inland ponds were sited primarily in garden settings and in homes much less opulent than the fishponds associated with seaside *villae maritimae*. The choice of a fishpond at these inland sites reflects the tendency of house and small villa owners to imitate on a reduced scale the luxury appointments found in the larger seaside villas.[35] It is logical to assume that any surplus from these ponds could be sold to generate some revenue, but for the owner of a small *piscina*, the possession of a private stock of fish would be useful for banquets and gifts.[36] The giving of a fish was one way by which the fishpond owner could show his wealth and status. Martial ridiculed the social climber Papylus who dines poorly at home but sends expensive fish (*mulli*) as gifts to make an important social impression.[37]

Small inland fishponds, typical of the new *piscinae* being built in the first century A.D., might have characterized the practice that Columella called "especially praiseworthy and respectable."[38] Such modesty is reflected in the smaller costs associated with building new but smaller enclosures or even repairing preexisting fishponds and would not have entailed the great cost associated with the large *piscinae* of the late Republic. As a consequence, pisciculture under the Empire did not attract the same degree of attention from ancient authors as the efforts of the *piscinarii* in the previous century. The very nature and style of the literary accounts illustrate this change. The anecdotal accounts of Varro, Cicero, and others contrast with the more technical treatment of Columella who describes the practice of raising fish almost a century after Varro. Building on the account of Varro, Columella is able to place Roman pisciculture in a historical framework, which included the humble beginnings of Rome's early history, the extravagances of the *piscinarii* during the Republic, and the respectability accorded the practice of raising fish in Columella's own day.[39] There is scant mention of fishponds or their owners in ancient literature after the first century A.D.[40]

Other factors appear to have a more direct bearing on the decline in popularity of fishponds. Policies instituted during the early principate tended to separate political from commercial elites. The costs associated with the maintenance of political status were hefty and there was little sympathy for those who squandered their resources.[41] In addition, under the principate, the senatorial order lost the power to conduct foreign policy, wage war, and oversee financial affairs—all lucrative sources of income under the Republic.[42] The extravagance associated with fishpond ownership did not fit this new model for the imperial political elite, although, despite growing imperial control, many continued to test these limits. A Lex Julia, which sought to set specific limits on the amounts lavished on banquets and dinners, illustrates the attempt by the emperor Augustus, albeit futile, to curtail behavior characteristic of the *piscinarii*. The display and consumption of pond-raised fish at banquets and private dinners directly communicated the advantaged status of owning a *piscina*. Eventually, the inefficacy of the Lex Julia was offset by the financial obligations required under the principate.[43] Tacitus observed, in his own day, that luxurious banquets had gradually declined in popularity when compared with practices in the Julio-Claudian period.[44]

In Italy, with the beginning of the principate, the popularity of the large *piscina* begins to wane. Any social or political benefit from owning these structures decreased with the recognition of a single power at the top of the Roman social pyramid. In the imperial period aristocratic power could be found increasingly in the provinces and was not centered in the Italian peninsula. The emperor, over time, discouraged such displays as building large artificial fishponds among the Roman aristocracy and gathered unto himself an exclusive right to such behavior. The emperor did not suspend the right to raise fish but rather undermined the foundation upon which pisciculture had operated in Roman Italy. Increasingly, the wealth of Rome's elite was regulated under the principate and with its monopoly on power traditional competition lost much of its significance. It was not a direct suppression that curtailed the activities of the *piscinarii* but the loss of the drive to compete.[45] In Rome senators were quick to alter their behavior while the republican form of self-advertisement continued for some time in the towns outside the capital. With the vast majority located away from Rome, *piscinae* lingered as part of villa architecture in Italy until economic pressures made large structures impractical.[46]

Still, the allure of these structures lingered in the stories recounted in the literature of the early Empire and smaller versions of the ponds of the *piscinarii* could be found in cities like Pompeii where owners sought on a reduced, and less threatening, scale to emulate the status of the nabobs of the late Roman Republic. The social correlation emphasized in the ancient literary record is substantiated by the archaeological remains.

Moreover, with the advent of Augustus, many of the sites where fishponds could be found ended up in imperial hands.[47] The banishments of Augustus's daughter Julia and Agrippa Postumus suggest imperial ownership of property at Surrentum (Sorrento) and control of the islands of Planasia (Pianosa) and Pandataria (Ventotene).[48] Throughout the first century A.D., despite some efforts on the part of Tiberius, the large seaside villas increasingly became part of imperial estates.[49] The emperor imitated or took over the senatorial pattern of villa life typical of the late Republic,[50] and as the villas with their fishponds were passing into the hands of the imperial household, the popularity of this type of architecture became restricted to structures of modest scale. The coincidence of decline of both large fishponds and Rome's traditional elite argues for an important social explanation rather than one determined solely by the marketplace.

This same social correlation appears significant in the design and setting of small inland ponds. The popularity of freshwater *piscinae* during the first century A.D. is based, in part, on the example set by the *piscinarii* of the late Republic and by the changing mode of social and political interaction.

The luxuriant life-styles of the republican elite fostered an image of success and wealth coveted by those of lesser means. Cicero, critical of the excesses of some of Rome's aristocracy, assailed L. Licinius Lucullus for the bad example he set for his neighbors.[51] At Tusculum, Lucullus's villa lay between two opulent residences belonging to his neighbors, an *eques* and a freedman. Lucullus complained that he should be entitled to at least the same luxury as his neighbors of lower station. Cicero replied that the neighbors' desire for luxury was Lucullus's own fault and that it was his example that was being imitated. As one of the *piscinarii*, Lucullus helped make the fishpond a symbol of financial and social success, a symbol copied by others.

Changes under the principate progressively eliminated the traditional avenues of aristocratic self-advertisement and placed more emphasis on local or private displays of status. Social and political power was wielded more and more through informal meetings, or contacts in private settings.[52] The symbolic importance of the fishpond continues into the early Empire. Distinctions in social status could be articulated not only

FISHPONDS AS EMBLEMS OF SOCIAL STATUS

by comparing one house to another but also by domestic interiors and access to various parts of the house.[53] Here, the placement and setting of the fishpond accentuated the relative status of the visitors while communicating the wealth and position of the owner. Placement of *piscinae* within Pompeian houses emphasizes the visual impact in both public and private settings. Viewed from the *atrium* or *tablinum*, the pond is a reminder of republican aristocratic privilege and high status and confers on the owner a measure of that prestige. Public acts, such as the *salutatio*, would take place in this atmosphere. Direct access would be restricted by the architecture of the house, thus reinforcing the social distinction between the casual visitors and the owner.

An invitation into the garden would move the visitor closer to the "corridors of power" and would be indicative of a higher station. The decorative refinements of the pond and the specific varieties of fish within could be observed upon close inspection of the *piscina*. Focus on the fishpond was maintained even in the most private of gathering places. The strategic placement of dining *triclinia, biclinia*, and *oeci* placed the *piscina* center stage during private meetings and banquets. Here, political and social peers could plan, deal, eat, or just amuse themselves while the owner basked in the trappings of aristocratic splendor. Fish taken fresh from the pond would add an exotic dimension to the meal and highlight the gastronomic taste of the owner.

In this private and domestic context, *piscinae* became more popular with a growing segment of the Italian population who had long aspired to the standards of luxury established during the late Republic. By the end of the first century A.D., wider dissemination of the fishpond tended to debase its social importance and to obscure its symbolism. The possession and use of fishponds were tied to the changes in the social climate that marked the transition from the late Republic to the early Empire. As a symbol of status and wealth, the fishpond becomes an informative social index for Roman Italy.

CONCLUSIONS

The cultivation of fish in Italy enjoyed a long tradition among the Romans. In particular, during the later Roman Republic and the early Empire, the practice of raising fish, pisciculture, reached a level of complexity previously unknown. This interest led to the development and construction of a range of buildings designed to facilitate the exploitation and enjoyment of fish. The ancient literary sources present a cursory account of the practice of raising fish. While verifying the Roman fascination in pisciculture, the literary record falls short in detailing the variety of architectural designs and the contexts in which fishponds are found. With the addition of information obtained by examining the archaeological remains of fishponds built in Italy during the late Republic and early Empire, a more vivid picture is created of the practice of raising fish in artificial enclosures.

Seaside *piscinae* were the most famous among ancient writers and most popular among the elite of ancient Rome. The association of fishponds with Rome's more wealthy citizens is confirmed by the remains of both large elaborate *piscinae* and the general opulence of the villas found in conjunction with these ponds. The high degree of architectural variation and the general complexity of most seaside ponds indicate that considerable resources were devoted to the construction of these structures.

The construction of fishponds also involved a considerable degree of technical expertise. The examination of the *piscinae* in Italy shows that the builders of fishponds considered the following diverse and often complex factors: the optimal site for constructing a *piscina*; the source of water and how to control it; the suitable construction technique, in particular, the facility of building with hydraulic concrete; the habits and behavior of fish; the importance of brackish environments to attract and maintain schools of fish; the decorative appearance of the pond; and the potential impact, whether social or economic, on the persons who owned and operated such structures.

The practice of building artificial fishponds in Italy had its period of greatest popularity from the first century B.C. until the end of the first century A.D. This was a time of dramatic social and political change in the Roman Empire. The artificial fishpond flourished then as a symbol of aristocratic wealth, tied to the social aspirations of Rome's elite. Possession of a fishpond demonstrated a control over nature and the resources with which to accomplish this in dramatic fashion. Aside from the practical advantage of having one's own source of fish, the construction and operation of fishponds constituted displays of conspicuous consumption — activities characteristic of Rome's republican elite.

The creation of the principate under Augustus began a process through which the active competition among the ruling classes was reduced and power as well as property was transferred in greater measure to the imperial household. Imperial controls on the financial activities of Rome's elite limited the resources that could be expended on fishpond construction and operation. During the early years of the Empire the large seaside villas increasingly became part of imperial estates.[1] As the large fish-producing structures gradually passed into the hands of the imperial household, the popularity of this type of architecture became restricted to structures of modest scale. In addition, Rome's

CONCLUSIONS

imperial elite became less and less Italian and preferred to build their leisure dwellings in other parts of the Empire.[2] The coincidence of decline of both fishponds and Rome's traditional elites argues for a social explanation rather than one determined by the marketplace. Despite the apparent potential for commercial profit, the construction of fishponds in Italy declined with the rise of imperial control and appears to have been linked to this social transformation. In the face of commercial competition from other parts of the western Mediterranean and the reduction of competition between Roman elites, the large seaside fishpond faded from the Italian scene, to be eclipsed by smaller, inland imitations of the ponds built by the *piscinarii* of the Republic.

These smaller ponds became popular under the Empire. Often built inland, in structure they were less pretentious than their larger cousins and certainly did not convey the sense of extravagance and opulence equated with the ponds of Lucullus, Hortensius, Hirrius, or Murena. Still, the desire to control nature remained an important motivation for owning and operating the smaller *piscinae*. In a fishpond, the owner found a structure that could be pleasing to the eyes and, at the same time, supply a prized source of food for his table and for others. These basic impulses led the owners of smaller houses and villas to imitate the grand *piscinae* of the late Republic.

During the two centuries, in which fishponds enjoyed their greatest popularity, open competition among the elite of the Republic led to civil wars, and eventually gave way to the autocratic rule of the Empire. The consolidation of power under the emperors, who discouraged the conspicuous display of wealth and status common in the Republic, parallels the gradual demise in the popularity of the fishpond in the first century A.D.

Cassiodorus, Latin secretary for Theodoric the Great and Athalaric, relished the Avernan oysters grown in ponds, which must have been in operation as late as the sixth century A.D.[3] His enthusiasm for fish raising is reflected in the ponds he had constructed at Vivarium near modern Squillace.[4] Before retiring to Vivarium, Cassiodorus collected manuscripts of classical literature that would be useful to the inhabitants of his monastic retreat. These included the works of Columella, whose treatise on Roman pisciculture would have been invaluable to the builder of Italy's last documented Roman fishpond.[5]

CONCLUSIONS

GAZETTEER OF FISHPONDS IN ROMAN ITALY

What follows is a descriptive inventory of the Roman fishponds from the late Republic and early Empire that survive in the Italian archaeological record. *Piscinae* from other locations in the Mediterranean are mentioned when they contribute information absent from the Italian examples. Description is confined to those enclosures designed for the confinement, cultivation, and harvesting of fish. Adjacent buildings are included when they clarify the contexts in which these *piscinae* were constructed and functioned. Monuments in this corpus are organized geographically, beginning in Etruria and proceeding southward (Fig. 7).

The islands of the Tyrrhenian Sea and the western coast of Italy, from opposite the island of Elba to the site of Paestum on the Gulf of Salerno, are littered with seaside and submerged architectural remains of the

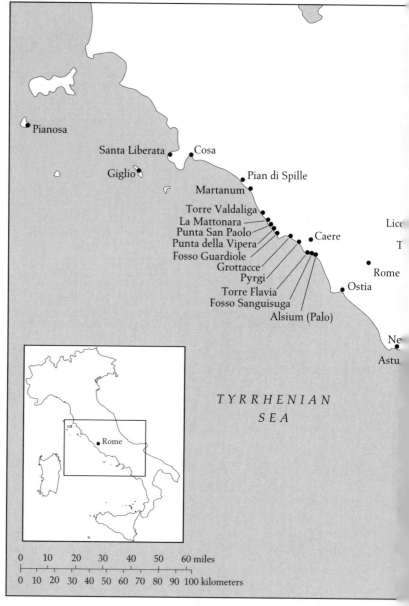

FIGURE 7. Map of Central Italy, with locations of the principal fishponds.

Roman epoch. Most of these are difficult to identify in terms of form or function and difficult to study due to the general rise in sea level over the past two millennia.[1] Many *piscinae* that lie inland have suffered due to subsequent construction, or remain buried among the ruins of Roman villas. The fishponds that best preserve details of their construc-

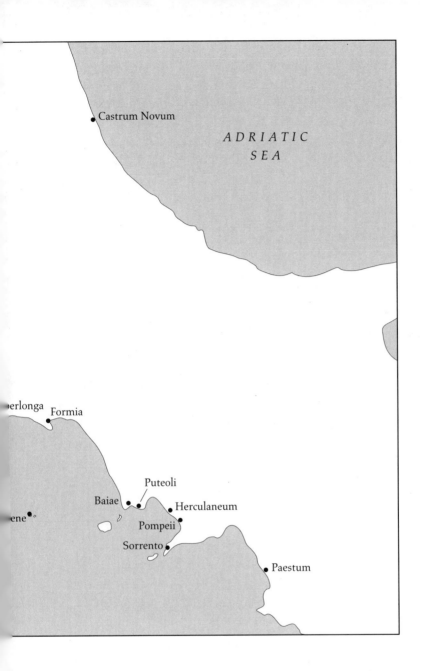

tion and function are the focus of this study. Other less informative remains are noted but receive less attention. Measurements and descriptions of the fishponds result from both on-site examinations and careful
study of published accounts. In the course of studying the remains in
situ, previously published data were verified or, in some cases, modified.

GAZETTEER OF FISHPONDS

The fifty-six sites included in this study are the locations of the major monuments in Italy that could be identified as having been designed to hold fish. In Roman Italy there are countless pools and basins that, conceivably, could have held fish. The vast majority of these probably held water for other purposes (i.e., drinking, bathing, swimming, etc.) and their designs reflect no special accommodation for fish. Consequently, many of these structures are not included in this study. Due to poor preservation or inaccessibility of the remains, the descriptions of the *piscinae* at Pian di Spille, Martanum, Punta San Paolo, Torre Flavia, Nettuno, Scauri, Capua, Pozzuoli, and Pausilypon are based entirely on published reports and plans.

The collection of monuments presented here is the most complete corpus of Roman *piscinae* in Italy. The fishponds noted by Giulio Schmiedt included only those which contributed to the understanding of the changes in sea level since antiquity and, as such, constituted a selective list, which ignored the numerous examples of inland *piscinae*. Systematic excavation was not possible within the scope of this study. Visual and graphic analyses were employed to render the most accurate and complete descriptions of the fishponds included in this book. The data collected in this gazetteer serve as a basis for the examination of the geographic distribution of Roman fishponds, their architectural design, techniques employed in their construction, how fishponds worked, what fish they held, and the chronological range of these buildings.

ETRURIA

Pianosa — I Bagni di Agrippa (Fig. 8)

The island of Pianosa, ancient *Planasia*, is located 20 kilometers southwest of the island of Elba off the western coast of northern Italy. Just northwest of the port of Teglia, positioned on the shore are the ruins of a *villa maritima* with remnants of two Roman fishponds situated in the sea. The villa is identified as that of the nephew of the emperor Augustus, Marcus Agrippa Postumus, who was exiled to the island in A.D. 7.[2] The remains were described for the first time in 1833 by Giuli and the first systematic study was undertaken by Chierici in 1874.[3] The action of the sea, time, and the construction of walls for a penal colony in 1955 have taken their toll on the ruins of this villa and its accompanying

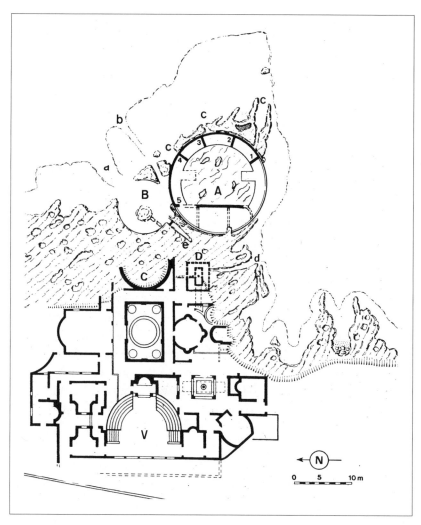

FIGURE 8. Pianosa—plan of the villa called I Bagni di Agrippa. **A** = large rock-cut fishpond with tanks 1–5; **B** = small rock-cut fishpond; **C** = *exedra*; **D** = cistern; **V** = villa; **a** and **b** = channels into fishpond B; **c** = openings into fishpond A; **d** and **e** = freshwater canals. (From G. Schmiedt, ed., *Il livello antico del Mar Tirreno* [Florence 1972] 42, pl. 38)

structures.[4] Long held to be part of an elaborate bath complex, the *piscinae* were first identified as fishponds by A. Olschki in 1970.[5]

These fishponds (A, B) are circular in plan and lie side by side on a rocky shelf which extends into the sea. The enclosures were cut from the rock, and concrete walls were added to complete the circular forms and to provide barriers dividing the pond interiors. Both fishponds are protected by the natural formations of rock, which form the arcing perimeters of the enclosures. These barriers are broken at irregular intervals by fissures in the rock which may have been used as channels, or *itinera* (a, b, c), permitting seawater to circulate through the enclosure. Today, the prevailing surf moves from northeast to southwest lashing the north and east sides of the rocky shelf which projects into the sea. The positions of the ponds on the shelf allow the force of the incoming surf to circulate seawater within both structures. Crude channels cut into the rocky shelf, two (a and b) on the north side and three (c) on the east side, permit communication between the open sea and both the large (A) and small (B) *piscinae*.

Fresh water was conveyed into these fishponds from a large cistern (D) in the adjacent villa (V) just to the west and a little above the ponds. The partly preserved remains of two rock-cut canals (e and d) are located between the cistern and the ponds, one (e) leading to the small *piscina* B and the other (d) running to the south. Canal "e," which appears to run from the cistern to the small fishpond, is in a better state of repair. It is 6.2 meters long, 70 centimeters wide toward its source, and widens to 1.2 meters as it enters the pond. The depth of the cutting is approximately 1 meter but precise measurements could not be obtained because the canal is filled with much debris. A small concrete barrier positioned inside this canal 60 centimeters from the pond and 30 centimeters below the top of the canal served to block the water's flow just long enough for sediment to fall and clean water to pass through.

The larger of the two ponds (A) is 17 meters in diameter with its deepest portion cut in a circle just inside its perimeter. This leaves the center higher and preserves the original rocky terrain in the pond's center. Allowing for the general rise in sea level since the pond's construction, this central area would have appeared as an island in the middle of the enclosure.[6] A broad concrete wall (approximately 80 centimeters wide) lines the inside of the seaward perimeter of the pond. Correcting for the change in sea level, this wall would have projected above the water level, providing both a barrier against the sea and a walkway around the *piscina*.

Following the line of the concrete wall, an arcing tank parallels a little over two-thirds of pond A circumference (the north, east, and south sides). This C-shaped tank is 2.3 meters wide on the north side of the enclosure and tapers gradually to a width of 1.6 meters at the pond's south end. Radially aligned walls, fashioned of hydraulic concrete, extend inward from the fishpond's perimeter and divide the arcing enclosure into five sections or tanks (1–5). The lower portions of these tanks are cut in the rocky shelf, and the upper walls were constructed of concrete, now badly eroded. The precise depth of this portion of the pond is impossible to determine due to the accumulation of debris. Measurable depths range from 80 centimeters to 1 meter below the level of the central island. The remaining third of the *piscina* is sectioned off by a wall running north to south. Chierici noted remains of three walls (shown in broken lines on the plan), now in ruin, which ran east to west and subdivided this portion into three separate tanks. Three openings (c) in the pond's perimeter (in the northeast and east sides of the enclosure) permitted seawater to circulate inside.

Pond B is approximately 10 meters in diameter and is in a poorer state of repair than pond A. There is no evidence for internal subdivisions like those in the larger *piscina*. The line of the pond's western half is discernible where it was cut into the rocky shore. Adjacent to the large fishpond (A), where the terrain falls away, the rocky surface was leveled, probably to support a wall of concrete. The natural rock rises to form the eastern side of the pond and again falls away to the northeast.

Two channels (a and b) cut into the shelf to the east and northeast of the pond eased the flow of seawater toward the enclosure. There are no remains of the perimeter protecting the northeast side of the pond. The opening in the fishpond's east side is preserved having been cut through the living rock. Fresh water was directed into the *piscina* from a cistern in the villa through a rock-cut canal mentioned earlier. Here too, loose rocks and architectural debris make accurate depth calculations impossible.

The villa (V) associated with these ponds was situated so as to take in a panorama of the sea. Its slight elevation (about 3 meters above the projecting shelf) affords an almost theatrical view of the water and the fishponds below. A small *exedra* (C), which may have supported cavea seating, faces the sea and is aligned directly with the small pond (B).

As the only known villa complex on the island, the structure is commonly connected with the exile residence of Postumus Agrippa.[7] The existence of a villa before A.D. 7 is implied by Varro.[8] The evidence of the villa's architecture allows for a pre-Augustan phase with a major rebuilding in the mid first century A.D.[9] Unfortunately, the building materials do not make clear to which phase the *piscinae* belong. The fondness for curvilinear forms in the villa's second phase however makes a first century A.D. date for the circular fishponds probable.

Santa Liberata—Villa Domiziana (Figs. 9, 10)

The promontory of Santa Liberata, on the Monte Argentario near Porto Santo Stefano, was the site of a Roman villa the remains of which are commonly called the Bagni di Domizio or simply the Villa Domiziana.[10] The villa was elevated 10 to 12 meters above the sea. Below the villa and extending out into the sea are the remains of a rectangular fishpond. The villa and its fishpond were first documented by Raffaele Del Rosso in 1905 (Fig. 9).[11] Since the study by Del Rosso, the fishpond at Santa Liberata was noted by Richard Bronson and Giovanni Uggeri in 1970,[12] and figured in the calculations of the historical changes in sea level by Giulio Schmiedt.[13] The remains of the villa or the fishpond have not undergone any systematic excavation or study since the beginning of this century.

The fishpond (Fig. 10) was constructed of concrete walls founded on a rocky shelf which forms a nearly level platform under the sea. The concrete included tufa rubble and ceramic shards as aggregate in a sandy mortar. A wide protective mole forms three sides of this rectangular pond; a thinner wall along the shoreline completes the enclosure. The concrete mole is more than 6 meters wide (the north side is 6.1 meters wide, the east side is 6.4 meters wide, and the west side is 7.2 meters wide) and rises nearly 1.4 meters from the ocean floor.[14] The resulting rectangle encloses an area 40.9 meters north-south by 28.1 meters east-west. The main pond was bisected by a wall 1.56 meters wide (A), which ran east to west 26.3 meters from the northern wall of the enclosure. Only 7.2 meters of this dividing wall remain connected to the west wall of the enclosure. The interior of the enclosure is littered with concrete debris, probably from the internal structures of the fishpond or the villa on the promontory above the pond. Del Rosso, who saw the pond in a better state of preservation, reconstructed a lozenge-shaped tank in the southern portion of the enclosure south of the dividing wall mentioned earlier. The poor state of preservation of the fishpond's southeast corner makes it difficult to reconstruct the dimensions of this section with any certainty.

In addition to the protective perimeter, the fishpond was provided with three blocklike piers (Fig. 9:B) arrayed to the west of the enclosure. These piers vary in size from 5.7 to 11.5 meters square and were posi-

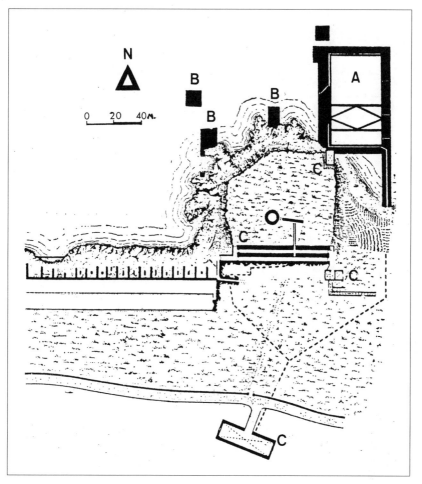

FIGURE 9. Santa Liberata—plan of the Villa Domiziana. **A** = concrete fishpond; **B** = piers; **C** = cisterns and subcisterns. (From R. Del Rosso, *Pesche e peschiere antiche e moderne nel-l'Etruria marittima* I [Florence 1905] 98)

tioned to break the force of the prevailing surf, which is from the west. It is possible that the piers had the additional purpose of providing points of anchorage for boats, which could serve the needs of the villa and supply the fishpond with fresh catch. This is the most plausible explanation for the pier located immediately off the northwest corner of the fishpond. Two other piers were anchored on the shore, while a fourth was located more than 77 meters directly to the west of the fishpond's western wall. These positions, while breaking the most deleterious waves, did not prevent the wave action from circulating seawater through the

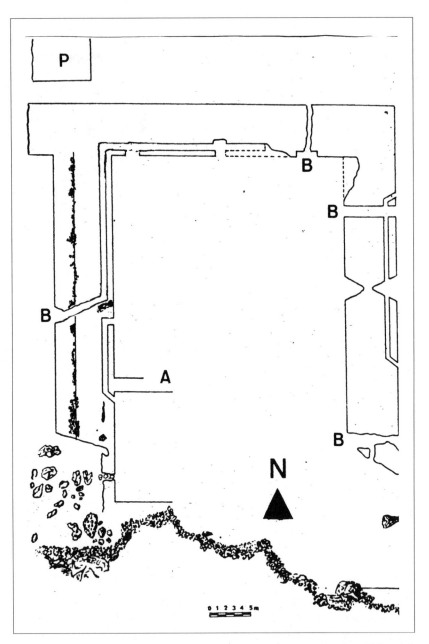

FIGURE 10. Santa Liberata—plan of the fishpond. **A** = remains of interior dividing wall; **B** = openings through the mole; **P** = corner pier. (From G. Schmiedt, ed., *Il livello antico del Mar Tirreno* [Florence 1972] 27, pl. 22)

fishpond. Thus, the three westernmost piers served more to calm the area west of the fishpond, which was amply protected by its own substantial moles.[15]

The circulation of water within the fishpond was accomplished by channels pierced through and conduits carried along the top of the perimeter mole of the enclosure. Del Rosso's plan of 1905 shows four openings to the sea, three through the east wall and one through the west. Today, it is possible to make out two openings in the eastern mole, one through the western mole and another, cut after construction, piercing the northern mole (Fig. 10:B). The best preserved opening or *iter* is the single channel, 1.2 meters wide and 6.4 meters long, that pierces the eastern side of the fishpond. The bottom of this channel is obscured by rocks and debris but is at least 70 centimeters below the top of the enclosure walls. The damaged state of the southeast corner of the enclosure has made impossible any reliable reconstruction of the two openings noted by Del Rosso. At the extreme southeast corner of the pond, a line visible in the concrete may be the only vestige left of the other channels on this side.[16] The faint traces of the channel through the west wall of the fishpond can be discerned today. This channel, approximately 80 centimeters wide, runs diagonally through the wall and stops 75 centimeters from the interior of the enclosure. Debris that chokes the channel makes a precise description difficult.[17] The concrete enclosure has many chunks missing from its walls and debris has made the seabed indistinguishable from the architecture.

The thick walls of the fishpond also were provided with conduits that distributed fresh water into the enclosure. The fresh water was conveyed from a system of cisterns incorporated into the villa on the promontory above (Fig. 9:C). The remains of the primary cistern lie on the slope of the hill 162 meters south of the fishpond. Del Rosso observed conduits running from this cistern to subsidiary cisterns serving both the villa and the fishpond. Once lowered from the promontory, fresh water was carried in wall-top channels along the southern and western walls of the enclosure. Today, it is difficult to discern the precise course of these channels because of the accumulation of sediment and debris along the mole.

On the promontory above the pond are the remains of vaults that supported the terraces of a seaside villa. This structure and the fishpond have been associated with the Domitii Ahenobarbi, thus the modern name of the site, the Villa Domiziana. Walls and tumbled remains of architecture faced in *opus incertum, reticulatum,* and brick attest to multiple phases of construction. By comparing the mortars in faced remains with that of the *piscina,* it is possible to associate the pond with walls faced in *opus reticulatum.* The mortar and tufo aggregate are not inconsistent with a late first century B.C. or early first century A.D. date.[18] The traces of brick and concrete on top of the protective mole of the pond appear to be modifications that were needed to keep pace with the general rise in the level of the sea. This and additional openings cut through the mole point to the continued use of the pond during subsequent phases of the villa.

Cosa — Ansedonia (Figs. 11, 12)

The port and fishery at Cosa were located on the Tyrrhenian coast of ancient Etruria. The promontory of Cosa was an important landfall and its proximity to the fishing lagoon to the east facilitated the commercial exploitation of fish. Fish were known to abound inside and outside the lagoon. Strabo tells us that the heights of Cosa were used to spot schools of tunny.[19]

The fishery was located in a coastal lagoon which is now largely silted over. Originally, the lagoon stretched for some 20 kilometers, from the promontory of Cosa, on its west end, to the Tafone River, to the east. Separated from the sea by a sand barrier, the lagoon was approximately 5 meters deep, nearly 800 meters across at its widest point, and 240 meters wide at the western end, where the fishery was located. Springs emanating from the Cosan or western end of the lagoon supplied fresh water, while several inlets, across the sand barrier and through the limestone promontory, allowed the intermixture of salt water.

Our understanding of the harbor and fishery at Cosa has benefited from the careful excavation and study carried out under the direction of Anna Marguerite McCann between 1965 and 1978.[20] These excavations, on land and under the sea, have documented the history of a large commercial fishery and postulate its relationship with the adjacent port.

The excavators believe it is probable that fishing, since the colony's earliest days, took place along the entire length of the lagoon. Cane or wooden enclosures, which generally do not survive as part of the archaeological record, can be imagined scattered in these brackish waters. More permanent architectural remains were found to be concentrated at the western end of the lagoon near the limestone promontory (Fig. 11). Here, freshwater springs and a conduit to the sea provided ideal condi-

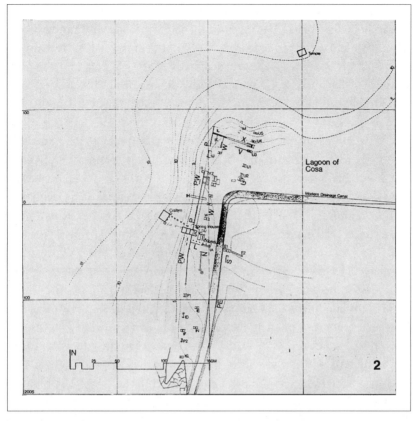

FIGURE 11. Lagoon of Cosa—plan of the excavated remains belonging to the fishery. (From A. M. McCann et al., *The Roman Port and Fishery of Cosa* [Princeton 1987] map 7)

tions for raising fish.[21] Communication with the sea through the sand barrier would have required constant maintenance. The Tagliata—a somewhat modified natural fissure in the promontory—provided a reliable connection between the sea and the lagoon. Seasonally, when the amount of rainfall varied, water would flow through this fissure at different rates. In time of little rainfall the prevailing current would run from the sea into the lagoon. Conversely, an influx of rainwater into the lagoon would direct the current out toward the sea. Migrating fish, attracted to the resulting changes in temperature and salinity, would swim through the channel and be caught easily in the narrows. The modern fisheries in this very lagoon and in the nearby Lago di Burano attest to the attractiveness of these brackish waters for raising fish. It is probable that some species of fish that migrated between the sea and lagoon would have been exploited by the ancient Cosans just as they are today.

GAZETTEER OF FISHPONDS

The excavators identified three phases in the life of the fishery at Cosa.[22] The first phase, dating from the late third and continuing probably into the early first century B.C., is not represented by remains of construction other than the scarped walls of the Tagliata and the adjacent canal. This first phase probably saw the use of cane enclosures with little modification of the natural conditions of the fishing lagoon. The second phase (Fig. 12), probably dating from the second quarter of the first century B.C. to the end of the century, saw major building activity centered around the port and the fishery. Concrete piers were placed in the water offshore possibly to provide safe anchorage, but they were spaced so as not to interfere with the complex system of tidal circulation.

The modifications of the natural conditions during the second phase were concentrated at the western end of the lagoon.[23] The principal natural fissure, the Tagliata, was equipped with sluice gates, which could regulate the flow of water and control the movement of fish. It is possible that some gate system was already in place during the first phase and simply modified in the second phase. Cuttings in the seaward end of this fissure point to the installation of mechanisms for the lowering and raising of the gates. The lowering of these gates had the effect of creating a holding tank within the southern portion of the Tagliata. The resulting enclosure was 10 meters long and 4 to 5 meters wide. The seaward opening faced the southwest, the direction of the incoming waves. Water, entering the main opening, could circulate through the enclosure and exit by way of a smaller channel, the Tagliata Piccola, back into the sea.

As already noted, the Tagliata facilitated the exchange of sea and lagoonal water. In the second phase of the fishery's development, polygonal retaining walls were constructed just to the east of the Tagliata to provide a second connection between the sea and the lagoon. These channels appear to have been linked to the lagoonal area that contained two large rectangular enclosures that ran along the western side of the lagoon. Selected excavation unearthed walls and stratigraphy suggesting that these two enclosures covered about 1.2 hectares. Internal subdivisions within these enclosures were likely, but their exact form is uncertain. Walls of the southern pond are higher (80 centimeters to 1.3 meters above the ancient sea level) than those of the northern pond (ca. 50 centimeters above the ancient sea level).

The position of the large concrete fishponds at the western end of the lagoon took advantage of the ready access to several freshwater springs.

GAZETTEER OF FISHPONDS

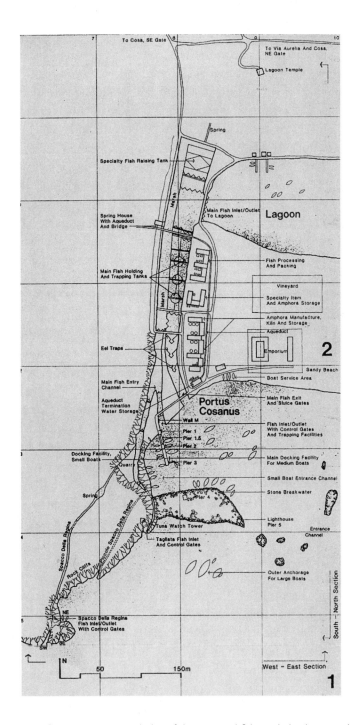

FIGURE 12. Cosa—reconstructed plan of the port and fishery during its second phase. (From A. M. McCann et al., *The Roman Port and Fishery of Cosa* [Princeton 1987] fig. VII-10)

A channel formed by two parallel walls carried water from a hillside spring to the northern enclosure. The width of this channel narrows as it approaches the tank. This hydraulic configuration increased the velocity of the water as it entered the pond and thus stimulated circulation. The second phase also saw the construction of a water-lifting device to make more fresh springwater available for the fishery and other port facilities. Some incomplete walls have led the excavators to hypothesize that the renovations of the fishing lagoon in the first century B.C. were never finished.[24] Excavation revealed large amounts of sea sand deposited within a short space of time. A severe storm or series of storms may have put a temporary end to activities in the fishing lagoon.

After a hiatus of nearly a half century, a third and final phase of construction began in the area of the port. The remains of vaults belonging to a *villa maritima* line the shore near the lagoon entrance. Repairs of several preexisting structures are evident and the Spring House was rebuilt during this phase, which lasts into the third century A.D.

During its heyday, the fishery appears to have been linked with the fortunes of the Sestii. Dates derived from the study of *amphorae* at the site suggest that commercial activity in the area of the port began with the earliest days of the colony in the third century B.C. The majority of the *amphorae* date from the late second through the first century B.C. During this floruit most stamped *amphorae* are associated with the Sestii.[25] Elizabeth Will has concluded that Cosa was the primary site where these *amphorae* were manufactured. The Sestii, who were wealthy plebeians, are amply attested in the ancient literary record and, along with the Domitii Ahenobarbi, of patrician lineage, were the most probable benefactors and beneficiaries of the port and fishery at Cosa.[26]

Orbetello Lagoon

There is evidence to suggest that the lagoons of Orbetello were used as fisheries by the Romans. Channels constructed of polygonal masonry have been observed at both the north and south ends of the Tombolo di Feniglia.[27] The remains of concrete walls have been seen in the water near the inner or northern shore of the Tombolo di Feniglia and at the south end of the Tombolo della Giannella.[28] The character of these finds is reminiscent of the remains unearthed at Cosa. The presence of modern fisheries in the lagoons of Orbetello lends credence to the idea of this area being exploited by the Romans in a like manner. The date and exact form of these lagoonal fisheries are impossible to determine. It must be assumed that enclosures built of perishable materials would have supplemented the permanent remains noted here.

Isola di Giglio—Bagno di Saraceno (Fig. 13)

The island of Giglio, ancient Igilium, is located off the Etruscan coast some 10 kilometers west of Monte Argentario and is mentioned in ancient itineraries.[29] Situated inside Giglio Porto, the ancient Roman port, are the remains of a Roman villa. The ruins of the villa line the edge of a small cove and are incorporated into houses of the medieval period. The cove, or Cala del Saraceno, is the site of a small fishpond known as the Bagno di Saraceno.[30]

The Cala del Saraceno is formed by two granite arms that leave an open connection to the sea on its east side. The rise in sea level since antiquity has obscured most of the pond's architectural details but enough remains visible to permit a general description.[31] The fishpond was designed to take advantage of the protected waters offered by the cove. The fishpond consists of a central tank which measures 15 by 15 meters (Fig. 13:A). The measurable depth, allowing for the change in sea level, is about 1.5 meters but this figure is not precise due to the accumulation of sediment and debris. The interior of the cove was provided with level platforms (B) around the perimeter of the enclosure which were cut into the granite or fashioned of concrete. The north and south sides of the *piscina* were lined with hydraulic concrete walls (C), which provide a narrow (80 centimeters wide) walkway. Both of these are backed by broader platforms cut from the rock and made even, where needed, by the addition of concrete.

The western side of the pond is fronted by a very broad platform cut into the rock and bisected by an opening (F), 2.7 meters wide, which was also cut into the rock. The eastern or sea side of the fishpond is formed by two projecting granite arms of the cove. Today, these arms stand high above the water (the north projects 1.9 meters and the south rises 6 meters). Both arms have been squared, creating a rectilinear opening to the sea 10.4 meters wide. Cuttings (E) in the facing ends of the seaward opening indicate the placement of wooden beams that would have spanned the opening and the northern seaward channel.[32] Correcting for the change in sea level would put these beams about 60 centimeters above the ancient level of the sea. It is probable that these beams supported nets or other such temporary barriers that would allow water to circulate while keeping the fish confined.

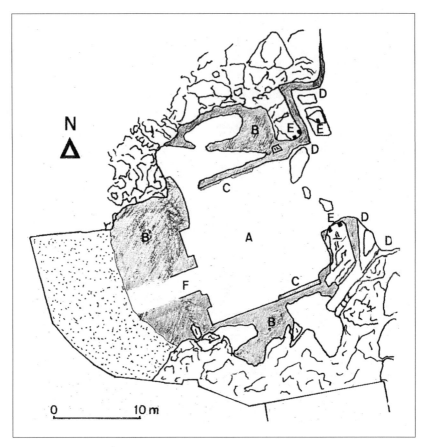

FIGURE 13. Isola di Giglio—plan of the villa called the Bagno di Saraceno. **A** = rock-cut basin; **B** = platform around pond; **C** = concrete walls; **D** = channels to the sea; **E** = beam cuttings; **F** = shoreside cutting. (From G. Schmiedt, ed., *Il livello antico del Mar Tirreno* [Florence 1972] 34, pl. 30)

Seawater circulated into the enclosure through two rock-cut channels (D); one, 1.07 meters wide and 6 meters long, was cut through the south-ern arm of the enclosure opening and branches into two smaller channels as it moves seaward, while the other runs along the northern arm and passes through the main opening into the pond. Two *cuniculi*, the re-mains of which can be observed on both the north and south sides of the cove, probably supplied fresh water to the fishpond.[33] The canal on the north side of the pond was founded on rock, constructed of concrete, and followed the edge of the enclosure. The *cuniculus* at the southern side of the cove emerges from a villa wall faced in *opus quasi-reticulatum*.

Though no direct connection to the pond remains, these canals, by their proximity, are to be associated with the fishpond.

The villa associated with the Bagno di Saraceno has walls faced in *opus quasi-reticulatum*, which suggests an initial date of the first century B.C. This is substantiated by the black-glaze pottery (Campanian A) with stamped decoration found scattered about the site.[34] The majority of the villa is constructed of walls faced in *opus reticulatum* that date to the first century A.D.[35] Some scattered brickwork has yielded stamps that point to repairs of the second century A.D. If the freshwater canal, emerging from under the early *opus quasi-reticulatum* wall, is to be associated with the Cala del Saraceno, then it is probable that fish were raised in these brackish waters as early as the first century B.C. However, the aggregate used in the concrete of the northern freshwater canal is identical to that which lines the enclosure and to that used in the *opus reticulatum* walls of the first century A.D., suggesting that this second phase of use saw the construction of the fishpond. Repairs to the freshwater canals with stamped *bipedales* attest to the continued use of this cove as a fishpond into the second century A.D.[36] The island of Igilium belonged to the Domitii Ahenobarbi and ships that were contributed to Caesar's cause by the admiral Domitius Ahenobarbus came from this location.[37] The dates of the activities of the Domitii in this area coincide with the phases represented in the construction at the Bagno di Saraceno.

Pian di Spille

Little remains of the fishpond at the site of Pian di Spille, which is located on the Etruscan coast 5.5 kilometers north of the ancient port of Gravisca. Approximately 400 meters north of the ruins at Martanum are the remains of an ancient seaside villa.

Today, the area is part of a military firing range, and the frequent bombardment has had a detrimental effect on the state of the Roman ruins along the shore. Some of these remains have been identified as those of a Roman fishpond. The *piscina* consists of a series of circular and rectangular tanks that extend from the shore out into the sea.[38] The walls of the fishpond are fashioned out of hydraulic concrete. The remains of a conduit, which conveyed fresh water from a nearby torrent to the area of this pond, have been noted by De Rossi. Fresh water emptied into a tank at an elevation above the fishpond and supplied the tanks below. This was probably accomplished by a system of clay tubing, remains of which are preserved in the concrete ruins at the site.

Concrete walls faced in *opus latericium* litter the landscape and point to a date no more specific than the first or second century A.D. It is interesting to note the remains of a black-and-white mosaic depicting an aquatic scene that includes a *mullus* and a *murena*.[39]

Martanum (Figs. 14, 15)

The site of Martanum lies 3 kilometers north of ancient Gravisca between the torrents that enter the sea at Pian di Spille to the north and the mouth of the Fiume Marta to the south.[40] In the water offshore are the remains of two *piscinae*, one of which consists of eroded concrete walls that suggest a rectangular enclosure; the other U-shaped pond is better preserved and is associated with the ruins of a *villa maritima*. The former offers little in terms of useful data and does not merit lengthy discussion. The latter presents more useful information. The plan of this fishpond (Fig. 14) consists of two parallel concrete moles, 27.5 meters long and approximately 2.0 meters wide, which project into the sea from the shore. These arms were connected on the shore by a third wall 14 meters long and about 2 meters wide. A portion of this side, 4.0 meters long, remains attached to the southeast corner of the *piscina* obscured by the accumulation of debris and sediment. The resulting U-shaped plan presented an open side toward the sea. Concrete remains inside the enclosure suggest that originally there may have been some form of internal subdivisions in the pond (Fig. 15).

The three sides which define the pond's perimeter carry a single channel, 1 meter wide and deep, which appears as a groove in the top of the U-shaped mole. The channel is closed at the southwest corner of the pond and does not connect to the sea. The analogous end at the northwest corner is in bad repair, making a precise reconstruction impossible. It appears that this channel was designed to carry fresh water, which was to be distributed within the enclosure. Remains of concrete walls extending inland from the northeast corner probably supported conduits that transported fresh water to the channel along the top of the *piscina* mole. The upper portions of the mole are badly eroded and do not preserve the upper finished edge of the pond. It is probable that small openings in this channel permitted water to circulate into the interior of the pond. Salt water was carried in and out by the action of the tide through the open seaward end of the pond. This end was probably closed by a net or gate fashioned from perishable materials.[41]

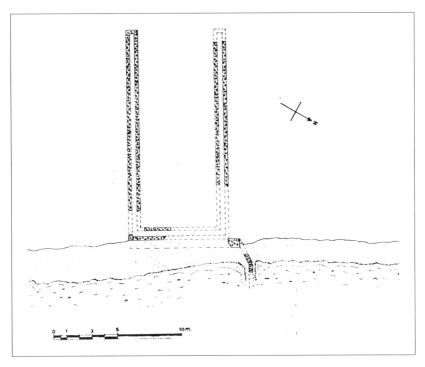

FIGURE 14. Martanum — plan of the fishpond. (From G. M. De Rossi, P. G. Di Domenico, and L. Quilici, "La Via Aurelia da Roma a Forum Aureli," *Quaderno dell'Istituto di Topografia Antica della Università di Roma* 4 [1968] fig. 316)

FIGURE 15. Martanum — concrete walls of the fishpond. (From G. M. De Rossi, P. G. Di Domenico, and L. Quilici, "La Via Aurelia da Roma a Forum Aureli," *Quaderno dell'Istituto di Topografia Antica della Università di Roma* 4 [1968] fig. 317)

The fishpond lies opposite a large rectangular precinct (700 by 430 meters), which has defined the limits of a large seaside villa. The U-shaped pond is situated on axis with the center of the rectangle. The remains of concrete walls can be seen all along the seaward side of the precinct. While consisting mostly of nondescript concrete cores, walls faced with brick suggest an imperial date.

Torre Valdaliga (Figs. 16, 17)

The site of Torre Valdaliga lies just north of the location of ancient Algae 4.5 kilometers northeast of Civitavecchia on the Etruscan coast.[42] The fishpond at Torre Valdaliga stands in the sea opposite a Roman villa situated on the shore. The villa was largely destroyed during the construction of the torre by Pope Paul V in 1616. The remains of the fishpond are located on a rocky shelf extending into the sea from the promontory of Valdaliga. The soft volcanic rock of this shelf or "panchina," eroded by the force of the sea, possesses many inlets, tidal basins, and coves. The natural terrain of the promontory of Torre Valdaliga also provided a cove large enough to serve as a private harbor for the villa. The *piscina* was constructed in one of the larger of these coves (Figs. 16:A, 17:A). The rock was cut to accommodate a rectangular plan, 39 by 19 meters. The inside of the cove was lined with concrete walls faced in *opus reticulatum*, which also served to close in the northwest or open side. These walls regularized the plan of the enclosure and provided walkways for those maintaining the fishpond. The action of the sea has done much to destroy the remains of the fishpond. The protective walls of the seventeenth-century tower have been undermined by the force of the surf, and the resulting tumble, along with accumulated sediment, has obscured the architectural details of the pond on the shore.

The pond was supplied with seawater from at least six points of entry. Three of these are channels cut through the rock on the seaward side of the pond. These channels (a, b, and c in Figs. 16, 17) are between 32.5 and 35 meters long and roughly 1 meter wide.[43] They enter the pond through three openings in the concrete walls that line the enclosure. These openings or *itinera* were equipped with runners designed for securing barriers or gates. A fourth opening aligns with a broad channel 6.5 meters wide and 27.4 meters long. This channel cuts through the rock directly west of the enclosure and was modified with concrete walls that would allow the channel to be closed at two points; thus fish could be trapped entering or leaving the pond. A fifth opening is positioned

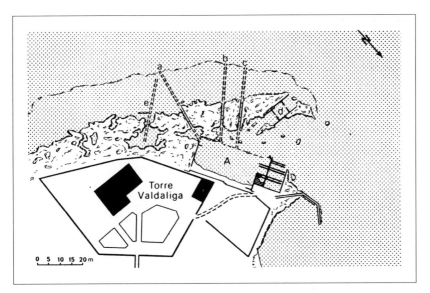

FIGURE 16. Torre Valdaliga—plan of the promontory. **A** = fishpond; **a, b,** and **c** = rock-cut channels connecting the pond to the sea; **d** = broad channel with concrete partitions; **e** = early rock-cut channel linking the small cove to the sea. (From G. Schmiedt, ed., *Il livello antico del Mar Tirreno* [Florence 1972] 65, pl. 65)

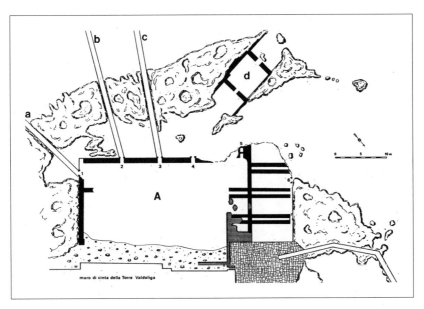

FIGURE 17. Torre Valdaliga—plan of the fishpond. **A** = fishpond; **a, b,** and **c** = rock-cut channels connecting the pond to the sea; **d** = broad channel with concrete partitions; **1–6** = openings into the fishpond. (From G. Schmiedt, ed., *Il livello antico del Mar Tirreno* [Florence 1972] 66, pl. 66)

near the western corner of the *piscina* and is fitted with slots for a movable barrier. This opening connects the open sea to the fishpond. The sixth visible opening is located in the northwest side of the enclosure at a point where the pond's wall meets the end of the rocky shelf.

Internal subdivisions are preserved only in the northwestern end of the pond and divide the enclosure into two parts: an open tank A to the southwest and a collection of smaller tanks in the remaining portion of the pond. *Itinera* 1, 2, 3, and 4 supplied seawater to the open side of the fishpond, while openings 5 and 6 did the same for the subdivided side.

The concrete walls in the northwestern third of the pond divide this area into three separate tanks. These tanks are divided from the open enclosure by a concrete wall faced in *opus reticulatum* that runs northeast to southwest across the pond. The dividing walls, 60 centimeters wide, were laid in pairs that run parallel to each other, leaving a 60 centimeter space between. The double walls form channels for distributing fresh water into the fishpond. The remains of concrete vaults and tessellated flooring at this end indicate that, in addition to water circulation, these walls supported a platform or veranda that covered nearly a third of the pond. The resulting shaded and more constricted waters were beneficial to fish trying to escape the heat of the sun or the appetites of their neighbors. Moreover, the veranda afforded easy access to the pond for the purpose of harvesting the catch or for simple enjoyment.

The site of Torre Valdaliga provides a notable example where the natural topography was gradually altered to facilitate the raising of fish. Southwest of the pond is a small natural cove, approximately 12 by 10 meters, with a narrow connection (about 1.5 meters wide) to the sea. During the first phase of the villa in the early first century B.C., a long channel (Fig. 16:e)—27.5 meters long and about 1 meter wide—was cut into the panchina to facilitate the circulation of salt water into the cove and to allow migrating fish to enter. Seasonally, this inlet received fresh water through rivulets caused by rainfall, which changed the salinity and temperature of the seawater in the inlet. The addition of fresh water helped keep the water inside the enclosure from becoming stagnant and unhealthy for the fish inside. The rock-cut channel also served to advertise the brackish conditions inside the enclosure and thus lure fish into the inlet. The depth of this channel is shallower than those which feed the fishpond nearby. This has led Schmiedt to deduce that channel e was cut when the villa was constructed in the first century B.C.[44] The general rise in sea level necessitated deeper channels when the fishpond was added to the villa later in the first century. The general characteristics of this small cove — closable, possessing an adequate circulating supply of salt and fresh water, and equipped with a channel — formed the basis for the design of the more elaborate fishpond.

The villa was first constructed in the early first century B.C. as is evidenced by scattered remnants of concrete walls faced in *opus incertum*. The small cove equipped with a rock-cut sea channel probably dates to this initial phase. A major phase of construction took place in the third quarter of the first century B.C. The distribution of architectural remains suggests the villa of this second phase covered over 3,000 square meters.[45] Concrete walls, faced with *opus reticulatum* using stone blocks for corners and quoins, are used in the remodeling of the villa and the construction of the fishpond. Brick-faced walls and vaults testify to restorations during the empire.

La Mattonara (Figs. 18, 19)

La Mattonara is a promontory that projects into the sea 3 kilometers northeast of Civitavecchia, ancient Centumcellae. The remains of a Roman villa are located on this spit of soft volcanic rock or "panchina." The natural coves and inlets allowed the villa owner to incorporate a private harbor and fishpond into his domestic complex (Fig. 18:A, B, C).[46]

The fishpond (Fig. 19) was largely cut from the rocky panchina, which forms the projecting shelf around the promontory and was finished with addition of concrete walls. The *piscina* is divided into three separate tanks. The main tank (Fig. 19:1) is a rectangular enclosure (25 meters east-west by 30 meters north-south) defined by the rock and walls faced in *opus reticulatum*. The remains of walls, both rock-cut and concrete, inside the main tank suggest that some sort of internal subdivisions was part of the original design. The other two tanks (2 and 3) are smaller, trapezoidal in plan, and are cut from the fissured rock west of the main tank.[47]

Two long channels can be made out cut from the rock. These conduits connect the western or seaward side of the enclosure to the sea. Channel A–B (34.8 meters long and approximately 1.3 meters wide) runs east-west and links the sea (A) to the southwest corner (B) of the larger trapezoidal tank (2). An opening in the same corner of the main tank (1) is probable and suggests that the current from this channel supplied both tanks (1 and 2).

Channel C–D (35.6 meters long and about 1.2 meters wide) connects the sea (C) to the main tank, through its west side (D), while passing

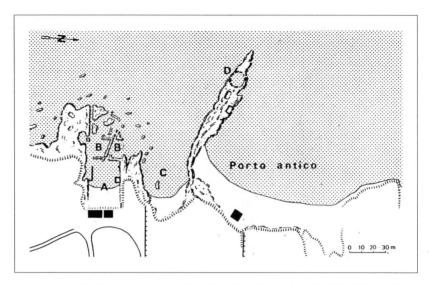

FIGURE 18. La Mattonara—plan of the shoreline. **A** = main tank of the fishpond; **B** = trapezoidal tanks; **C** = private harbor; **D** = circular pond called "La Buca di Nerone." (From G. Schmiedt, ed., *Il livello antico del Mar Tirreno* [Florence 1972] 68, pl. 69)

between both trapezoidal tanks. An opening in the rock wall at the northeast corner of tank 2 could be an original link, though the eroded condition of the walls makes any definite reconstruction difficult. The small trapezoidal tank (3) was probably supplied with seawater either through its north side or by way of the channel C–D.

Three sides of the main tank are visible, and exhibit use of both rock-cut and concrete architecture. The fourth side or landside is obscured by the accumulation of sediment and debris. The natural formation was sufficient to form the north, west, and most of the south sides of the main enclosure. On shore and in line with the pond's north side are the remains of a wall, which suggest that the east side of the enclosure included concrete walls. At the southwest corner, where the panchina is lacking, concrete walls faced in *opus reticulatum* were added to complete the tank. The remnants of four parallel concrete walls (about a meter wide), similarly faced, abut the north side of the enclosure. Two of these spurs are barely 60 centimeters apart and thus resemble a double-walled channel system designed for the distribution of fresh water. The alignment of these walls also could support a floor that would create a shaded area with the tank and allow a platform from which fish could be harvested or viewed.

GAZETTEER OF FISHPONDS

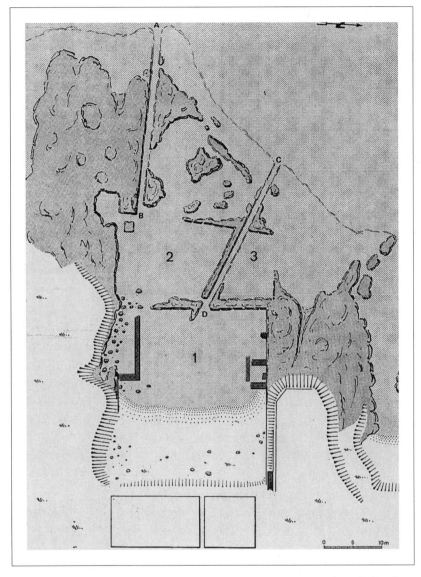

FIGURE 19. La Mattonara—plan of the fishpond. I = main rectangular tank; **2** = large trapezoidal tank; **3** = small trapezoidal tank; **A–B** and **C–D** = rock-cut channels. (From G. Schmiedt, ed., *Il livello antico del Mar Tirreno* [Florence 1972] 74, pl. 79)

Just inside the southwest corner of tank 2, part of the panchina was worked into an isolated square (1.7 by 1.8 meters). The precise function of this element is uncertain. It is possible that this pier was part of a mechanism that could close the sea channel at point B or isolate the small inlet that opens off the southwest corner of the trapezoidal tank 2.

This element might also have served as a support for a corner tower used by a watcher directing *piscatores* in the harvest of fish. This location would be well suited for spotting fish attempting to leave the main tank so that they could be trapped in the large trapezoidal tank (2). The smaller trapezoidal tank (3) seems to be designed as a holding tank perhaps for the confinement of select fish or shellfish.

In addition to the fishpond, the natural formations at La Mattonara permitted the creation of a small port protected by a long rocky arm (115 meters long) that juts out into the sea. Near the end of this arm is a circular rock-cut pond (7.6 meters in diameter) called the Buca di Nerone, which could have been used to hold fish.

The date of the *piscina* at La Mattonara, like Torre Valdaliga, is derived from the walls faced in *opus reticulatum* used in the construction of the enclosure. The construction is dated to the third quarter of the first century B.C.[48]

Punta San Paolo (Fig. 20)

The site of Punta San Paolo lies on a spit of land 1.7 kilometers north of Civitavecchia. The area has suffered much as the result of the construction of a large oil refinery between the Punta San Paolo and the Punta del Cimitero.[49] In the sea just off the south end of the point are the remains of a square fishpond divided into four tanks by two walls (Fig. 20:A). The pond was partially cut into the rocky shelf and finished with concrete walls. The surrounding protective mole is nearly 3 meters wide and each side is approximately 25 meters long. The internal subdivisions are made of concrete walls about 60 centimeters wide. The resulting subtanks are nearly 10 meters square.

The positions of openings, which would permit seawater to circulate within the enclosure, are difficult to locate with any certainty. An opening in the west side of the enclosure is visible but it is impossible to determine if this was the result of damage to the *piscina* in the centuries since its construction or part of the original design. The northwest corner of the fishpond is buttressed by a concrete pier 3 meters square. This element probably served as an anchorage for boats stocking the pond or the pier may have been a support for a corner watchtower.

Little can be said concerning the date of this fishpond. The villa on the shore, now destroyed, yielded little useful information. Prior to the Second World War Bastianelli noted the remains of a large seaside villa decorated with mosaics many of which possessed marine scenes.[50]

FIGURE 20. Punta San Paolo—aerial view of promontory, with the square fishpond (**A**) to the right. (From G. Schmiedt, ed., *Il livello antico del Mar Tirreno* [Florence 1972] 61, pl. 63)

Punta della Vipera (Figs. 21–23)

The site of Punta della Vipera is located between Civitavecchia and Santa Marinella, 1.5 kilometers north of Torre Chiaruccia in the Località Sogno.[51] The hard stone shelf, which extends beyond the point, was cut to accommodate a large rectangular fishpond. The pond has weathered well and the ruins provide much useful information (Figs. 21, 22).

The plan of the rectangular pond measures approximately 55 meters by 34 meters. The three sides of the enclosure, which face the sea, are formed by a thick mole (Fig. 23:a) made of *opus caementicium* or concrete. The northern side of this mole is 3.12 meters wide, the west side is 2 meters, and the south side is 2.25 meters wide.

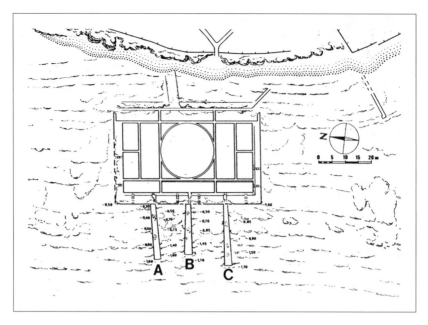

FIGURE 21. Punta della Vipera—plan of the fishpond and its position along the coast. **A, B,** and **C** = rock-cut channels. (From G. Schmiedt, ed., *Il livello antico del Mar Tirreno* [Florence 1972] 77, pl. 83)

FIGURE 22. Punta della Vipera—aerial view of the fishpond. (From G. Schmiedt, ed., *Il livello antico del Mar Tirreno* [Florence 1972] 76, pl. 82)

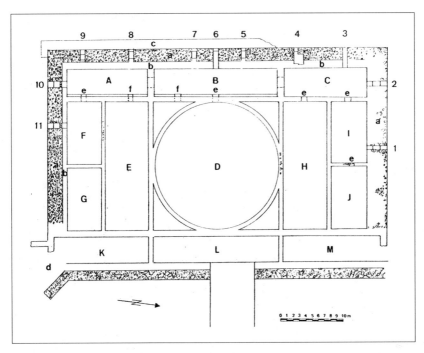

FIGURE 23. Punta della Vipera—schematic plan of the fishpond. **A–M** = internal tanks; **a** = protective mole; **b** = partition walls and walkways; **c** = external buttress wall; **d** = possible freshwater canal; **e** = original openings between tanks; **f** = brick arched openings; **1–11** = openings in the mole. (Adapted from G. Schmiedt, ed., *Il livello antico del Mar Tirreno* [Florence 1972] 79, pl. 84)

The architecture inside the pond was fashioned after the completion of the perimeter mole. These concrete walls are faced in *opus reticulatum* and stand nearly 1 meter below the height of the moles. Two of these concrete walls (b), about 1 meter wide, were built along the inside of the west and south moles. These brought the total thickness of the perimeter on these sides to the magnitude of the north mole.[52] Allowing for the rise in sea level since antiquity these lower walls would have stood just above the water and provided walkways around the inside of the enclosure.

Additional concrete walls (50 to 80 centimeters wide) subdivided the enclosure into several tanks. Two walls, running east-west, divide the pond into three large sections. The central rectangular section (20.2 by 30.2 meters) is dominated by a circular tank (D) inscribed within its center. The open zones east and west of the circular tank were made into separate tanks (B and L) by the construction of north-south walls tangential to the circle. The areas between the outside edge of the circle and these rectilinear walls form four roughly triangular-shaped tanks.[53]

The two sections, north and south of the large central portion, are divided into five tanks each (tanks E and H measure 20.2 by 6.9 meters; tanks A and C measure 3.7 by 13.4 meters; tanks F, G, I, and J measure 5.6 by 9.5 meters; and tanks K and M measure 3.9 by 15.4 meters).

In many of the tanks openings (e) that permit communication within the enclosure are preserved. These are formed by stone quoins and voussoirs.[54] Inside tanks A and B, along their east sides, is a small buttress wall around 30 centimeters wide and 80 centimeters below the top of the interior walls of the pond. The buttress walls are pierced by two brick arched openings (f), one in tank A and one in tank B. The openings link tanks A and B to tanks E and D respectively. The small walls and their openings appear to be an addition or repair to this part of the fishpond.[55]

The perimeter of the fishpond is pierced by at least eleven openings. Three of these (4, 6, and 8) are fed by long channels cut into the rock shelf west of the enclosure; the northernmost channel is 18.8 meters long and 1.8 meters wide; the middle channel is 18.6 meters long and 1.8 meters wide where it meets the pond and widens to 2.8 meters as it moves away from the shore; the southernmost channel is 20 meters long and 1.8 meters wide where it contacts the pond, widening to 2.5 meters where it opens to the sea.[56]

The southwest corner of the fishpond is in a good state of repair and provides the most complete details as to the structure of the protective mole and how seawater entered the enclosure. It is apparent that a buttress wall (c), 95 centimeters wide, lies around the base of the mole on the seaward side of the pond about a meter below the top. The openings through the mole (best exemplified by numbers 10 and 11) that allow the sea to circulate within the pond are approximately 80 centimeters wide and are designed with a catch basin built into each. The basins measure 1 meter by 80 centimeters and are a little over half a meter deep. Immediately after leaving the basin, water would pass through a fenestrated opening (20 centimeters high and 80 centimeters wide) and empty into the pond. Variations of this arrangement (inlet, catch basin, and fenestrated opening into pond) were used in the other openings.[57] The association of these openings to the circulation of seawater is obvious enough. It is possible that conduits, carried atop the mole, could have distributed fresh water through the same openings.

In their original state, the three long channels, which were cut from the shelf of hard stone (*pietraforte*), were covered with concrete vaults (Fig. 21:A, B, C). Rock excavated in the construction of the channels was used for the aggregate in the concrete vaulting.[58] The covered channels helped relay the brackish conditions inside the enclosure to points far out to sea without having the salinity altered by contact with the sea. The channels led to arched openings into the fishpond (85 centimeters wide and about 1 meter high). These three channels served the dual function of facilitating circulation and providing an entrance for migrating fish attracted by the change in salinity. At some later point the opening from the southernmost channel was closed with rock and debris. This may correspond with construction of the additional openings in the southwest corner of the pond.

The east or shoreside wall of the *piscina* has been damaged by the construction of modern villas. It is possible to discern that both corners, the northeast and southeast, are incomplete. At the southeast corner, the east wall turns shoreward at an angle of 45 degrees. This connection to the shore could play a role in the conveyance of fresh water into the fishpond. Later, both shoreside corners were opened and connected with crude semicircular enclosures arranged one at each corner.[59]

The construction of the fishpond at Punta della Vipera after the middle of the first century B.C. is suggested by the use of concrete faced with *opus reticulatum* employing stone quoins and voussoirs. This date is supported by the history of the nearby Etruscan sanctuary. The buildings of the sanctuary were destroyed by the mid first century B.C. and materials from this site were used in the construction of the villa opposite the fishpond.[60] The villa has phases which last into the third century A.D. The brick used in the modifications of the fishpond point to a date of the first century A.D. or later and suggest that the pond continued to be used in the later phases of the site.

Fosso Guardiole (Figs. 24, 25)

The località di Fosso Guardiole lies immediately northwest of Santa Marinella and southeast of Punta della Vipera. In the sea, stretching for some 400 meters along the shore, are the submerged remains of two Roman fishponds: one apsidal and the other rectilinear (Fig. 24:A, B).[61] Both ponds sit in the sandy shallows, where the water from the Fosso (F) empties into the sea, and are not cut from rock.

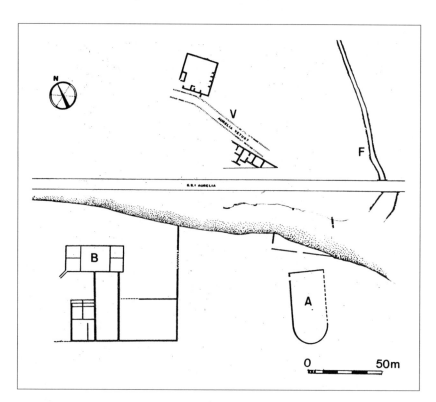

FIGURE 24. Fosso Guardiole—schematic plan of the shoreline. **A** = apsidal fishpond; **B** = rectangular fishpond; **F** = Fosso; **V** = villa along the Via Aurelia. (From P. A. Gianfrotta, *Castrum Novum*—*Forma Italiae* 7.3 [Rome 1970] fig. 234)

The apsidal pond (A) lies closest to the mouth of the Fosso delle Guardiole. The long sides of this enclosure, a little over 1 meter wide and 32.2 meters long, run parallel to each other 21 meters apart. These concrete walls are connected by a straight wall, about 21 meters long, near the shore and by an arching wall seaward, thus creating an enclosure 38.7 meters long, down its axis, and 21 meters broad. Much of the pond's east side has been destroyed by the constant erosive forces from the Fosso. What remains preserves a single opening (about 2 meters wide) through the perimeter at the pond's northwest corner. Portions of the walls still retain their *opus reticulatum* facing.

The rectangular fishpond (B) is situated some 65 meters northwest of the apsidal enclosure. This complex is protected by an L-shaped mole (Fig. 25:A) to the southwest, south, and southeast. The remains of the mole extend about 75 meters out to sea and then turn west, 90 degrees, for another 70 meters. The breakwater was constructed primarily of

GAZETTEER OF FISHPONDS

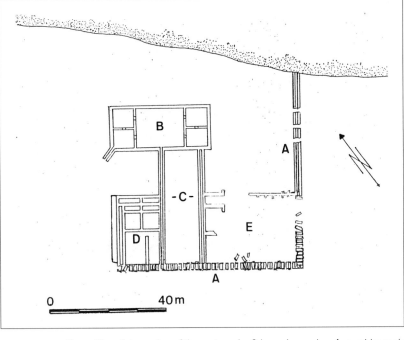

FIGURE 25. Fosso Guardiole—plan of the rectangular fishpond complex. **A** = ashlar mole with remains of a freshwater canal; **B** = fishpond; **C** = twin canals supplying the fishpond; **D** = fishpond(?); **E** = anchorage. (Adapted from G. Schmiedt, ed., *Il livello antico del Mar Tirreno* [Florence 1972] 88, pl. 93)

sandstone ashlars, 1.5 to 2 meters in length, laid with their long sides parallel to each other and with interstices that allow some water to flow through the mole. This protective barrier appears to stand on the ruins of an earlier harbor built by the Etruscans or, perhaps, during the foundation of the Roman colony of Castrum Novum in the third century B.C.[62]

At a later date, the early mole was connected to the shore by a concrete addition. This modified mole protected an area covering nearly half a hectare. Within this sheltered zone are the remains of concrete walls, which form a complex assemblage of tanks, channels, and anchorages associated with a Roman fishery.

The best-preserved remains lie near the center of the protected area. This rectangular fishpond (Fig. 25:B), which is further protected by its own molelike perimeter, encloses an area 35.1 by 15.6 meters. The perimeter of the pond is formed by a concrete wall approximately 2 meters wide. The enclosure was subdivided into five interconnected tanks. The largest, in the center, measures 16.1 by 12.7 meters. Flanking this tank, to the east and west, are four tanks, two to a side, each of which measure 7.3 by 5.8 meters. The tanks are linked to those adjacent by openings approximately 1 meter wide.

Seawater entered the enclosure by means of an opening in the south-west corner of the fishpond that faces the open sea. Two short parallel walls (around 5 meters long and 2 meters apart) extend out from this opening and form a channel through which water and fish could enter and leave the pond. This channel was equipped with at least one set of vertical slots for a sliding barrier.[63]

Fresh water was supplied to the pond by means of a canal, carried from the shore atop the outer protective mole. This conduit is around 80 centimeters wide and 1 meter deep. Once at the end of the mole fresh water was transferred to two additional canals (C), which were formed by closely parallel concrete walls, 80 centimeters wide and less than 1 meter apart. These two canals fed directly into the central and eastern portions of the rectangular fishpond. The mixture of salt and fresh water would have provided the enclosure with a brackish environment.

The remains of concrete walls east and west of the freshwater canals are difficult to describe with precision. It is possible to make out a third canal parallel to the other two at the western end of the outer protective mole. On the seaward side of this third canal there appears to be a wide concrete wall (less than 3 meters wide), which would shelter the canal and the area to its east and south of the rectangular fishpond. There is a high concentration of concrete remains in this location and it would seem probable that they are the remains of another fishpond (D).[64] East of the freshwater canals (E) the situation is less clear. There appears to be no attempt to make this area secure for the confinement of fish. The interstices between the ashlars of the mole were left open and the use of concrete walls was kept to a minimum. Some blocks which could have served as mooring stones suggest that this part of the complex functioned as an anchorage for boats.

A villa (Fig. 24:V) on the shore along the Via Aurelia and opposite both fishponds was constructed in the late first century B.C. or early first century A.D. and then remodeled later in the first century.[65] The facing (opus reticulatum) used in the apsidal fishpond fits with either phase. The absence of brick in the construction of both fishponds suggests a connection to the villa's Augustan phase.[66]

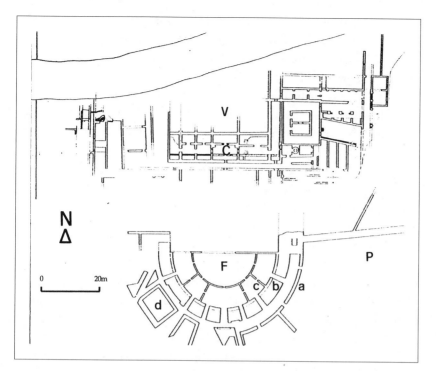

FIGURE 26. Grottacce—plan of the villa and fishpond. **F** = semicircular fishpond; **a** = outer ring of walls, piers, and tanks; **b** = protective mole; **c** = interior tanks; **d** = exterior tank; **V** = villa; **C** = cisterns; **P** = private port. (From A. Bufalo in G. M. De Rossi, P. G. Di Domenico, and L. Quilici, "La Via Aurelia da Roma a Forum Aureli," *Quaderno dell'Istituto di Topografia Antica della Università di Roma* 4 [1968] fig. 152)

Grottacce (Fig. 26)

Grottacce is located 2.5 kilometers east of Santa Marinella, ancient Punicum.[67] A luxurious Roman villa (Fig. 26:V) was constructed on a point of land which stands about 10 meters above the sea. The villa was explored by the Soprintendenza alle Antichità dell'Etruria meridionale in 1952. Below the villa in the sea are the remains of a large semicircular fishpond (F).[68]

The fishpond was constructed on a platform of hard volcanic stone (*pietraforte*), which extends into the sea around the point of Grottacce. The pond is semicircular in plan, with a diameter of approximately 55 meters, and comprises a system of concrete piers, moles, and walls. The pond can be divided into four concentric sections. The outer ring (a) of this enclosure consists of a curvilinear wall which runs from the shore, on the east side of the pond, around the eastern half of the pond. This outer wall is approximately 1 meter wide and pierced at three points by openings which allow seawater to circulate within the enclosure. Two concrete walls that radiate seaward from the outer wall may be the remains of separate tanks or slips for the mooring of boats.

The outer ring, which surrounds the western half of the fishpond, is formed by piers and small enclosed tanks. The three irregularly shaped piers appear to have been designed to direct the flow of water to prescribed parts of the pond. The other two elements in this outer ring are small tanks: one square (d) in plan 8.6 by 9.8 meters, the other is trapezoidal in plan 8.6 meters by 5.5 and 7.4 meters (the seaward side of this tank no longer remains). The isolated tanks would have kept certain fish segregated from the rest of the fishpond and performed the same function as the piers, helping direct water into the enclosure.

A channel, which ranges from 3.1 to 1.2 meters in width, separates the outer ring from the primary protective mole of the fishpond (b). This concrete wall is 4.3 meters wide and is pierced at seven locations by openings, or *itinera*, which allow seawater to reach the inner portion of the fishpond. Behind the mole the pond is divided into six tanks: a ring of five (6.5 meters wide) just inside the mole and a single semicircular tank (20.9 meters in diameter) at the pond's center.

The position of the fishpond allowed the designers to rely on the winds and waves to circulate seawater. Fresh water was supplied to the pond from cisterns, fourteen of which were found in and around the villa. Too many for solely alimentary purposes, some of the cisterns must have stored water for the fishpond in the sea below the villa.

The villa at Grottacce encompassed an area of about 1.6 hectares (200 meters by 80 meters). The central building was designed with vaulted cisterns (C) in its lower level and a second story or piano nobile from which the seaside panorama could be enjoyed. Along the shore east of the pond are the remains of a concrete wall 2.15 meters wide which could have served as a landing quay for a small private port (P).

The date of the entire villa complex is uncertain. The concrete walls of the villa are faced with *opus reticulatum*, which suggests a date of the first century A.D. for the initial construction. Bricks, bearing stamps of the first century A.D., were used in the first phase of the villa.[69] A second phase, which included some remodeling, is hypothesized for the late second or early third century A.D.[70] The fishpond appears to belong to the initial phase of the villa in the first century A.D. Many of the villa's cisterns were converted into storerooms during the second-century phase and as such could not have supplied fresh water to the fishpond. The mortar and aggregate used in the villa's first phase are identical to that employed in the construction of the *piscina*.

Pyrgi — Santa Severa

The site of Pyrgi was one of the ports for the Etruscan city of Caere. In the water, founded on a long rock jetty which projects into the sea, are the remains of a square enclosure thought by Schmiedt to have been a fishpond.[71] The enclosure measured 24 meters to a side and is formed by a wall 2.5 meters wide (best preserved on the north and west sides). There are the ruins of concrete walls inside the enclosure, which, according to Schmiedt, may have been part of internal subdivisions similar to those in the *piscina* at San Paolo. Subsequent study by John Oleson has cast some doubt on this identification.[72] According to Oleson, concrete fragments found inside the enclosure are the remains of pavement and not the partitions for separate tanks. The preservation of the wooden framework that was used to form the concrete suggests that the interior of the square was filled in shortly after the construction of the walls rather than being left open as a pond. The square was probably the foundation of a tower, which stood watch over the harbor area. The existence of towers in this city is suggested by its name, which means towers (*pyrgi*) in Latin.

Torre Flavia (Figs. 27, 28)

The fishpond near Torre Flavia is located 1.3 kilometers northwest of the Torre.[73] Partially buried in the sand along the shore is a *piscina*, circular in plan, 22.2 meters in diameter (Figs. 27, 28). The perimeter of the pond is formed by two concentric concrete walls faced in brick or *opus testaceum*. Each wall is 75 centimeters wide and spaced 3.65 meters apart. The remains of concrete walls can be observed lying within the confines of the pond. A single opening pierced the southwest portion of the inner ring. This configuration may have divided the pond into separate tanks or created a channel, around the pond's perimeter, for the purpose of distribution of freshwater. The northeast side of the enclosure was reinforced by a concrete wall (95 centimeters wide), which was added after the initial construction of the pond, making use of discarded building materials and aggregate.

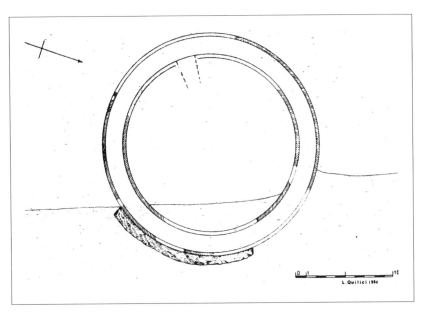

FIGURE 27. Torre Flavia—plan of the circular fishpond. (From G. M. De Rossi, P. G. Di Domenico, and L. Quilici, "La Via Aurelia da Roma a Forum Aureli," *Quaderno dell'Istituto di Topografia Antica della Università di Roma* 4 [1968] fig. 143)

FIGURE 28. Torre Flavia—concrete walls of the fishpond's northern perimeter. (From G. M. De Rossi, P. G. Di Domenico, and L. Quilici, "La Via Aurelia da Roma a Forum Aureli," *Quaderno dell'Istituto di Topografia Antica della Università di Roma* 4 [1968] fig. 144)

FIGURE 29. Fosso Sanguisuga—east end of the *euripus* faced in *opus reticulatum*. (From G. M. De Rossi, P. G. Di Domenico, and L. Quilici, "La Via Aurelia da Roma a Forum Aureli," *Quaderno dell'Istituto di Topografia Antica della Università di Roma* 4 [1968] fig. 127)

Fosso Sanguisuga (Fig. 29)

Immediately east of the town of Ladispoli and the Fosso Sanguisuga lie the remains of a large Roman villa. Scattered concrete walls faced in *opera reticulatum* and *testaceum* cover an area 200 meters square. Situated 20 meters inland and running parallel to the shore are the ruins of a long narrow pond or *euripus*.[74]

The pond was at least 39 meters long, 5.4 meters wide, and oriented east to west along the shore.[75] The east end of the pond is formed by a semicircular or apsidal wall, now half visible (Fig. 29). The west end is in poor repair and the foundations are still buried but a similar apsidal wall is possible. The concrete walls are approximately 50 centimeters thick and preserved mostly at the level of the foundation. Hard stone pyramids found in situ at the pond's east end indicate that the walls were faced with *opus reticulatum*.

Palo—Alsium (Figs. 30, 31)

The village of Palo, 2 kilometers south of Ladispoli, is associated with the ancient site of Alsium, a port of Caere.[76] The site is occupied by a fifteenth-century Orsini castle, now called the Castello Odescalchi, and the nearby seventeenth-century Villa La Posta. Excavations, beneath the Villa north of the castle, carried out by the Soprintendenza alle Antichità dell'Etruria meridionale in 1966 have unearthed remains of a Roman villa with an U-shaped plan. Visible in the sea opposite the ancient villa are the concrete ruins of two enclosures which could have functioned as fishponds: one rectangular in plan, the other curvilinear. A shelf of soft stone platform or panchina projects beyond the shore and forms the basis on which the ponds are built.

Best preserved is a large rectangular pond (Fig. 30) which measures approximately 110 by 50 meters and is protected on its three seaward sides by a wide concrete mole. The fourth side supports the seventeenth-century villa. The seaward walls are about 4 meters wide and emerge as much as 2 meters above the present level of the sea. Though the concrete mole is badly eroded at least three openings through the thick walls can be identified.

The second curvilinear pond, located just north of the rectangular pond, is difficult to make out today. A sketch drawn by Rodolfo Lanciani in 1890 (Fig. 31) depicts an enclosure formed by two walls at right angles to each other with a curved quarter circle completing the pond.[77] Lanciani noted that the walls of this enclosure were about 3 meters wide and faced in *opus reticulatum*.

Architecture used in the construction of the ancient villa includes walls faced with *opera reticulatum* and *testaceum*. Mosaics, with polychrome geometric designs, were uncovered during the excavations in the 1960s, and have been dated to the third or fourth century A.D.[78] These finds attest to several building phases, beginning as early as the second half of the first century B.C. and lasting until the late antique period. The use of reticulate masonry supports the placement of at least the curvilinear pond in the earliest history of the villa during the late Republic.[79] An inscription found at the site suggests that this property came into imperial hands by at least the second century A.D.[80]

ROME AND LATIUM

Rome — Grottarossa (Figs. 32 – 34)

The site of Grottarossa is located along the Via Flaminia 7.5 kilometers north of Rome. Between the hill of Grottarossa and the Tiber is a plain

FIGURE 30. Palo—aerial view of the rectangular enclosure. (From G. M. De Rossi, P. G. Di Domenico, and L. Quilici, "La Via Aurelia da Roma a Forum Aureli," *Quaderno dell'Istituto di Topografia Antica della Università di Roma* 4 [1968] fig. 117)

dominated by the concrete cores of two large *tumuli*.[81] West of the ancient road and immediately south of the western *tumulus* are the remains of two *piscinae*.[82]

The first fishpond consists of three long enclosures lying side by side and oriented east to west (Fig. 34: foreground). Each tank is 3.5 meters wide and around 30 meters long. The entire complex covers an area measuring 12.5 meters by 30 meters. The walls (50 centimeters wide) were built of concrete faced, in most part, in *opus reticulatum* and are preserved to a maximum height of 1 meter. Some of the walls (near the southwest corner) have no facing but bear the lines of wooden forms or shuttering. A small portion of flooring (cocciopesto) still in situ in the southwest corner of the southernmost tank and what appears to be a finished top edge of the wall suggest that the maximum depth of this pond was not much more than a meter. The top of the pond is at a level just below the surface of the ancient road. Given its depth the pond could have been supplied by the nearby Tiber or from other sources (cisterns or aqueducts), which originate at a higher elevation.

Four meters south of the rectangular pond are the much restored ruins of an ornate fishpond whose plan has the shape of the Greek letter

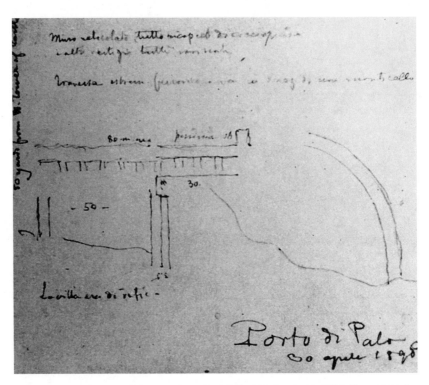

FIGURE 31. Palo—curvilinear pond sketched by Rodolfo Lanciani in 1890. (From G. M. De Rossi, P. G. Di Domenico, and L. Quilici, "La Via Aurelia da Roma a Forum Aureli," *Quaderno dell'Istituto di Topografia Antica della Università di Roma* 4 [1968] fig. 119)

phi (Figs. 32 – 34). The plan with its curvilinear walls and internal subdivisions recalls, on a smaller scale, some of the larger seaside fishponds. The central portion of the *piscina* is formed by a circular tank nearly 20 meters in diameter. Appended to the north and south side of the circle are rectangular tanks, one to a side, which measure approximately 4 by 10 meters. The walls of the pond are constructed of concrete around 45 centimeters wide. The interior of the walls is faced in *opus reticulatum* and covered with a layer (3 to 4 centimeters thick) of concrete. The exterior is faced with ashlars of tufa in a sort of *opus quadratum*. Many of the blocks have been robbed from the walls of the pond and are most complete on the circle's east side and along portions of the rectangular tanks (Fig. 32). The exterior facing appears to be only a single course and the haphazard nature of the placement of these blocks points to their reuse.

The eastern side of the circular tank is formed by double semicircular walls, which are laid out on slightly different centers. The intervening

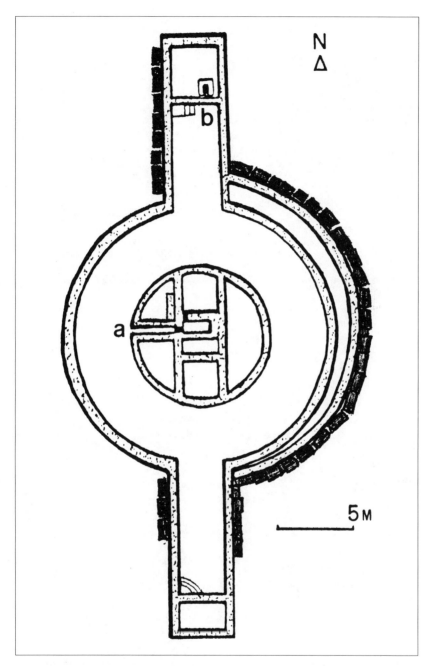

FIGURE 32. Grottarossa—plan of the phi-shaped fishpond. **a** = freshwater channel; **b** = location of drain. (Plan by J. Higginbotham)

FIGURE 33. Grottarossa—phi-shaped fishpond from the south, with walls of rectangular pond in front of the *tumulus*. (Photo by J. Higginbotham)

FIGURE 34. Grottarossa—phi-shaped fishpond from the north, with walls of the rectangular pond in the foreground. (Photo courtesy of the Fototeca Unione)

space is filled stones and debris. This arrangement could have resulted from a repair to this side where the original or inner wall needed shoring. The similarity between the concrete and the facing suggests that the repair was effected soon after the original construction.[83]

The floor of the pond is mostly intact and lies 1.2 meters below the top of the pond. Like the walls, the floor of the fishpond is covered with a layer of concrete 3 to 4 centimeters thick.

Small sections at each end of the rectangular parts of the pond were walled off and filled to form small platforms. The cross-walls do not bond with the sides of the pond and seem to have been added after the original construction. The materials of construction and the similarity of facing suggest that this modification was effected soon after the initial building phase. The northern platform measured 4 meters square while the one at the south end measured 2 by 4 meters. Small sets of stairs were set against each platform and permitted access into the pond. The steps at the north end are rectangular and those at the south are curved.

Inside the main portion of the pond is a circular island (9.25 meters in diameter) which is subdivided into six tanks. The concrete walls are faced in *opus reticulatum* and are about 50 centimeters wide. The western side of the island is pierced by a channel (Fig. 32:a), which carried fresh water into a small catch basin and then, by way of small openings, water is circulated into the other tanks.

The exact means by which water was conveyed to this pond is difficult to determine. The location of the channel in the central island supports the hypothesis that fresh water was brought in from the west side of the enclosure.[84] This position also strengthens the notion that water came from sources other than the Tiber which lies to the east. The pond could be cleaned by flushing sediment through a round opening (40 centimeters in diameter) located at the bottom of the north wall of the enclosure (b). The opening lies at the bottom of the stairs, which lead down into this end of the pond, and was covered, when not in use, by a lead access panel (in situ). On the platform above this drain is a square (30 centimeters to a side) access port. This arrangement seems designed to allow those cleaning the pond to help move sediment out of the tank and into the drain.

Both fishponds are sited where a branch of the Via Flaminia moves west towards the heights of Grottarossa. Perhaps one of the nearby villas operated these ponds.[85] The spacious flats near the river allowed sufficient space to build fishponds while still being accessible to the villa (by way of the branch road to the Flaminia) and to potential markets in Rome (by way of the Flaminia or the Tiber).

The use of concrete faced with regular *opus reticulatum* and the total absence of brick suggests a date in the late first century B.C. or the early first century A.D.

Rome—Monteverde (Figs. 35, 36)

Early in this century, during the construction of the Nuovo Ospedale della Vittoria on Monteverde in Trastevere, a Roman fishpond was unearthed.[86] The pond was designed to have the tops of its walls flush with the surrounding ground. The enclosure was rectangular in plan measuring 42.1 by 19 meters and 2 meters deep. The walls were constructed of concrete (80 centimeters wide) faced in *opus incertum* covered by a layer of plaster (4 centimeters thick). The floor of the pond was formed by a stratum (approximately 15 centimeters thick) of cocciopesto.

The plan included platforms (5.6 meters wide) that extended (4.8 meters) into the pond from both short sides of the pond (Fig. 35:B). Incorporated into the fabric of the pond's wall were ten large ceramic storage vessels or *dolia*. The *dolia* were laid on their sides in the wall so that their rims were flush with the wall's inside surface and their bodies buried in the concrete and the fill that surrounded the pond (Fig. 36). Each *dolium* was 1.6 meters tall, 1.3 meters in diameter at the shoulder with a rim that provided an opening 65 centimeters in diameter.[87] Three *dolia* were placed into each projecting platform and two positioned in each of the pond's long sides. These vessels provided shady retreats where fish could escape the heat of the sun or other fish.

In the center of each long side were small recesses: a circular niche on the west side and a square recess on the east side. These appear to be points where water emptied into the enclosure. At the northeast corner of the *piscina* a flight of stairs was included to facilitate entry into the pond.

A second phase of construction saw the addition of a circular tank to the center of the pond (Fig. 35:A). This tank (11 meters in diameter and 2 meters deep) was positioned slightly west of the north-south axis and its construction cut through the cocciopesto floor of the original pond. The circular wall was made of concrete (90 centimeters wide) faced in rough *opus reticulatum* and reinforced at four points by buttresses

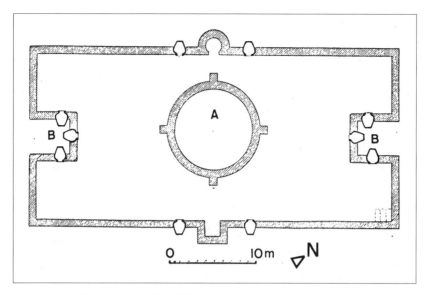

FIGURE 35. Monteverde—plan of the fishpond. **A** = circular tank; **B** = projecting platforms with *dolia*. (From G. Mancini, "Roma. Recenti trovamenti di antichita nella citta e nel suburbio," *NSc* 21 [1924] 54, fig. 6)

FIGURE 36. Monteverde—remains of projecting platform, with *dolia* in place. (Photo courtesy of the Fototeca Unione)

(90 centimeters square and 2 meters high).[88] In addition, these buttresses could have served to support temporary walkways which would permit access to this central tank. The inside and outside of the tank were coated with plaster. Iron spikes were inserted into the circular wall to help hold the plaster to the faced surface.

The original construction of the pond used concrete faced in *opus incertum*. This would support a date for the original construction no later than the early first century B.C. The second phase saw the addition of a circular tank, which was built with concrete faced in rough *opus reticulatum*. This same method of facing was used in the branch of the Aqua Alsietina, the remains of which were unearthed near the fishpond.[89] According to Frontinus,[90] the Alsietina was brought into Rome in 2 B.C. to supply the Naumachia built by Augustus. The association of the aqueduct with the pond's second phase leaves the question of the fishpond's original water source unanswered.

Rome — Domus Tiberiana (Figs. 37, 38)

The Domus Tiberiana occupies the northwestern portion of the Mons Palatinus. Built into the southwest corner of the platform, which supported the palace, are the remains of an oval fishpond (Fig. 37). The pond has been known since it was uncovered during the excavations of Pietro Rosa at the behest of Napoleon III when the French emperor took possession of the Farnese gardens in the 1860s.[91]

The fishpond is oval or elliptical, measuring 11.8 by 8 meters (Fig. 38). The pond was constructed of concrete walls (50 centimeters wide) faced with courses of brick (triangular and broken). The interior of the pond was lined with cocciopesto, the majority of which is no longer preserved. Access to and around the pond was afforded by a pavement riveted with tiles and marble, which ran up against the top of the pond.

The bottom of the pond was designed with two steps that lead down to a channel running along the long axis of the pond. The first step lies 1.2 meters below the top of the wall, is 1.5 meters wide, and rings the pond broken only at both the east and west ends by the channel. The second level begins 50 centimeters below the first and is bisected by the channel leaving approximately 1.5 meters on either side.

The last level is 50 centimeters below the second and is occupied by a channel, 1 meter wide. At each end of the channel are openings in the *piscina* wall that discharge into a drain below. There is a curious notch in the channel along its south side. The space afforded by the notch, barely 50 centimeters square, might have been provided so that a worker, standing in the channel, could assist the flushing of the pond while not impeding the flow of water and sediment. Water was supplied through a single arched aperture (60 centimeters wide and 50 centimeters high) at

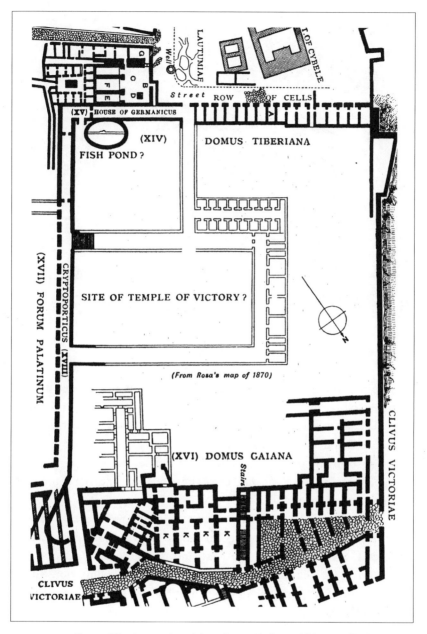

FIGURE 37. Domus Tiberiana—plan of the palace, with the oval fishpond. (From P. Rosa's plan of 1870 reproduced in R. Lanciani, *The Ruins and Excavations of Ancient Rome* [London 1897] fig. 54)

FIGURE 38. Domus Tiberiana—oval fishpond from the west. (Photo courtesy of Fototeca Unione [Archivio Fotografico Vaticano VI-20-12])

the top of the west end of the ellipse. This system allowed sediment to settle at the bottom of the pond without fouling the rest of the enclosure. The steps permitted workers, periodically, to sweep detritus into the channel and, when this was filled, completely flush the pond by forcing the sediment out the bottom drains. The drains were probably equipped with panels that could close these openings during routine operation of the fishpond.

The location of the pond in the Domus Tiberiana has tended to date the enclosure to the early first century A.D.[92] However, the exclusive use of brick-faced concrete and the curvilinear plan does fit better in the repertoire of forms common later in the century.[93] Modifications to this section of the Palatine by Nero and Domitian may have included the addition of the fishpond.[94]

Rome—Domus Augustana (Figs. 39, 40)

The architect who designed the Flavian residence on the Palatine made ample use of the fresh water supplied by a branch of the Aqua Claudia. Along with the fountains and nymphaea, one pool has characteristics that suggest that it was designed as a fishpond. The pond is located in the

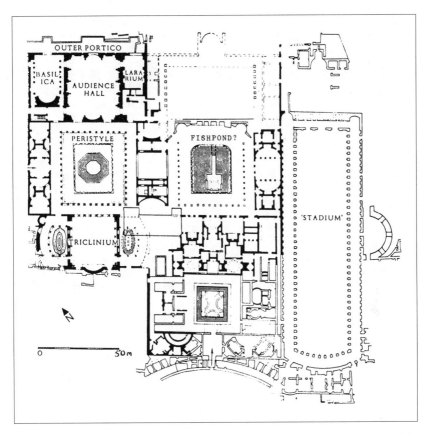

FIGURE 39. Domus Augustana—plan of the Flavian palace, with the location of the fishpond. (Adapted from J. B. Ward-Perkins, *Roman Imperial Architecture* [Harmondsworth 1970] pl. 36)

center of the upper peristyle court of the Domus Augustana, the private residence of the emperor. The area was cleared and excavated by Bartoli but never fully published before his death in 1957.[95]

The *piscina* in the upper peristyle is the largest structure in the palace constructed to hold water (Figs. 39, 40). The pond is basically rectangular in plan measuring approximately 32 by 24 meters. The two corners of the side away from the private quarters of the palace (the northeast) are rounded while the other two are square. The enclosure was constructed in brick-faced concrete lined with cocciopesto and then revetted with marble. The remains of marble flooring near the walls indicate a depth of just over 1 meter. The sides of the pond were provided with a continuous series of recesses that consisted of a repeating pattern of

FIGURE 40. Domus Augustana—aerial view of the fishpond. (Photo courtesy of the Fototeca Unione)

semicircular, triangular, and rectangular niches. The entire arrangement consisted of at least eighty recesses around the interior of the pond. This design, while aesthetically appealing, provided retreats for the fish. The pond, in the center of the upper peristyle, was constructed as part of Rabirius's Flavian palace, which was inaugurated in A.D. 92.[96]

A second phase of construction saw the addition of an island, which was connected to the northeast side of the pond by a bridge. The island and the connected bridge were positioned slightly off center lying closer to the southeast side. Both structures were built of concrete faced with courses of brick. The bridge is 7.4 meters long, 1.05 meters high, 2.4 meters wide, and supported by seven arches.[97] The piers of the bridge sit right on the pond floor with no foundation. The solid concrete island measures 10.1 by 9 meters and is 1.45 meters high. Foundations on this island appear to have supported a small temple or *aedicula*. This addition is dated by a brick stamp, which provides a *terminus post quem* of the late third or early fourth century A.D.[98]

Tivoli—Villa of Quintilius Varus (Figs. 41–43)

On a spur of the Colle Piano southwest of the Chiesetta dei Cappuccini, Madonna di Quintiliolo, are the remains of a large Roman villa identified with the Quintilii or Quinctilii Vari. The site was first excavated by

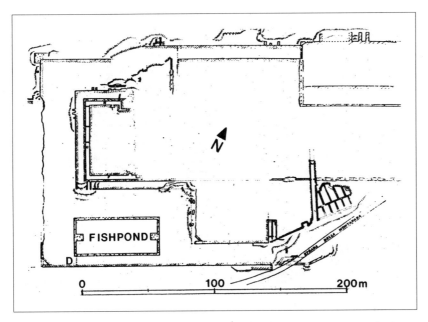

FIGURE 41. Tivoli—plan of the Villa of Quintilius Varus, with fishpond on the lower terrace. **D** = drain. (From C. F. Giuliani, *Tibur—Forma Italiae* I.7 pars prima [Florence 1970] fig. 425)

Pirro Ligorio in 1567 at the behest of Ippolito II, Duca d'Este. Later in that century, Giovanni Zappi first suggested that the pond on the lower terrace was designed for the raising of fish.[99] The pond is now the site of a privately owned olive grove.

The villa was built on a two large terraces that overlooked the Roman Campagna to the west and commanded a breathtaking view of the Sanctuary of Hercules Victor, which was located across the Anio River in ancient Tibur. The villa covers an area measuring 270 by 152 meters or roughly 6 hectares.[100] The south corner of the lower terrace, which was supported by walls constructed of concrete faced in *opus incertum*, is occupied by a fishpond (Figs. 41, 42).[101]

The fishpond is rectangular in plan and measures 62.8 by 24 meters and is about 1.5 meters deep. The walls of the *piscina* were constructed of concrete faced in *opus incertum* just as the walls of the lower terrace. The top of the walls were 1.5 meters wide and flush with the floor level of the terrace. Attached to the middle of the pond's short sides are single platforms (4.8 meters wide) which project 6.45 meters in toward the center of the enclosure. Each platform is supported by piers formed by

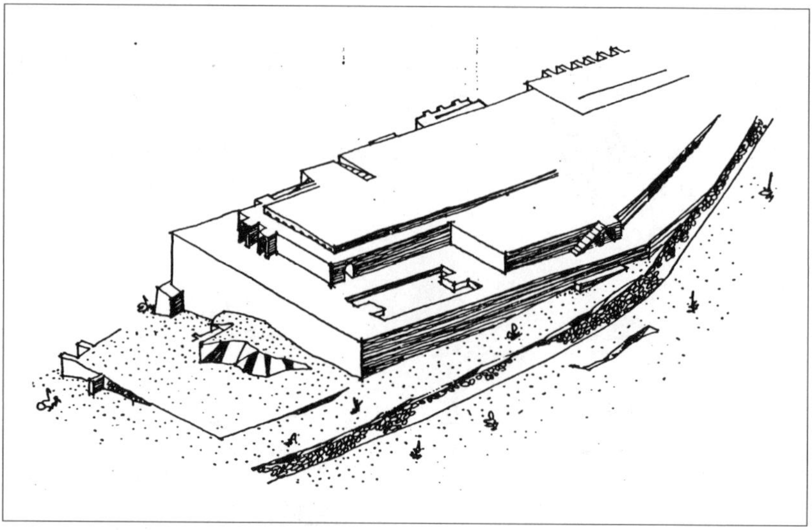

FIGURE 42. Tivoli—schematic reconstruction of the Villa of Quintilius Varus. (From C. F. Giuliani, *Tibur—Forma Italiae* 1.7 pars prima [Florence 1970] fig. 426)

the intersection of five small barrel vaults: three through the long sides of the platform, two through the front side. Each platform possessed eight arched openings (75 centimeters wide and 1.1 meters tall), which allowed fish to enter and escape the heat or the appetites of other fish (Fig. 43).

Around the fishpond the terrace supported a broad esplanade. The pond and the terrace, where it sits, are framed on two sides (northeast and northwest) by the substructures of the upper terrace (Fig. 42). From here it would have been possible to view the fishpond as well as the panorama beyond.[102]

The villa was supplied with water from a large cistern positioned higher on the Colle Piano 200 meters to the east.[103] This cistern was fed by two aqueducts which conveyed water from the upper course of the Anio River. It is logical to infer that water from the cistern could have supplied the *piscina* as well.[104] Overflow from the pond was carried through a canal that emptied from an outlet in the terrace below the southern corner of the pond (Fig. 41:D).[105] It is clear that the terrace with its pond was planned as a unit. The accommodation of the pond's overflow in the fabric of the terrace and the similarity of construction method support this contention. The *opus incertum* used in the construction of the terrace and the pond is dated to the late second or early first century B.C.[106]

GAZETTEER OF FISHPONDS

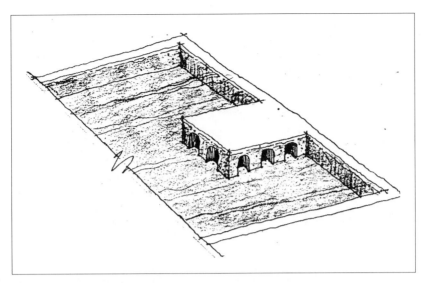

FIGURE 43. Tivoli—schematic reconstruction of the fishpond's east end, with projecting platform. (Sketch by Linda Cook)

The site has been associated with the Quintilii since at least the tenth century.[107] This tradition has been used to bolster the notion that this villa belonged to Quintilius Varus who was a friend of Virgil and Horace.[108] Varus was known to have had property in the vicinity of Tibur, but his lifetime may have been a little late for him to be considered responsible for the original construction. This does not preclude the likelihood that this villa was in the hands of the Quinctilii Vari, whose line included P. Quinctilius Varus, consul in 13 B.C. and general at the disaster in the Teutoburg Forest.[109]

Tivoli—Villa of Manlius Vopiscus (Figs. 44, 45)

On the cliffs of the Monte Catillo, immediately west of the falls where the Anio drops into the valley north of Tivoli, are the remains of a Roman villa on the grounds of the nineteenth-century Villa Gregoriana. The ancient villa follows the contours of the cliff, oriented southwest to northeast. The precipitous drop of the hill necessitated a plan built on a narrow terrace supported by concrete vaults faced, primarily, in *opus incertum*.[110] In the southern half of this villa are three interconnected rooms that were designed for raising fish.[111]

The fishpond consists of three adjacent rooms constructed of concrete faced in *opus incertum* and covered by concrete vaults (Fig. 44). The

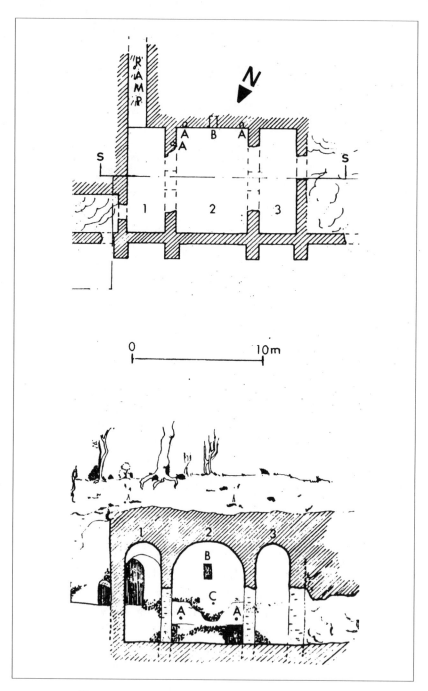

FIGURE 44. Tivoli—plan of vaulted fishpond in the Villa of Manlius Vopiscus (top), with cross-section (bottom). **1–3** = principal tanks of the fishpond; **A** = locations of *amphorae*; **B** = water inlet; **C** = overflow drain; **S–S** = location of cross-section. (From C. F. Giuliani, *Tibur—Forma Italiae* I.7 pars prima [Florence 1970] fig. 329)

FIGURE 45. Tivoli—schematic reconstruction of vaulted fishpond (right) and adjacent terrace (left). (From C. F. Giuliani, *Tibur—Forma Italiae* I.7 pars prima [Florence 1970] fig. 342)

central room (2), which measures 5.3 by 8 meters in plan, is larger than the two lateral rooms (1 and 3) which measure 2.95 by 8 meters. The vaulted ceilings of all three rooms stand 7.8 meters above their floors.[112] All three rooms of this complex were connected by openings in the two sidewalls, which divide the vaulted tanks of the pond. The exact form of these openings is impossible to determine due to the poor condition of the walls.

The complex was built against the hill, which was cut back to accommodate its construction. Concrete was used to complete the rooms which were enclosed on all sides save for the front wall. This side, facing the gorge of the Anio, was formed by three walls which closed off the open ends of the vaults.[113] This arrangement left a clerestory at the top of each vault, which would allow air and light into the confines of the pond.[114] In addition, the side walls, which divide the three rooms, extend beyond the line of the cross walls. Thus, they form four buttresses, which support the pond on the steep slope of the hill (Fig. 45).

No access was provided between the fishpond and rooms on the same terrace. With the three rooms of the fishpond isolated, entrance was afforded by way of a ramp (1.5 meters wide and 3.2 meters high), which connected the upper level of the villa to the fishpond. The ramp opened on to the back of the easternmost room (Fig. 44:1) 3 meters above the level of the floor. Cuttings, in the walls below the ramp access, attest to the placement of wooden stairs that would lead to the floor of the room.

An aqueduct, which is cut into the hill behind the pond, supplied water to the *piscina* as well as other parts of the villa. Water entered the pond through a rectangular opening (60 centimeters wide and 1.1 meters high) that was placed in the back wall of the central room (2), 4.8 meters above the floor (B). This room was coated with cocciopesto to a line height of 3.15 meters above the floor of the room. In the back wall, just above this line, a circular opening served as the overflow drain, which empties behind the wall (C). A diagonal cutting in the back wall of room 2 probably carried a small conduit that conveyed water from the aqueduct, past the main room, and emptied into room 3.

Three large *amphorae* (A), laid horizontally, were incorporated into the fabric of the concrete walls of the central room or tank 1.6 meters above the floor: two in the back wall, one in the east wall that separates room 2 from room 1. The rims of these *amphorae* are flush with surfaces of the walls. These *amphorae* are positioned below the apparent water line of the pond and served as receptacles for fish to lay eggs or to escape predacious neighbors.

For a long time, these remains have been associated with the villa of Manlius Vopiscus mentioned by Statius.[115] Manlius Vopiscus was a wealthy philanthropist during the reign of Domitian. Excited by Statius's description, Lady Compton began excavating the site in 1825.[116] Construction of a villa by Pope Gregory XVI in 1835 and the Strada delle Cascate in 1847 exposed more remains.[117] It is probable that the ruins in the Villa Gregoriana are part of the famous Villa of Vopiscus— the remainder probably lies between the Palazzi Pacifici and the Ristorante Sirene, the exact limits of which have been obscured by later construction.

The *opus incertum* used in the construction of the vaulted fishpond points to a date in the late second or early first century B.C. These republican ruins are probably part of a villa which, later, formed a nucleus of the celebrated villa of Manlius Vopiscus.

Licenza—Villa of Horace (Figs. 46 – 48)

The villa, commonly connected with the writer Horace, is sited near the city of Licenza (ancient Digentia) in the località Vigne di San Pietro, which is around 50 kilometers northeast of Tivoli. The site has been known since at least the seventeenth century.[118] Excavations of the villa began under Angelo Pasqui in 1911, passed to the direction of Giuseppe Lugli, and continued, intermittently, until the 1930s.[119]

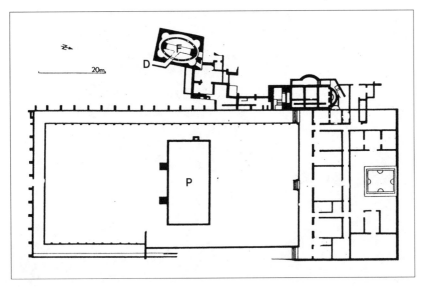

FIGURE 46. Licenza—plan of the Villa of Horace. **F** = fishpond; **D** = main drain; **P** = early fishpond? (Adapted from G. Lugli, "La villa sabina di Orazio," *MonAnt* 31 [1926] pl. III)

The villa is positioned on a small hill and is composed of three parts: living quarters to the north, a large quadriporticus to the south, and a bath complex added to the western side of the villa, which included a *piscina*. The fishpond (Fig. 46:F) is located in the southern extremity of the western annex.

The pond is oval in plan (10.4 meters in length along its long axis, 6.8 meters along its short axis) and enclosed within a rectangular building (Fig. 47). The bottom of the pond was laid out on two steps. The first level lies 1.3 meters below the top of the pond and forms a bench (up to 2.5 meters wide) on either side of the long axis. The second level is actually a channel (1.3 meters wide, 80 centimeters deep) which connects to a large drain (Fig. 46:D) that exits from the southeast side of the pond. Attached to the north and south ends of the pond, along the long axis, are small platforms that project 1 meter into the center. Each platform is 1.3 meters wide and is aligned with the central channel below.

The fishpond is constructed of concrete faced in courses of brick. The walls of the *piscina* are 45 centimeters wide and pierced by ten openings; nine are nichelike openings or *specus*, the tenth is the large arched opening into the drain. The small niches (1 meter high and 50 centimeters wide) have gabled tops and floors that slope up to small rectangular openings in the floor around the pond (Fig. 48). These recesses were

FIGURE 47. Licenza—oval fishpond from the west. (Photo by J. Higginbotham)

FIGURE 48. Licenza—perspective drawing and cross-section of gabled *specus*. (From G. Lugli, "La villa sabina di Orazio," *MonAnt* 31 [1926] fig. 43)

provided to allow fish to escape the sun's heat and predacious fish. The large arched opening (1.5 meters high and 1 meter wide) leads to a drain, which runs down the west side of the villa, and must have been closable during normal operation of the pond. Sediment could accumulate in the channel without fouling the rest of the pond. When it was deemed necessary to clean the fishpond thoroughly, this channel could be opened and the sediment flushed down the drain.

Water, from a nearby spring (Fonte degli Oratini), was supplied through a circular opening that runs through the northern platform just below the top of the wall. This opening carried a lead or ceramic pipe, which probably formed part of a hydraulic pressure system. Lugli, pointing to curved channels on each platform and calcareous accretions in the gabled niches, postulated that this system could have piped water to each of the rectangular openings above the niches.[120] This would have produced an impressive visual effect as the pond was filled from all sides by water jets and, in addition, would have greatly aided the circulation of water inside the pond. Circulation within the recesses of fishponds was a particular concern of Columella.[121] Having water circulate through the niches is a clever solution to the problem of stagnation.

During normal operation overflow was drained from the pond by way of a triangular aperture which runs through the southern platform. The position of this drain (40 centimeters below the top of the wall) would have kept the water level high enough to cover completely the gabled *specus* around the pond. A second rectangular opening was positioned in the angle immediately west of the southern platform.[122]

The pond was surrounded by a building which is rectangular in plan. The interior walls of the building are curved to match the shape of the pond while leaving 1.3 meters of floor space around the *piscina*. Four semicircular niches, corresponding to the corners of the building, complete the plan of the pond's decorative enclosure. The walls of the building were fenestrated in order to allow light and air into the pond.

The majority of the villa is built of concrete faced in *opus reticulatum*, which dates to the third quarter of the first century B.C.[123] Though this date supports the ancient literary tradition that has Maecenas giving a villa to the writer Horace between 33 and 32 B.C.,[124] the association of this particular villa with Horace is not secure.[125] The western annex and its fishpond, which employed brick-faced concrete, were added in the late first or early second century A.D.[126]

Nettuno (Figs. 49–51)

On the coast between Anzio (ancient Antium) and Astura, in the vicinity of Nettuno, are the remains of three coastal villas with fishponds. Coastal development and the destructive force of the sea, which has destroyed much of the remains, has made study difficult. At the beginning

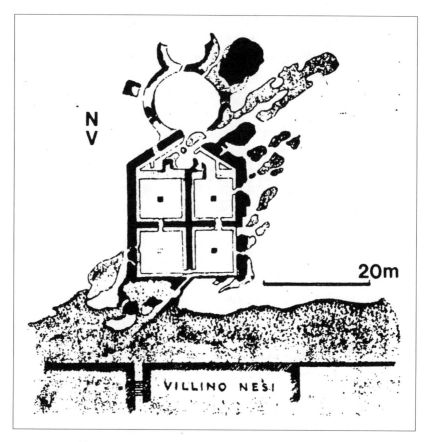

FIGURE 49. Nettuno—plan of fishpond A. (From L. Jacono, "Nettuno—*Piscinae in litore constructae*," *NSc* 21 [1924] 335, fig. 1)

of this century, when the remains were in better condition, Luigi Jacono was able to document the plans of these fishponds.[127]

The first of the fishponds (Fig. 49, pond A) was located in the water opposite the Villino del Adolfo Nesi, which was founded, in part, on the walls of an ancient villa.[128] The pond was founded on a sandstone shelf that extends into the sea beyond the promontory. The pond was located 15 meters from the Villino and covered an area which measured, roughly, 42 by 22 meters. The *piscina* consisted of several tanks of varied shapes and sizes which were protected by a thick mole, 1.5 to 2.7 meters wide. The pond was cut from the sandstone shelf and completed by the addition of concrete.

The plan of the pond consisted of a rectangular tank near the shore with a triangular tank on the seaward or south end. Appended to the apex of the triangle were two circular tanks, the last of which (southern-most) is incomplete. The main house-shaped section is divided into five tanks: four roughly square (measuring 8 meters square) and one triangular (22 meters along its base with the other sides 12 meters long). Remains of walls within the triangle suggest the presence of more subdivisions in this tank. The partition walls, which subdivide the pond, appear to be approximately 90 centimeters wide and fashioned primarily from concrete. Walkways (70 centimeters wide) were constructed around the inside of the moles and the partition walls at a level just below these walls. Small piers (1 meter square), which were located in the center of each square tank, were probably supports for temporary walkways that allowed access to the centers of these tanks. Four openings or *itinera* were positioned between some of the tanks and permitted the movement of water and fish within the subdivided enclosure. The apparent depth of this pond increased as it moves farther from the shore: 1 meter in the square tanks, 1.3 meters in the triangular tank, and 2 meters in the first circular enclosure.

The triangular tank, which was linked to the southwestern square   **133**
tank, was connected to the open sea through a channel at its apex and to the circular tank immediately to the south. The circular tank (13 meters in diameter) was a simple enclosure with no apparent walkways or partitions. The remains of the second curvilinear tank suggest an enclosure 11 meters in diameter. Its southern or seaward side, where the sea floor falls off, has been destroyed.

Seawater entered the pond through at least two points: the channel to the apex of the triangular tank and the circular enclosures. The pond was also supplied by a freshwater canal, which entered the center of its shoreside wall. The canal was 40 centimeters wide and ran on a diagonal course northeast to southwest. Its ultimate source is unknown.

Along the east side of the large circular tank was a square concrete pier, which measured 3 meters square. This pier could have served as an anchorage for boats or as a base for a tower to direct harvesting in the pond. Fish, attracted by the brackish environment inside the pond, would first enter the circular tanks at the seaward end of the pond. Here, harvesting could take place, with fish to be consumed separated from those to be confined in the main partitioned section of the pond.

The second *piscina* (Fig. 50, pond B) was positioned on a sandstone shelf in the sea below the walls of the Castello del Sangallo.[129] The pond was located 22 meters south of the castle walls and covered an area

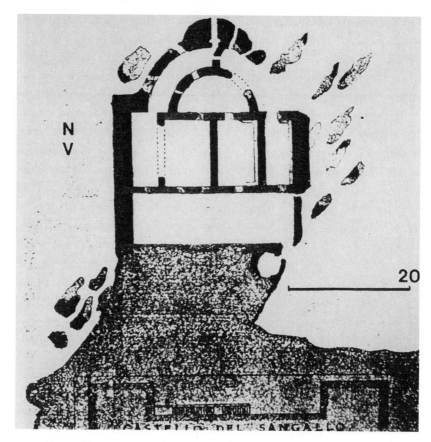

FIGURE 50. Nettuno—plan of fishpond B. (From L. Jacono, "Nettuno—*Piscinae in litore constructae*," *NSc* 21 [1924] 336, fig. 2)

measuring 32.5 by 37.5 meters. The enclosure was cut from the sandstone and finished with walls of concrete. The plan of the *piscina* consisted of a rectangular section, which was closest to shore, with a semicircular section on the southern or seaward side of the pond.

The fishpond is surrounded by protective moles which form the east and west sides of the enclosure. The landward side of the pond was obscured by the beach sand and the walls of the castle. The seaward side of the pond was enclosed by an arching mole approximately 2 meters wide and based on a circle 25 meters in diameter. The mole thickens to 5 meters at the pond's southern extremity where it is pierced by a channel to the sea, which was 75 centimeters wide and 5 meters long. Vertical slots in this channel suggest the placement of a movable barrier or gate. Two additional openings, through the semicircular mole, were noted by Jacono lying either side of the main channel. Others probably were positioned on the pond's western side where the force of the surf had rendered any detailed reconstruction impossible.

The interior of the *piscina* was divided into at least eight tanks: one large rectangular tank (26.5 by 8 meters) along the shore, a line of four smaller rectangular tanks (two measuring 10.5 by 4 meters and two measuring 10.5 by 7.3 meters) adjacent to the large tank, and at least three tanks that occupy the semicircular end of the pond. The remains of interior walkways (50 centimeters wide) are noted in the two western-most of these tanks and probably could be restored in the others. The semicircular part of the pond was partitioned by a wall concentric with the mole. This arrangement resulted in an inner semicircular tank (approximately 12 meters in diameter) and two narrow tanks (about 3 meters wide) just inside the mole. Many of the dividing walls were pierced by openings to allow the movement of water and fish between tanks. The apparent depth of this pond increased as it moved farther from the shore, ranging from 1 to 2 meters.

The third *piscina* (Fig. 51, pond C) was located at the east end of the city 24 meters from the line of the walls of Nettuno.[130] Pond C was designed with a square plan, which measured 22 by 22 meters, and was constructed entirely of concrete. The walls of the pond were uniformly a meter wide and partitioned the enclosure into nine separate tanks six of which were intact and three which were possible to reconstruct.[131] The area in which the fishpond was located was protected by a concrete mole (3 meters wide and stretching for at least 36 meters), which ran east to west 11 meters south of the pond. This mole made unnecessary the construction of a thick perimeter wall similar to that employed in ponds A and B at Nettuno.

Astura—La Saracca (Figs. 52, 53)

The site of Astura lies at the mouth of the river of the same name along the Tyrrhenian coast 11.5 kilometers east-southeast of Anzio and 54 kilometers southeast of Rome. The location is recorded by several ancient writers and geographers who mention the river and an island, and testify to the residences in the area.[132] Along the shore are the remains of three *villae maritimae* which possess fishponds: the semicircular pond at La Saracca, the rectangular pond near La Banca, and the large insular *piscina* at Torre Astura.[133]

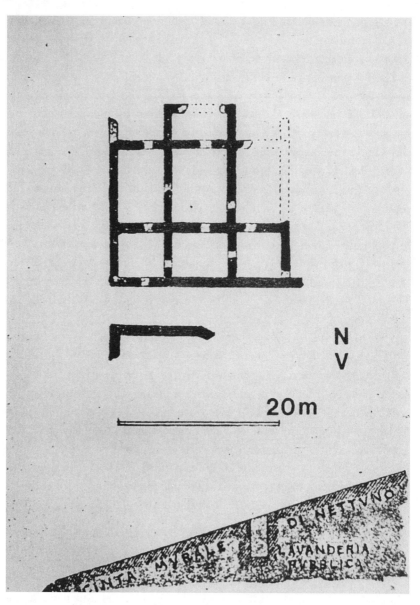

FIGURE 51. Nettuno—plan of fishpond C. (From L. Jacono, "Nettuno—*Piscinae in litore constructae*," *NSc* 21 [1924] 338, fig. 3)

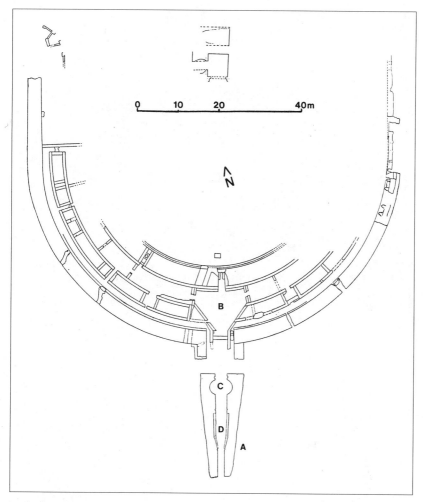

FIGURE 52. Astura, La Saracca—plan of semicircular fishpond. **A** = channel; **B** = hexagonal tank; **C – D** = traps inside channel. (Adapted from F. Piccarreta, *Astura—Forma Italiae* I.13 [Florence 1977] fig. 124)

The site of Astura was continuously inhabited since antiquity and is mentioned, in connection with fishponds, in documents from the tenth century.[134] Scholarly interest in the Roman remains and, in particular, their relationship to the Asturan villa owned by Cicero, dates from the seventeenth century.[135] This interest has continued up to the present with more attention to the details of the topography and architecture.[136]

The villa and fishpond at La Saracca are located 2.1 kilometers northwest of Torre Astura (Figs. 52, 53).[137] Sand dunes cover most of the villa

FIGURE 53. Astura, La Saracca—aerial view of fishpond. **A–D** as in Figure 52; **I–III** = concentric rings of tanks. (From G. Schmiedt, ed., *Il livello antico del Mar Tirreno* [Florence 1972] pl. 122)

and part of the fishpond. The *piscina* was constructed on a rock shelf, which projects from the shore, and was linked to the villa on shore. The pond is semicircular in plan, the perimeter of which was protected by a concrete mole 3.5 meters wide and based on a circle 90 meters in diameter.

The mole was pierced by at least five openings, or *itinera* (four small and one large), which allowed seawater to circulate within the enclosure. Vertical slots, visible in the sides of three of these openings, attest to the placement of movable gates. The main opening into the pond was through the center of the semicircular perimeter. This *iter* was positioned on the central axis of the pond and left a gap 6.6 meters wide in the mole. This opening aligned with an external channel, which extended beyond the confines of the pond to the south. From the shore along the pond's east side are the remains of a freshwater aqueduct, which would have supplemented the supply inside the enclosure and created a brackish environment.

Just inside the mole (leaving a channel 1.8 meters wide) are three rows of rectangular tanks (Fig. 53:I–III) that follow the curve of the mole. Each row of tanks (approximately 4 meters wide) is formed by walls of concrete (60 centimeters wide) which are just below the height of the perimeter mole. The accumulation of sand has obscured the remainder of the pond but it appears that there were no other major subdivisions behind the three rows of tanks.

The most interesting feature of this fishpond is the group of structures that dominates the center of the enclosure. Inside the pond and aligned with the principal opening through the mole is a hexagonal tank (B), which interrupts the first two rows of tanks (I and II) while abutting the south wall of the third ring of tanks (III). Closable openings in the east and west sides of this tank link it to the second ring of tanks. The south end of the hexagonal tank virtually plugs the main opening through the mole while leaving small channels (90 centimeters wide) between the walls of the tank and the mole.

Outside the mole, two spur walls (4 meter long and 2.3 meter wide) extend the walls of the main *iter* and align with the walls of the external channel (A). This channel was positioned 3.6 meters south or seaward of the spurs attached to the *piscina* mole. It was formed by two large moles 25 meters long and up to 4 meters wide while leaving a channel 2.5 meters wide. The moles of the channel taper as they move out to sea. Inside the channel are three sets of vertical slots for the placement of movable gates. In place they would form two zones within the channel: one rectangular (D, 2.5 meters wide and 6 meters long) and the other (C, 8 meters long, 2.5 meter wide, and 5 meters wide at the circles) augmented by two semicircular recesses. Another set of gates would have closed the gaps between the channel (A) and the perimeter mole of the pond.

The function of the channel (A), with its closable tanks (C and D), and the hexagonal tank (B) is twofold: circulation of water and the capture of fish. The force of the surf and tides would cause water to enter the channel (A), at its south end, and direct it through the narrow channels either side of the hexagonal tank (B). The constriction of the water's pathway would increase the force of the flow and thus facilitate the exchange of water within the pond.

The harvest or capture of fish (euryhaline species) was dependent on the tides and the salinity of the water. During high tide the primary force of flow would move into the enclosure, while at low tide the flow would reverse. Adult fish, responding to the instinctual need to make for open sea in order to spawn, swim against the flow toward water with a higher degree of salinity. These conditions were best approximated during high tide when flow into the pond and the salinity would increase.

Migrating fish, attempting to leave the *piscina* would be directed through the tanks in the second row (II) where they could be trapped in the closable tanks or herded into the hexagonal tank (B) and there harvested. During low tide, when flow would reverse and brackish water inside the fishpond was forced out of the enclosure, the external channel acted as a lure and a trap (*excipula*) for fish. After spawning, fish returning to sheltered brackish waters would be attracted by the torrent of less salty water issuing from the channel. Once inside this channel selective gates could be closed, trapping fish for harvest or transfer to the holding tanks inside the fishpond.

The perimeter of the fishpond joins the sides of the villa on shore. The walls of the pond and the villa share the same concrete core but on land the walls are faced with *opus reticulatum*. The walls of the pond reveal impressions of wooden shuttering, which stop once the walls leave the water and could be faced in a conventional fashion. A small concrete wall, which was built on top of the perimeter mole, was decorated with attached columns arranged in pairs. Though only preserved on the pond's east side it is possible that they decorated the entire arc of the pond accentuating the pleasing shape of the *piscina*.

The villa, on the shore north of the pond, was planned and constructed at the same time as the *piscina*. The remains of the villa are scanty but suggest a structure built on a vaulted platform (100 meters by 50 meters) which would have afforded an attractive view of the pond and the sea beyond. The vaulted rooms, and terrace, all of which were constructed of concrete faced in *opus reticulatum*, provide a date for the original construction of the villa and pond of the late first century B.C. or early first century A.D. Repairs and additions to the villa during the later Empire are attested by concrete walls faced in brick and tufa blocks (*opus vittatum*).

Astura—La Banca (Fig. 54)

The fishpond at La Banca is located 1.6 kilometers northwest of Torre Astura (Fig. 54). The *piscina* is positioned at the end of a small point founded on a rock shelf that extends beyond the point.[138] The pond is rectangular in plan (33.2 by 20.3 meters) and was subdivided into at least two roughly square tanks (the south being 10.8 meters square; the north, 10.8 by 9.2 meters). Concrete was used to construct the enclosure, which was built in a sequence of stages. The perimeter of the pond, which measures between 4.7 and 6.8 meters wide, is formed from sev-

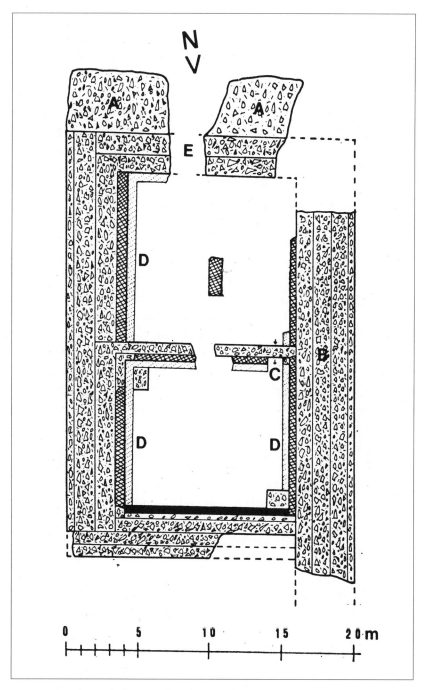

FIGURE 54. Astura, La Banca—plan of rectangular fishpond. **A** = initial pier; **B** = composite mole; **C** = opening between tanks; **D** = interior walkways; **E** = possible opening to the sea. (Adapted from F. Piccarreta, *Astura—Forma Italiae* 1.13 [Florence 1977] fig. 120)

eral walls laid side by side to create a wider barrier. The positions of these walls vis-à-vis each other suggest the following sequence of construction: south pier, west side, north side, east side, interior facing, and partitions.

The first element to be fashioned was the rectangular pier (54:A), which originally measured 20.3 by 4.2 meters, at the seaward or southern end of the enclosure.[139] The second stage saw the construction of long lateral walls on the pond's west side (B). These four walls would have abutted the original pier and continued to shore. The exact length of these walls is unknown because they disappear into the sand dune along the shore and presumably connected with the villa buried here. It appears that all four parallel walls (three of these walls were 1 meter wide, the fourth outer wall 44 centimeters) that make up this side of the enclosure were constructed rapidly, one after the other, in a single building phase.

Shuttering was probably extended from the sheltered side of the pier to the shore. After the concrete of the first wall had set the remaining three were added with the thin outer wall completing this section of the pond's perimeter. This thin outer segment was probably the position occupied by the original shuttering where heavy braces were needed to withstand the force of the sea. With the concrete walls in place, the shuttering was removed and the thin outer area was filled in. The completed west mole, when joined to the original pier, created a sheltered area, behind which the remainder of the pond could be completed in relative calm. In addition, the completed walls provided convenient walkways to facilitate subsequent construction.

With this link established, the other walls were added to complete the enclosure. Again, walls were constructed side by side to create a wide mole or barrier. Once the rectangle was complete and the interior isolated from the sea, the partition walls and walkways were added. Remains of the walkways are best preserved along the pond's east side (D). Some of these were built of concrete faced in *opus reticulatum*, which indicates that the interior of the pond was drained of water for the final sequence of construction.

Seawater probably entered the fishpond through an opening in the southern or seaward mole (E). The exact location of this aperture is impossible to fix due to the eroded condition of this portion of the enclosure. A small opening (C) through the west end of the central partition wall permitted circulation within the pond. It is probable that fresh

FIGURE 55. Torre Astura—aerial view of island fishpond and harbor moles. (From G. Schmiedt, ed., *Il livello antico del Mar Tirreno* [Florence 1972] 109, pl. 113)

water was supplied to this pond. The long western wall, which disappears into the dune, may have supported the canal that brought fresh water from reserves in or near the villa.

The use of concrete faced in *opus reticulatum* suggests a date of the late first century B.C. or early first century A.D. Additions to the pond faced in brick attest to the use of this enclosure in the later years of the Empire.

Torre Astura (Figs. 55 – 61)

The third fishpond at Astura is sited off the southern extremity of the Punta di Astura 1 kilometer south of the mouth of the river Astura (Figs. 55 – 61). A large maritime villa is located on the point and connected by a bridge to an artificial island offshore. This site has been the location of almost continual occupation since antiquity and has attracted scholarly attention since the seventeenth century.[140] Early study was prompted by the desire to connect the remains with the villa owned by Cicero, who wrote several of his letters to Atticus from Astura.[141] Interest in the architecture formed the focus of research in this century culminating in a most thorough study by Fabio Piccarreta, published in 1977.[142]

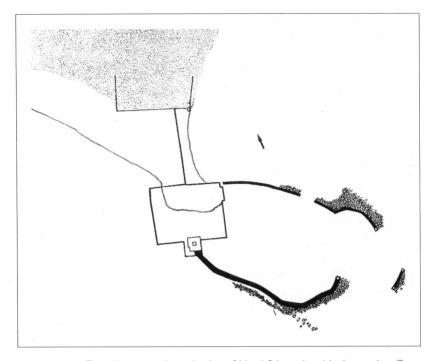

FIGURE 56. Torre Astura—schematic plan of island fishpond and harbor moles. (From F. Piccarreta, *Astura—Forma Italiae* 1.13 [Florence 1977] fig. 112)

The fishpond at Torre Astura was part of an elaborate *villa maritima*. The residential buildings on the shore were connected to an artificial island fashioned from hydraulic concrete (Figs. 55, 56, 60). The island, to the south, was reached by way of a concrete bridge, approximately 130 meters long, which carried a roadway (4 meters wide) and the channel of a freshwater aqueduct. The bridge led to a roughly rectangular terrace (82 meters square) supported on concrete vaults. This part of the complex was positioned in the center of the north side of a large rectangular enclosure given over to the raising of fish (Fig. 60).

The fishpond, which surrounded three sides of the raised terrace, measured 172 meters (east-west) by 125 meters (north-south). The perimeter of the fishpond was formed by a concrete mole 2.4 meters wide, which was pierced at at least five points so that seawater could circulate within the enclosure (Fig. 57:G). Four of these apertures were simple *itinera*, barely a meter wide, that cut through the east and west walls, two to a side.

The fifth opening was a large gap (41 meters wide) in the southern or seaward wall of the *piscina*. The two walls that constitute the southern

144

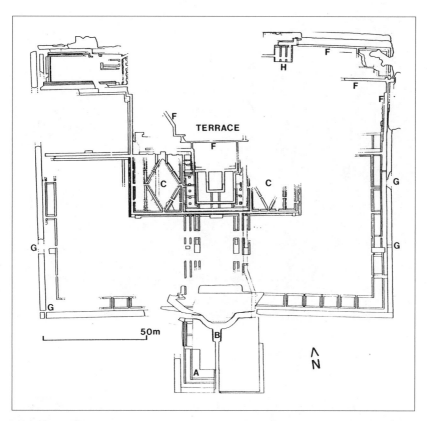

FIGURE 57. Torre Astura—plan of the fishpond. **A** = exterior structure with tanks; **B** = primary sea channel; **C** = lozenge-shaped tanks; **F** = freshwater canals; **G** = openings through the perimeter mole; **H** = cistern. (Adapted from F. Piccarreta, *Astura—Forma Italiae* 1.13 [Florence 1977] fig. 36)

boundary of the pond do not lie on a single line but on slightly different axes. This has led Piccarreta to suggest that there was a preexisting structure in the gap between these walls, a lighthouse perhaps, which precluded the construction of a continuous wall and prevented any accurate siting of these walls.[143]

A rectangular structure (42.6 meters wide and projecting 37.5 meters) was positioned just south of this gap outside the principal enclosure of the fishpond (Fig. 57:A). Most of this projecting element was used as the foundation of the medieval Torre and cannot be reconstructed with complete certainty. The ruins, which are visible, suggest an area protected on three sides by its own perimeter mole (2.5 meters wide) and bisected by a channel (running north to south) that linked the sea with the fishpond (B). The channel is forced to branch as it moves around the obstacle

FIGURE 58. Torre Astura—aerial view of fishpond from the south. (From F. Piccarreta, *Astura—Forma Italiae* 1.13 [Florence 1977] fig. 11)

FIGURE 59. Torre Astura—detail of an opening in the western lozenge-shaped tank, with vertical slots for a movable gate. (Photo by J. Higginbotham)

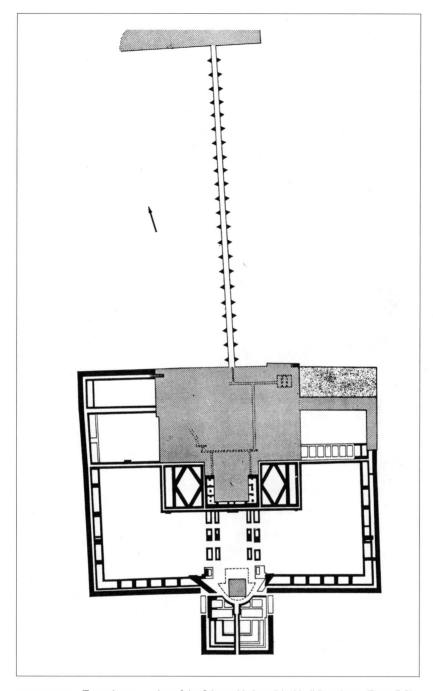

FIGURE 60. Torre Astura—plan of the fishpond in its original building phase. (From F. Pic-carreta, *Astura*—*Forma Italiae* 1.13 [Florence 1977] fig. 90)

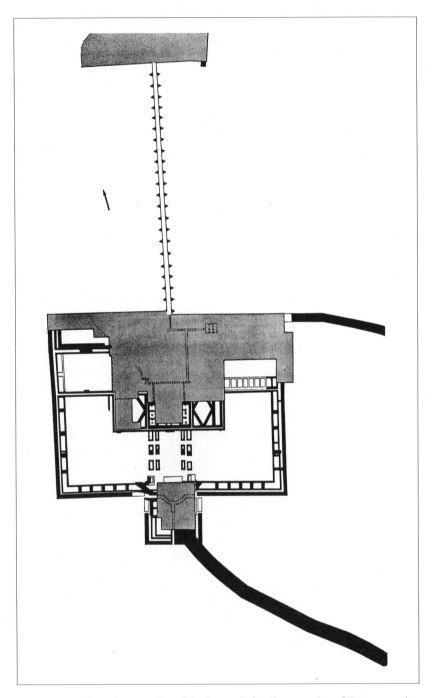

FIGURE 61. Torre Astura—plan of the fishpond after the expansion of the terrace platform and addition of the harbor moles. (From F. Piccarreta, *Astura—Forma Italiae* 1.13 [Florence 1977] fig. 94)

(lighthouse?) in the middle of the pond's southern wall. Either side of the channel the rectangular structure appears to be subdivided by at least two concentric walls of concrete.

It is possible to reconstruct this external element as the main sea channel into the pond where migrating fish could be caught as they try to enter or leave the pond. In addition, the channel funneled seawater into the enclosure (around the lighthouse?). In the pond's original phase this channel and its branches were probably open to the air. The tanks on either side of the channel could have been used to segregate and confine fish harvested in the channel (A). Subsequent construction, which may have involved the expansion of the lighthouse, caused the channel to be vaulted and the lateral tanks to be used as foundations for the expansion.

The majority of the fishpond was left open and without partitions. At least 19 small rectangular tanks (5 meters wide and between 7.5 and 15.3 meters long) were arranged inside the perimeter of the pond on three sides (east, south, and west). A space, 2.2 meters wide, was left between these tanks and the perimeter mole. The result was a channel that ran just inside the perimeter and distributed seawater brought in through the perimeter. Remains of slanting walls, located just inside the pond opposite the external channel structure, confirm that incoming seawater was directed to the east and west of the central channel and into the perimeter channel.

Two double rows of twelve small tanks (three in a line and isolated from each other) were arrayed down the north-south axis of the pond. They link the southern wall of the pond with the complex arrangement of tanks around the raised terrace at the north side of the island. Some of the tanks were partially vaulted to provide shade for fish confined inside. It is probable that these tanks joined with those that line the perimeter of the pond; but this area along the center of the pond's southern wall has been obscured by the construction of the Torre. The effect was to divide the fishpond into two large sections, east and west, which were delineated by the lines of small tanks and left with their centers largely open. The small tanks probably served to segregate varieties of fish by species or age. In addition, they would have provided convenient support for temporary walkways, which would facilitate the movement of service personnel about the fishpond.

To the north, the double rows of tanks join with an inner enclosure, which is rectangular in plan (measuring 82.5 by 31 meters) and fronts the raised terrace at the center of the island's north side. This inner enclosure is divided into three parts: a central area of narrow tanks built around a projecting platform of the terrace, and two flanking areas characterized by the imposition of lozenge-shaped tanks.

This inner zone was enclosed by three concrete walls, just over a meter wide, echoing the main fishpond; a channel was left between the perimeter and the walls of the tanks. The central section was built around a platform (19.4 meters east-west by 23 meters north-south) that projects from the center of the terrace's southern wall. The narrow tanks are 5.5 meters wide and 14.7 meters long, on either side of the platform, and 2 meters wide and 15.3 meters long in front (to the south). The tanks flanking the platform were equipped with small piers (80 centimeters square) down the center (five to a side), which probably supported wooden walkways or balconies. Lining these two tanks are narrow concrete walkways (50 centimeters wide).

East and west of the small platform and the central area of narrow tanks are two sections dominated by lozenge-shaped tanks (Fig. 57:C).[144] These sections enclose rectangular areas measuring 23.5 meters (east-west) by 26.2 meters (north-south). The extreme east and west ends of these sections—those which border the open fishpond—are designed with a rectangular tank measuring 4.5 meters wide and 26.2 meters long. The remaining area (19 by 26.2 meters) was divided into five tanks by the imposition of a lozenge-shaped tank measuring 14.2 meters to a side. The lozenge- and the four triangular-shaped tanks are lined with narrow walkways (50 centimeters wide) that stand below (60 centimeters) the dividing walls of the tanks. Openings in the walls of these tanks link the three main sections of the inner enclosure and most of the tanks they possess. Most of these openings were fitted with sets of vertical slots that permitted the placement of movable gates (Fig. 59). These openings would help regulate the movement of fish and the circulation of water in these tanks.

The raised terrace at the north end of the island was built on concrete vaults faced, in their original phase, with *opus reticulatum*. The terrace stood about 3.5 meters above the level of the pond and probably supported buildings from which the view of the sea and the ponds could be enjoyed. The bridge provided direct access from the shore to this villa adjunct. Sets of stairs led from the terrace down to the level of the pond and also to a boat landing, paved in cocciopesto, which was located at the northeast corner of the terrace.

The fishpond was supplied with both salt and fresh water to create a brackish environment. Salt water was forced through openings in the perimeter mole by the force of the tides and waves. As was noted earlier, the principal opening to the sea was by way of the channel through the wall of the pond. Water from this channel was directed to another channel, which ran around the perimeter of the enclosure. Fresh water was conveyed by an aqueduct, which ran from the shore, across the bridge, and into the island terrace. Here, a system of canals and cisterns distributed fresh water to the various sections of the fishpond as well as storing some water for alimentary uses (Fig. 57: F, H).[145]

At some point in its history, the island at Astura was equipped with two long moles which enclosed a harbor (Figs. 55, 56). The moles were anchored to the island; one abutted the pond's southeast corner and the other was attached to the projecting structure which was located in the middle of the southern wall of the enclosure (Fig. 61). The mole was founded on a rock shelf and on deposits of boulders and stones laid in the water. The concrete moles ranged between 6 and 12 meters in width and probably were carried on a series of arches. The concrete remains are faced in brick and suggest that the mole was added in the first century A.D. or later.[146] Though an earlier port might have existed, no physical remains support this contention.[147]

Pliny's mention of the *insula* at Astura can only be a reference to the artificial island constructed off the Punta di Astura.[148] The original phase of construction of the artificial island employed concrete faced in *opus reticulatum*, which is somewhat carelessly laid with slightly irregular pyramids. This building style suggests a late republican date, perhaps early Augustan. This date is supported by ancient literary evidence. In a letter to his friend Atticus, Cicero expresses his wish to erect a monument (*fanum*) for his deceased daughter in a place whence one could view Antium (Anzio) and Circeo.[149] The only site that affords this view is the Punta di Astura where the island fishpond is located. Cicero does not mention a villa, island, port, or fishpond at this site. This evidence suggests that the villa at the Punta di Astura was constructed sometime after Cicero wrote to Atticus and thus provides a terminus post quem of 45 B.C.[150]

Later phases saw additions to the terrace platform on the island, at the expense of the fishpond, and repairs to the bridge. Concrete structures used in these later phases were faced in brick and a combination of brick and tufa blocks (*opus vittatum*) indicating dates well into the later Empire.

GAZETTEER OF FISHPONDS

Circeo—Piscina di Lucullo (Figs. 62 – 65)

Along the canal, which connects the sea to the Lago di Paola (Sabaudia), are the ruins of a circular fishpond commonly called the Piscina di Lucullo. The enclosure was first studied by Giuseppe Lugli early in this century and at that time it was still used as a fishpond.[151] In the 1960s the structure was drained and the architecture was examined in great detail by V. Ginetta Chiappella.[152]

This pond lies within a rectangular terrace that is delimited by a concrete wall 1 meter high, 40 centimeters wide, and enclosing an area measuring 61.6 (north-south) by 56.1 meters (east-west). The terrace is earth-filled and creates a surface that runs up to the top edge of the pond.[153] Access to the pond was provided from both the north and south sides. The north entrance was a simple corridor (3.5 meters wide and 10.7 meters long) that leads up to the pond's edge. On the enclosure's south side, a short corridor (6.5 meters long and 3.2 meters wide) leads to a broad platform (Fig. 62:P) which measures 8.5 meters wide and 18.1 meters long and projects 5.8 meters into the circular pond.

Inscribed within the rectangular enclosure, the circular pond measures 32.5 meters in diameter and is divided into four sectors of unequal size (1 – 4). The northern and southern tanks (1, 3) are larger than the other two (2, 4). The sectors, or tanks, are delineated by radial walls that join the perimeter of the pond with a small circular tank (5.15 meters in diameter) at the pond's center. These dividing walls (60 to 80 centimeters wide) are pierced at several locations (a) by rectangular openings (approximately 20 by 30 centimeters), which facilitated the circulation of water within the *piscina*.

Appended to the northeast and northwest sides of the circular pond were two trapezoidal tanks (5, 6). Tank 5 extends 4.6 meters from the pond's perimeter and measures 8.4 meters wide, widening to 14 meters where it joins the pond. Tank 6 extends 3.5 meters and measures 9.3 meters, widening to 11.2 meters where it meets the pond. Depth, as measured from the top of the walls to the floor, was 2.75 meters in the trapezoidal tanks and 2.45 meters within the main pond.

The partition walls widen toward the bottom of the pond so as to provide walkways (70 to 80 centimeters wide) on either side of the dividing walls below their tops. Similar steps were constructed on the east and west sides of the projecting platform and inside the trapezoidal tanks (Fig. 63).

GAZETTEER OF FISHPONDS

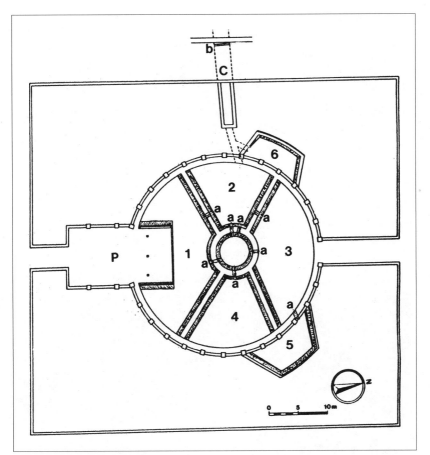

FIGURE 62. Circeo—plan of the Piscina of Lucullus. l – 4 = interior tanks; **5** and **6** = trapezoidal tanks; **P** = projecting platform; **C** = canal to the sea channel; **a** = openings between tanks; **b** = position of sluice gate. (Adapted from V. Ginetta Chiappella, "Esplorazione della cosiddetta 'Piscina di Lucullo' sul lago di Paola," *NSc* suppl. [1965] fig. 2)

The platform (Figs. 64, 65), which projects into the southern tank (Fig. 62:1), is carried on three parallel vaults: the central vault is 3.4 meters wide, 2.4 meters high, and 9.85 meters long, the two lateral vaults are 1.3 meters wide, 2.4 meters high, and 6.9 meters long.[154] These vaults (as they appear today) would have been submerged beneath the water level of the pond and were designed to provide a shady refuge for the fish kept in the *piscina*. Above the vaults was a broad platform, surrounded by a small parapet (Fig. 64, left side of photograph), which would have provided a convenient vantage point from which to view the pond.[155]

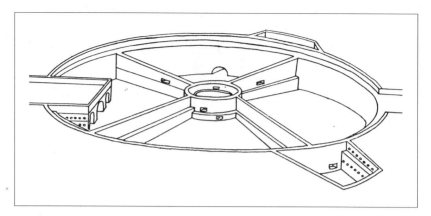

FIGURE 63. Circeo—axonometric drawing of the Piscina of Lucullus. (From V. Ginetta Chiappella, "Esplorazione della cosiddetta 'Piscina di Lucullo' sul lago di Paola," *NSc* suppl. [1965] fig. 3)

FIGURE 64. Circeo—Piscina of Lucullus, with platform at left. (Photo by J. Higginbotham)

Included in the design of the pond was the placement of numerous *amphorae* in the fabric of the walls. These vessels, minus their necks, rims, and handles, were placed laterally in the walls so that the open ends faced the interior of the pond. *Amphorae* were placed inside and outside the vaults of the platform and in the sides of the trapezoidal

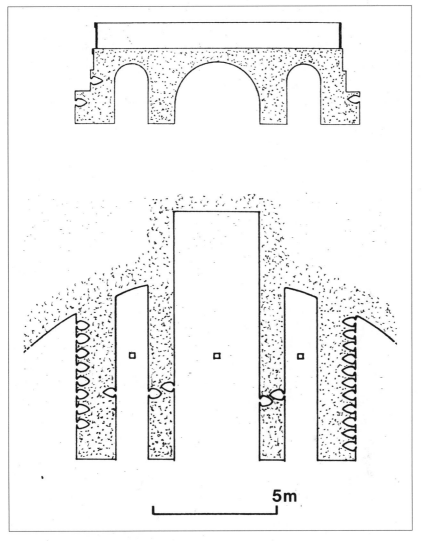

FIGURE 65. Circeo—elevation and plan of vaulted platform in the Piscina of Lucullus. (Adapted from V. Ginetta Chiappella, "Esplorazione della cosiddetta 'Piscina di Lucullo' sul lago di Paola," *NSc* suppl. [1965] figs. 5, 6)

tanks. The resulting *specus* (55 centimeters long and 35 centimeters high) presented a more constricted hiding place for the fish.

The *amphorae* were placed on the east and west sides of the platform barely 75 centimeters from the bottom of the pond: on the eastern side they were arranged in two rows of eight each, while on the western side there was a single row of eleven. In addition, a few vessels were placed inside the vaults: two in the eastern and central vaults, and one in the western vault (Fig. 65). The northeastern trapezoidal tank (Fig. 62:5) was equipped with thirty-four *amphorae* arranged in double rows on both of the tank's short sides. The northwestern tank (6) was similarly designed with thirty-one *amphorae*. Tanks 1, 5, and 6 were designed to meet different specifications than the other tanks. It would seem that the inclusion of *amphorae* meant that these tanks were intended to hold a particular species of fish, probably eels (*murenae*).

The *piscina* was supplied by a canal (Fig. 62:C), which carried brackish water from the channel connecting the Lago di Paola to the sea. The course of the canal covered the 31.5 meters distance from the channel and entered the pond's west side. The canal begins at the sea channel as a vaulted gallery 3.7 meters high and 1.6 meters wide, which covers a channel 65 centimeters wide. Upon passing the terrace wall of the pond, the canal is open to the air and continues for 6.75 meters before going underground once again for the final 4 meters to the edge of the pond. The final vaulted section of the canal (30 centimeters wide and 60 centimeters high) empties into the west side of the pond (2) while a branch feeds the adjacent trapezoidal tank (6). The water supply was augmented by a freshwater spring which bubbled through the floor of the western side of the pond (2).[156] An opening (20 centimeters by 1.5 meters) in the top of the covered gallery (b) permitted the opening and closing of a sluice gate, which could regulate the flow and the salinity of the water into the fishpond.[157]

The building history of this pond is very confused due to the continued use of the enclosure as a fishpond. Subsequent repairs and additions made use of ancient materials, and, consequently, ancient phases of construction are difficult to distinguish. This is particularly true of the upper courses of the pond. The structure was constructed of concrete laid out below ground level in order to allow the level of water in the sea channel and the spring to fill the enclosure.

The lower portions of the *piscina* including the perimeter wall, the partition walls, and the projecting platform were built of concrete faced in *opus incertum*. The trapezoidal tanks, though added after the construction of the circular perimeter, appear to have been built originally with *opus incertum*. This includes the system of *amphorae* encased in these walls. An examination of the walls shows that the trapezoidal tanks and the platform do not bond with the walls of the pond's perimeter. However, the similarity of construction and materials indicates that all of these elements were built within a short period of time and may have been part of the same initial phase. This original phase dates to the late Republic during the early to mid first century B.C.[158]

Subsequent repairs and modifications employed walls of concrete faced in *opus reticulatum* and brick, and the reuse of these same materials in later phases. These materials were used on repairs to the upper courses of the walls (including the fourteen small pilasters that ring the pond), the rectangular terrace, and the vaulted gallery that protects the canal. The latter two of these point to problems with the stability of the ground in which the pond was originally built. Erosion of the soil around the pond would have undermined the structural integrity of the walls and possibly caused their collapse. The shoring-up of the ground surrounding the pond and protecting its canal would have offered logical areas of modification, while the upper walls and vaults also were receiving repairs.[159] Subsequent repairs could correspond to the building activity, documented in this area, during the reigns of Augustus,[160] Nero,[161] and Domitian.[162] Public financed activity, in this area of the Lago di Paola, is attested by an early imperial inscription found in the area that refers to work in the lake and its connection to the sea. It is interesting to note that the *quattuorvir* responsible for this effort was L. Faberius Murena, who bears the cognomen of an illustrious *piscinarius* and whose name means eel.[163]

Circeo — Torre del Fico (Fig. 66)

The remains of a fishpond were noted by Giuseppe Lugli at the beginning of this century but are no longer visible.[164] Lugli placed the pond just below the Torre del Fico on the east side of Monte Circeo. His brief description recorded a system of walls and channels in the sea, basically rectangular in plan, measuring 40 meters (north-south) by at least 30 meters (east-west). The portion closest to shore was best preserved in Lugli's day and records a perimeter mole (2.3 meters wide) enclosing a zone divided into three rectangular tanks: a large central tank and two smaller flanking tanks with a circular tank (8.2 meters in diameter) inscribed within (Fig. 66).

Channels formed by parallel walls can be made out, along the north and south sides of the pond, and continuing seaward (to the east). It is likely that these walls enclosed a large area of sea for the purpose of raising fish. The channels, which emerge from the beach, would have

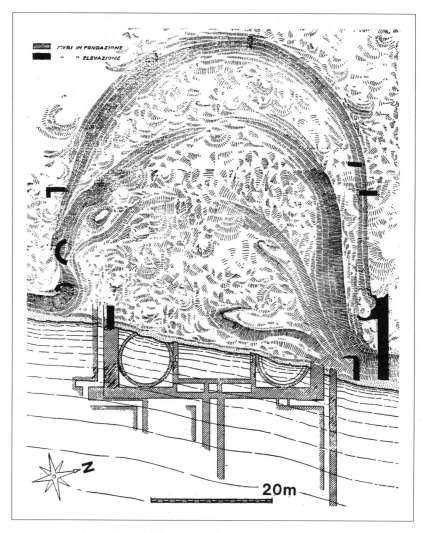

FIGURE 66. Circeo, Torre del Fico—plan of the fishpond. (From G. Lugli, *Ager Pomptinus. Circeii—Forma Italiae* 1.1 pars secunda [Rome 1928] fig. f)

conveyed fresh water from the shore to the outlying tanks of the fishpond. The arrangement of partitioned tanks (*piscinae loculatae*) close to shore with a less differentiated enclosure farther out to sea would correspond to designs best exemplified by the great *piscina* at Torre Astura.

Concrete walls, faced in *opus incertum*, were observed in the ruins of the villa on shore and in the upper structures of the pond. This would suggest a late republican date.

La Salette

The site of La Salette lies on the Lido di Fondi 2 kilometers northwest of Sperlonga immediately southeast of the Lago Lungo.[165] In the water are the much battered remains of a rectangular fishpond. The enclosure measures approximately 10 meters square and was delimited by a perimeter mole just over 1 meter wide. The remains of concrete walls inside the pond suggest that the interior was divided into separate tanks.

There are no ruins to suggest the existence of a villa on the shore near this *piscina*. The closest structures lie several hundred meters inland on the hills that rise above the sea. Several concrete platforms that supported hillside villas can be seen. These residences are positioned near the track of the Via Flacca, which ran along the sea, high above the marshy lowlands, and connected the Via Appia to coastal Campania. It has been suggested that the pond at La Salette belongs to the Villa Prato (sometimes known as the Villa Lago San Puoto), which is located 800 meters northeast 20 meters above the level of the sea.[166] The area between the villa and shore should be imagined as part of a single *praedia* and would have been cultivated on a series of terraces leading down to the sea.[167] The date for the construction of the pond is uncertain but if it belongs to the Villa Prato then a late republican date would be probable.

Sperlonga — Grotto of Tiberius (Figs. 67 – 70)

The so-called Grotto of Tiberius is located 1.3 kilometers southeast of the city of Sperlonga. Positioned inside and in front of the grotto are the ruins of a fishpond. The grotto was long associated with the emperor Tiberius and the name Sperlonga is certainly derived from the toponym, *Spelunca*, noted by Latin authors.[168]

The grotto was first excavated in 1957 during the construction of the modern Via Flacca.[169] The grotto was cleared by the engineer Erno Bellante in the course of a fortnight in 1957 (September 11 – 25). Mindful of the armaments stored here during the Second World War, Bellante recovered 554 "significant" fragments of sculpture and nondescript fragments numbering in the thousands. In addition to the sculpture, Bellante revealed the ruins of a circular *piscina* inside the grotto connected to a rectangular pond outside (Figs. 67 – 69). The ruins were first published by Giulio Jacopi in 1963.[170]

The complex consisted of a circular pond (Fig. 68:A) inside the cave, which measured 21.2 meters in diameter and was formed by circular

FIGURE 67. Sperlonga, Grotto of Tiberius. (Photo by J. Higginbotham)

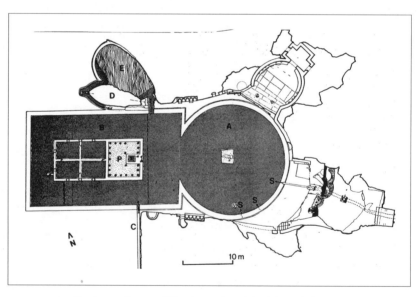

FIGURE 68. Sperlonga, Grotto of Tiberius—plan of the fishpond. **A** = circular pond; **B** = rectangular pond; **C** = sea channel; **D** = rock-cut prow of a ship; **E** = small grotto; **P** = dining platform; **S** = freshwater springs. (From E. Ricotti, "Il gruppo di Polifemo a Sperlonga," *RendPontAcc* 42 [1969–70] pl. 1)

FIGURE 69. Sperlonga, Grotto of Tiberius—marshy ground around the fishpond. (Photo by J. Higginbotham)

concrete wall 90 centimeters wide. The center of the circular pond was equipped with a roughly square pedestal (2.5 meters square) which would have stood just below the surface of the water. Connected to the west side of the circular pond was a rectangular enclosure (B), which measured 31 (east-west) by 19.3 meters (north-south). This section was also delimited by a concrete wall approximately 90 centimeters wide. The depth of both ponds is approximately 1.5 meters.

The center of the rectangular pond was dominated by an insular element, also rectangular in plan, which measures 17.6 (east-west) by 7.9 meters (north-south). The east end of this island was designed as a dining pavilion or *triclinium* (P). The rectangular platform, which measures 7.2 (east-west) by 7.9 meters (north-south), was arranged so that the couches would face the grotto. In addition, the platform was sheltered by a canopy or *pergula*, which was supported by twenty-two small brick columns (35 centimeters in diameter and of unknown height) positioned around the perimeter of the dining platform.

The remainder of the island, which measures 10.4 (east-west) by 7.9 meters (north-south), is divided into four rectangular tanks of roughly equal dimensions (5.2 by 3.8 meters). The cross walls and perimeter walls of the island bond with each other and were therefore constructed

FIGURE 70. Sperlonga, Grotto of Tiberius—north wall of the island with *amphorae* in the sides. (Photo by J. Higginbotham)

in a single phase. Each small rectangular tank is linked to the large rectangular pond and to the adjacent tanks by openings (50 centimeters wide) equipped with sets of vertical slots for the placement of movable gates.[171]

The rectangular pond (B) was equipped with many *amphorae* incorporated into the fabric of the concrete walls. These vessels, minus their necks, rims, and handles were laid horizontally with the open ends facing the pond's interior. The *amphorae* were concentrated in the tanks enclosed by the rectangular island and the walls at the rectangular pond's east end (Fig. 70), and no *amphorae* were used in the circular pond.[172]

Access to the island probably was afforded by a temporary gangway from the side of the rectangular pond to the dining platform. The remains of two walls, which attach to the western and southern walls of the island (submerged at the pond's southwest corner and difficult to see), probably supported walkways to this portion of the *piscina*.

A small grotto (Fig. 68:E) opens off the north side of the rectangular pond and forms a roughly oval pond (12.7 meters long and 6.9 meters wide). The northeast wall of this little grotto is lined with a row of twelve niches, which would have been partially submerged when the pond was full of water. These cells could have provided some refuge for the fish confined there. A small concrete wall (40 centimeters wide) lined the interior of the small grotto, now only preserved on the enclosure's northern and western sides. The small grotto is set off from the main pond by a wall of natural rock cut into the form of a ship's prow (D).[173]

The pond was supplied with fresh water from springs within the grotto, three of which are located along the circular pond's southeast side (S). A single channel (C) connected the south side of the pond with the sea. Together these sources would have created a brackish environment within the pond. In addition, the seaward channel provided a conduit that advertised the conditions inside the pond and enticed migrating fish into the enclosure.

The walls of the pond, both the circular and rectangular components, were constructed of concrete faced in a very irregular *opus reticulatum* or *quasi-reticulatum* (Fig. 70). Tufa reticulate pyramids and quoins were used throughout the construction and then covered with plaster (best preserved within the circular pond). This same building technique was employed in the construction of the pedestal in the middle of the circular pond within the grotto. This method of concrete facing places the construction of the *piscina* in the grotto near Sperlonga before the middle of the first century B.C.[174]

Surrounding the pond outside the grotto is a low marshy area that would have been flooded at high tides. This area is bound by the grotto on the east, and walls faced in *opus incertum* on the north and west sides. The *incertum* walls supported a portico and dining pavilion. These structures indicate that the grotto was a focal point before the construction of the fishpond. The fishpond with its *triclinium* provided the optimum viewing platform from which the cave with its sculptural decoration could be enjoyed.[175]

Formia (Figs. 71, 72)

Formia (ancient *Formiae*) is located at the north end of the gulf of Gaeta and was accessible by the Via Appia and from the sea. This coast was a favorite site for villas during the Roman Republic.[176] Martial refers to these residences at Formia during the Empire with special mention of the famous fishponds.[177] At the beginning of this century the remains of four fishponds were visible along the shore. These were noted for the first time by Luigi Jacono in 1913.[178] Since that time there has been much construction along this shore and the fishponds have been mostly reburied or destroyed.

The largest residential remains belong to the so-called Villa of Cicero located on the grounds of the Villa Rubino. The *villa maritima* was constructed on three terraces that step down toward the sea. The villa was built at the end of the second century B.C. and amplified during the first century B.C.[179] In the water, along the 150 meters of shoreline occupied by this villa, are the remains of two large concrete enclosures. These structures, now largely destroyed, were probably designed as fishponds. The ruins belong to two rectangular enclosures adjacent to each other. The western pond measures 75 meters (east-west along the shore) by at least 45 meters (north-south) and is divided into three roughly equal sections by two north-south walls. Two channels, one at the west and one at the east end of this enclosure, probably distributed fresh water into the pond from supplies on shore.[180] Openings in the pond's walls, which would have allowed seawater into the enclosure, are impossible to identify given the condition of the ruins.

The second enclosure is located 25 meters east of the first. It stretches for 56 meters along the beach and is of indeterminate width. Remains of walls inside this pond suggest the existence of internal subdivisions. Vestiges of a freshwater conduit can be traced on a course from the villa to the center of this pond. Openings to the sea are impossible to identify with any certainty.

The best-preserved *piscina* is sited in the sea off a small promontory which is now occupied by the Giardino Publico (Fig. 71).[181] The Giardino is built upon the ruins of a villa that dates to the late Republic.[182] The ancient villa provided an elevated platform from which the pond and the sea could be viewed.

The fishpond is rectangular in plan measuring 59.4 by 29.7 meters and is divided into three rectangular sections. The depth of the pond was estimated by Jacono to be about 3 meters.[183] The height of the perimeter walls and the interior dividing walls is the same. The central section was designed with rectilinear partitions while the two lateral sections were divided by lozenge-shaped tanks inscribed within the rectangle. The perimeter of the pond is protected by a mole 2.5 meters wide on the south and west sides and 2.9 meters wide on the east side. The fourth side, along the shore, was equipped with seven rectangular notches

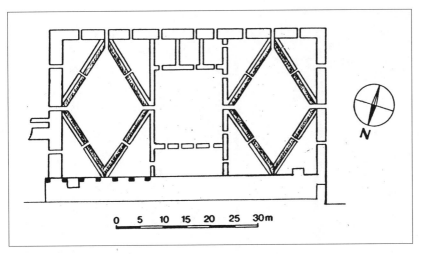

FIGURE 71. Formia—plan of the fishpond near the Giardino Publico. (Adapted from L. Jacono, "Note di archeologia marittima," *Neapolis* I [1913] fig. 2)

(85 centimeters square), which were arranged along the easternmost section of the enclosure. These notches probably supported small pillars that held an awning or other roofed structure.

The central section is rectangular in plan and encloses an area measuring 14.8 (east-west) by 28 meters (north-south). The north and south ends of this section are partitioned by walls (90 centimeters wide and 5.7 meters from the perimeter of the pond) and pierced by openings that would allow the circulation of water within these tanks.

The two lateral sections are also rectangular in plan measuring 18.9 (east-west) by 28 meters (north-south). These sections are partitioned by lozenge-shaped tanks measuring 15.6 meters on a side. The result of this design was to divide each flanking section into five separate tanks. The walls that divide these tanks are 60 centimeters wide and are equipped with walkways (1 meter wide and 50 centimeters below the top of the walls) that line the interior of each lozenge-shaped tank.

All tanks are linked by openings (approximately 80 centimeters wide) pierced through the dividing walls and many of these were designed with sets of vertical slots for movable gates.[184] The four openings, which connect the lozenge-shaped tanks to the open sea, are equipped with two such gates arranged in series. This configuration would allow migrating fish to be trapped while either leaving or entering the pond. In addition, the gates helped regulate the level and salinity of the water inside the

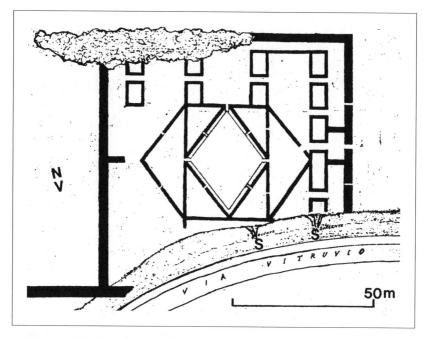

FIGURE 72. Formia—plan of the fishpond near the Via Vitruvio. (Adapted from L. Jacono, "Note di archeologia marittima," *Neapolis* I [1913] fig. 3)

enclosure. The fishpond's water supply was probably augmented by fresh water from sources on shore. The remains of parallel walls, which extend from the east wall of the pond, once formed a channel that could have conveyed fresh water.

The date of this pond is derived from the date of its associated villa. This structure, which underlies the Giardino Publico, was constructed of concrete faced in *opus reticulatum* that dates to late first century B.C.

On this same stretch of beach, further to the east, where the Via Vitruvio nears the sea, were the ruins of a large *piscina loculata* (Fig. 72). This pond was visible early in this century but has since been destroyed by recent port construction.[185]

The fishpond was square in plan measuring 89.5 meters to a side. The enclosure was protected by a concrete perimeter mole approximately 3 meters wide. There appear to have been at least two openings to the sea through the west side of the pond. Freshwater springs (S) augmented the supply of salt water and created a brackish environment inside the pond. The interior of the enclosure was partitioned by the at least eleven separate rectangular tanks (measuring about 6.5 by 8.5 meters) arranged around the perimeter of the pond: four rows of tanks (at least five to a row) with the two center rows interrupted by triangular and lozenge-shaped tanks at the pond's center.[186]

The center of the pond was divided by a rectangular tank, measuring 28 (east-west) by 40 meters (north-south), with an inscribed lozenge-shaped tank (measuring 22.5 meters on a side). A walkway, 1 meter wide, lined the inside of the lozenge. Triangular tanks were appended east and west of the central rectangle. All walls appear to have been 1 meter wide and were pierced by openings that permitted circulation between tanks.

The construction of this fishpond, which can only be inferred from its similarity to the nearby pond below the Giardino Publico, probably was built in the late first century B.C.

Scauri

The site of Scauri is located on the coast 7 kilometers east of Formia. Since at least the tenth century, the site was linked to M. Aemilius Scaurus, and the seashore was known as Porto Scauritano. The medieval torre at Scauri was built on the ruins of a villa that dates to the first century B.C. In a cove west of the Torre Scauri are the remains of a fishpond, which were first recognized in the 1920s.[187] The cove within which the pond was constructed was lined with concrete walls and subdivided into at least five tanks. Two of these tanks were cut into the rock surrounding the cove forming small grottoes. Two long moles helped channel water into this enclosure. These walls were constructed of concrete faced in *opus reticulatum*. Construction of a modern port has destroyed most of the remains and has made measurement impossible.

PONTINE ISLANDS

Isola di Ponza (Figs. 73 – 78)

The island of Ponza, ancient Pontia, is located off the west coast of Italy, 36 kilometers south of Monte Circeo, and forms the nucleus of the Pontine island group. The island was the site of a Latin colony, which was founded in 312 B.C., and contributed men and ships to Rome during the Second Punic War.[188] Little is known of the subsequent history of the island but it must have passed to imperial hands during the reign of

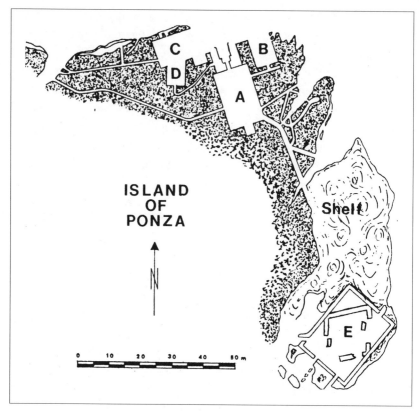

FIGURE 73. Ponza—fishponds of the Punta della Madonna. **A**, **B**, **C**, and **D** = fishponds in grottoes; **E** = open-air fishpond. (Adapted from G. Schmiedt, ed., *Il livello antico del Mar Tirreno* [Florence 1972] pl. 160)

Augustus.[189] Ponza became the site of many villas and the home of imperial exiles.[190] The most extensive villa remains lie at the south end of the island above the cliffs of the Punta della Madonna. Below the villa and connected to the sea is a complex of five fishponds almost completely carved from the living rock. Cut into the face of the cliffs, below the Punta della Madonna, are artificial grottoes that house four fishponds (Fig. 73 : A – D).[191] Linked to these by a long rock-cut corridor is another fishpond (E) built into a rock shelf and open to the air. The *piscinae* on Ponza were first studied by Luigi Jacono at the beginning of this century.[192] Additional study was carried out by Giulio Schmiedt with a focus on the sea level necessary for the ponds' operation.

The four artificial grottoes are in the form of half cylinders, rectangular in plan, and equipped with walkways that line their interiors. These covered ponds are connected by a system of channels and corridors that make use of the inlets and fissures typical of this shore. The complex centers on the largest grotto (A) with the smaller ponds (B, C, and D) flanking to the east and west.

Pond A opens off the north face of the cliff presenting an arched facade to the sea. The grotto (Fig. 74) is rectangular in plan and measures 11.5 meters wide and 18.2 meters long. The opening of the grotto is leveled in the form of a broad vestibule measuring 8.5 by 6.5 meters. The level of the vestibule continues inside the grotto, forming a walkway approximately 1.5 meters wide that runs around the perimeter of the pond (B). The roof of the grotto rises about 3.1 meters above this level; the ceiling is slightly lower at the grotto's entrance. Two steps (40 centimeters wide and 25 centimeters high) lead down to the rectangular pond, which measures 13.6 meters long, 6.8 meters wide, and descends to a depth of at least 2.35 meters.

The pond was equipped with five channels that linked the enclosure to the sea or to other ponds. The principal opening to the sea was through the platform of the vestibule at the grotto's entrance. This channel (C) bisected the floor of the vestibule before passing beneath the perimeter walkway and emptying into the pond. Channel C is 5.4 meters wide and over 3 meters deep, at its seaward end, and narrows by stages to an opening 85 centimeters wide and 50 centimeters high when it enters the pond. This configuration helped funnel water into the pond. The narrowing of the channel would increase the rate of flow as water entered the enclosure and facilitate circulation within. The channel was designed to be shut off by a sliding gate, which could be closed where the channel enters the pond. Two basalt blocks (a), cut with vertical grooves, were inserted into the sides of the channel so that the top of the gate was even with the lower step around the pond.[193]

In addition to the main channel (C), four other rock-cut channels (1–4) were positioned around the pond. Channel 1 opens through an arched portal on the west side of the broad vestibule in front of the fishpond. The traces of an opening beneath the floor of the vestibule (denoted by dotted lines) may indicate that this channel had an opening on the seaward side of the pond, though it is impossible to reconstruct this with any certainty. Channel 1 is linked to the rear wall of pond D and thus helped to carry the force of the surf, which hit the exposed entrance of pond A, to the more sheltered pond (D) next door.

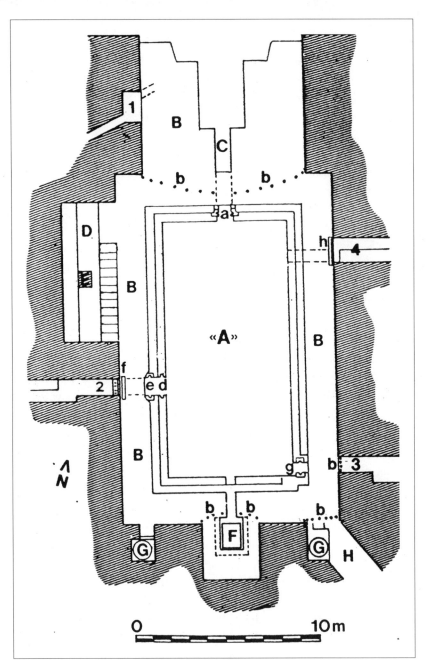

FIGURE 74. Ponza—plan of pond A. **B** = rock-cut walkway around pond; **C** = principal channel to the sea; **D** = gallery; **E** = square column; **F** = niche tank; **G** = specialty tanks; **H** = corridor to open-air pond (E); **I** = channel linked to pond D; **2** and **3** = channels to the sea; **4** = channel linked to pond B; **a, d, e, f, g,** and **h** = vertical slots for closable gates; **b** = holes for temporary barriers. (Adapted from G. Schmiedt, ed., *Il livello antico del Mar Tirreno* [Florence 1972] pl. 161)

Channel 2 entered pond A through the middle of its west side. The top of this channel appears as an arched portal cut into the side of the grotto. However, water from this channel traveled along the lower 70 centimeters of the rock-cut conduit and entered the pond from beneath the floor of the perimeter walkway (through an opening 60 centimeters wide and 70 centimeters high). Channel 2, by way of a meandering course over 65 meters long, connected pond A to an inlet of the sea west of the pond. A raised sidewalk inside this channel permitted relatively dry travel through this passage.

The channel was equipped with three separate positions where gates could be imposed to control the flow of water and restrict the movement of fish (d–f). A narrow opening (1.25 meters long and 20 centimeters wide), which was cut into the floor of the walkway next to the wall of the grotto, permitted the placement of a gate (f) in the course of the channel. The positions of the second and third gates (d and e) are indicated by the vertical slots positioned in sides of the channel at the level of both steps into the pond. These gates are indicative of at least three phases of the pond's operation and the gradual rise of sea level. The first gate (d) was placed at the position of the lower step inside the pond. As the level of the sea rose, the gate position had to be raised. The second gate (e) was constructed using basalt stone inserts, which were cut with vertical slots for the gate. Part of the perimeter walkway had to be cut away to allow for the placement of this gate. When the sea level exceeded the level of the second gate, water would have flowed over the walkway and into the pond. A small tufa wall was built across the upper portion of the channel above the level of the walkway. This wall (70 centimeters high) was pierced by two rectangular openings to allow the orderly flow of water from the channel. The slot cut in the floor of the walkway permitted the placement of a third barrier or gate (f) that would insure the complete closure of these upper openings.

Channel 3 enters the pond's east side near its southeast corner. The top of the channel appears as an arched portal in the wall of the grotto while the water entered the pond from beneath the floor of the perimeter walkway. This channel linked pond A to an inlet of the sea east of the pond and was closable by a slotted gate placed at the level of the lower step into the pond (g). The runners of this gate are cut into basalt inserts placed in the sides of the channel.

Channel 4 opens onto the east side of the pond and connects pond A to the back wall of pond B. The top of the channel appears as an arched portal in the east wall of the grotto but enters the pond from beneath the floor of the surrounding walkway (B). The channel was designed with a raised sidewalk (as in channel 2) and could have been closed by a gate inserted into a slot (h), 1.4 meters long and 20 centimeters wide, cut through the floor of the walkway.

Cut into the back wall of the grotto is a large niche with an arcuated top. The niche is 3 meters wide, 3 meters high, and 3 meters deep. A small tank (F), which measures 1 meter by 1.3 meters and is at least 2.35 meters deep, was cut into the floor of the niche. This tank is linked to the main pond by a channel, which runs beneath the perimeter floor of the *piscina*. A small niche (80 centimeters wide, 1.3 meters high, and 30 centimeters deep) was cut into the back wall of the larger niche and was probably intended to hold a statuette or bas-relief.

Symmetrically arranged in the corners at the back of the grotto are two circular tanks (G), one on either side of the large niche. These tanks are approximately a meter in diameter and a meter deep. They were not designed with any channels or conduits and were probably filled by hand or from the surf at high tide. The precise function of these tanks is unclear; they probably confined fish intended for special uses.[194] The western tank is accessible through an arched portal and the eastern tank was adjacent to the entrance of the corridor (H) which opens on the southeast corner of the grotto.

This large corridor (H), which is approximately 3.5 meters high and averages 2 meters in width, stretches for over 32 meters and links pond A to the rock shelf into which the uncovered fishpond (Fig. 73:E) was built. Cut into the walls of the corridor, immediately after leaving pond A, are two large vertical grooves (20 centimeters wide, 50 centimeters deep, and over 1 meter high), which would allow this corridor to be closed. At the south end of the corridor, a small wooden bridge was probably built to span the chasm between the southern end of the corridor and the shelf.[195]

The western wall of the grotto near the entrance was excavated to form an elevated gallery (Fig. 74:D) which was reached by a flight of stairs from the perimeter walkway (B).[196] The gallery was 1.6 meters deep, 2.5 meters high, and 5.5 meters long and bisected by a rock-cut pillar (E), which spans the distance between the floor and ceiling of the gallery. Placed behind the pillar was a rock-cut bench (1 meter wide and 1 meter high) running the entire length of the gallery. The exact purpose of this gallery is uncertain, although it probably afforded a good vantage point from which to enjoy the pond or to witness rituals involving the fish confined there.

Modifications that saw the addition of successively higher gates to channel 2 necessitated the placement of temporary barriers around the pond in order to compensate for the rise in sea level. By the time of these final additions, the floors of the vestibule and walkway would have been awash at least at high tide. Small circular holes (b) were placed in lines across the entrance to the grotto, in front of the niche tank (F), and blocking the openings to channel 3 and corridor H. These holes appear to have been intended to fasten a wood or cane barrier, possibly supporting a net, which would prevent the escape of fish from the grotto and keep those species in the niche segregated from the fish in the main pond.

Pond B lies east of the main pond and is oriented so that its entrance faces to the north (Fig. 73). The grotto in which the pond is housed is rectangular in plan, measuring 7.2 meters wide and 9.6 meters long (Fig. 75). The cave is lined on three sides (west, south, and east) by a rock-cut walkway 60 centimeters in width (a). The roof of the grotto was cut in the form of a half cylinder and stands about 3 meters above the level of the walkway. The resulting pond, which measured 6 meters wide and about 9 meters in length, was 3.5 meters deep. The seaward side of the pond is impossible to reconstruct with any precision.

The pond probably was supplied with water through an opening in the grotto's entrance, though no traces of such a channel remain. Two channels 60 centimeters wide (c) were cut through the eastern wall of the enclosure and connected the *piscina* directly with the sea.[197] A third channel (4) appears as an arched portal and enters pond B through its back (south) wall, cutting through the floor of the walkway.[198] Vertical grooves cut in the sides of the channel allowed this conduit to be closed. Three circular holes, which were positioned above the arch of the channel probably secured a mechanism by which the gate could be lowered and raised.[199]

Ponds C and D (Fig. 76) were built into the same grotto that lies west of the main pond A. Pond C is housed in a rectangular grotto (12.7 meters long and 9.2 meters wide) and is covered by a semicylindrical ceiling just under 3 meters high. The entrance to pond C faces the east at a right angle to the entrances of ponds A and B. The pond was equipped with a rock-cut walkway (a) approximately 60 centimeters wide that ran around the inside of the grotto. The northern and seaward (eastern) sides are poorly preserved but the remains of concrete in the water sug-

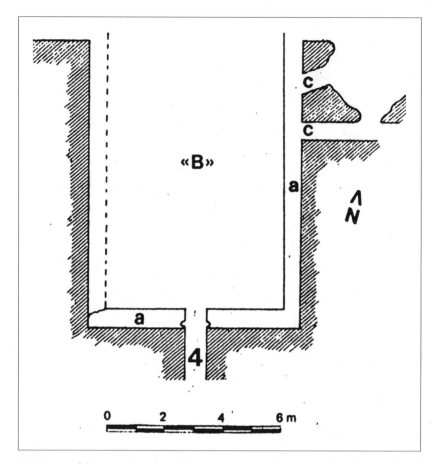

FIGURE 75. Ponza—plan of pond B. **a** = rock-cut walkway around pond; **4** = channel linked to pond A; **c** = channels to the sea. (Adapted from G. Schmiedt, ed., *Il livello antico del Mar Tirreno* [Florence 1972] pl. 169)

gest that architecture was employed to complete the enclosure. The southern side of pond C is pierced by large openings which permit access to pond D and tank h. The approximate depth within these ponds is in excess of 4.5 meters.

Channels were cut through the western and northern sides of the enclosure. Seawater was probably supplied by a channel through the grotto's entrance, but no traces remain. The largest channel enters the pond's west wall and is connected to the sea west of the grotto (d). This arched channel (1.8 meters wide, 2.1 meters high, and 43.4 meters long) was equipped with a raised sidewalk (85 centimeters wide) running down one side, while the other side was left free for the circulation of

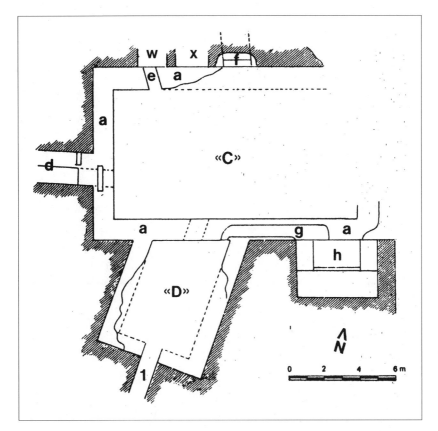

FIGURE 76. Ponza—plan of ponds C and D. **a** = rock-cut walkway around ponds; **I** = channel linked to pond A; **d**, **e**, and **f** = channels to the sea; **g** = small canal linking pond D to tank **h**; **w** and **x** = portals. (Adapted from G. Schmiedt, ed., *Il livello antico del Mar Tirreno* [Florence 1972] pl. 172)

water. Two meters before reaching the pond, the water was funneled into a smaller conduit (80 centimeters wide and 1 meter high), which passed beneath the floor of the walkway and into the pond. This channel was closable by a gate that could have been inserted through a slot (30 centimeters wide and 1.3 meters long) cut through the floor of the perimeter walkway.

The remaining two channels (e, f) were cut through the thin (just over 2 meters wide) north wall of the grotto, providing direct access to the sea. Channel e (70 centimeters wide and at least 1 meter high), which is located near the northwest corner of the pond, cuts through the walkway at an oblique angle aimed at the entrance to pond D. Channel f (1.5 meters wide and about a meter high) cuts through the wall of the grotto where there has been a lot of interior damage, and little can be said about its exact form. Above these channels are two large openings (w, x), cut at different heights in the wall. Portal w (1.36 meters wide and 2.9 meters tall) opens at the level of the interior walkway (a) and appears to have been an entrance into the pond. This portal was walled up later with tufa blocks and mortar to adjust for the rise in sea level. Portal x (1.8 meters wide and 2.2. meters high) was placed much higher in the wall (2.6 meters above the walkway) and appears to have functioned more as a window or lightwell.

Pond D opens off the south wall of pond C and is oriented on a north-south axis, but not at right angles to pond C. Pond D is rectangular in plan (8 meters long and 6 meters wide) and is covered by a rock-cut vault just less than 3 meters high. The pond was surrounded by a rock-cut walkway (approximately 80 centimeters wide) which is at the same level and contiguous with the walkway around pond C. Jacono reported that traces of marble revetment, painted stucco, and mosaics were still in situ on the walls of pond D, but nothing remains of this decoration today.[200]

Seawater is supplied to pond D by way a channel (1) that enters through the back of the grotto. This channel is connected to the vestibule of pond A where the incoming surf is more vigorous than in the recesses of ponds C and D. A small arched canal (1 meter high, 1 meter wide, and 1.25 meters long) connects both ponds and allows the circulating system within pond C to operate in conjunction with the system in the other pond (D).

Pond D is linked to the rectangular tank (h) that was carved out of the south wall of pond C near its entrance. The tank is housed in a rock-cut vault 4.3 meters wide, 3.3 meters deep, and over 2 meters high. The vault was equipped with a walkway around three sides: the southern 1.45 meters wide, and the western and eastern 1 meter wide. The tank is 1.7 meters deep and connected to pond D by a canal (g) cut into the top of the walkway (60 centimeters wide, 30 centimeters deep, and 6 meters long).

A stairway, which ran down the outside of pond C, connected the fishponds to the villa above on the Punta della Madonna.[201] According to Jacono's reconstruction, this stairway led to the portal (w) in the side of the grotto. Once inside the complex the system of channels could be used to travel between ponds. The raised sidewalks in some of these channels attest to their dual function. Access was also possible by way of boats, which could land right at the ponds' entrances.

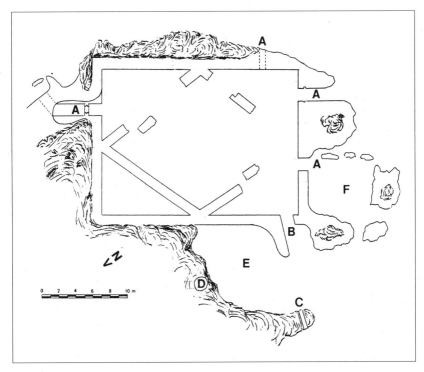

FIGURE 77. Ponza—plan of pond E. **A** = openings to the sea; **B** = freshwater inlet; **C** = rock-cut conduit; **D** = access to canal; **E** = small cove (tank?); **F** = exterior tank. (Adapted from G. Schmiedt, ed., *Il livello antico del Mar Tirreno* [Florence 1972] pl. 180)

Pond E, the last in this complex, was set away from the cluster of grottoes and accessible by a corridor (Fig. 73) that linked pond A to the rock shelf into which pond E was cut. In contrast to the other *piscinae*, pond E (Figs. 77, 78) was constructed so as to be open to the air. The rock was cut to form a rectangular enclosure (23.8 by 18.7 meters) surrounded by a broad walkway 1.2 meters wide. The interior of the pond was excavated to a depth of 2.5 meters leaving some of the rock to form internal partitions. These interior walls (1 meter wide) were designed to form a diamond- or lozenge-shaped tank (12.6 meters to a side) in the center of the enclosure. The apexes of the lozenge touch the middles of the walls forming the rectangular enclosure. The result was to divide the pond into five separate tanks.

The pond was pierced by five openings that allowed the circulation of water within the pond. Four openings (Fig. 77:A) connect the pond to the open sea and each is approximately a meter wide. Two of the aper-

FIGURE 78. Ponza—pond E. (From G. Schmiedt, ed., *Il livello antico del Mar Tirreno* [Florence 1972] pl. 181)

tures (located on the northeast and southwest sides of the enclosure) were equipped with vertical runners cut into basalt blocks, which could hold movable gates. It is probable that the other openings were similarly designed but no trace of the sluicing system remains.

The southwest side of the pond was cut to form a broad platform (at least 7 by 10 meters but now badly eroded). Remains of concrete on top of this platform suggest some sort of superstructure. A small rectangular area adjacent to this platform has the appearance of a rough enclosure (F) and may have been a series of external holding tanks. Jacono noted three tanks built of blocks held together by metal clamps.[202] No evidence of this construction is visible today.

Northwest of the pond between the enclosure and the cliffs is a small cove (E) in which Jacono reconstructs a small lozenge-shaped tank. Again the ravages of time have made verification of these details impossible. The cove was fed by two conduits: one (D) emerges from under the shelf at the base of the cliff and empties into the cove; the other (C) is attested only by a narrow cutting that appears to have been designed to carry a pipe. This cutting aligns with an opening in the western corner of the pond.

With no natural springs on the island, Ponza depended on great cisterns cut into the hills, which distributed water by aqueducts and other conduits.[203] It is probable that conduits (possibly C and D) carried fresh water from cisterns in the cliffs above and distributed the water into both the cove and the pond. This arrangement would have created a brackish environment within these areas. The *piscinae* on Ponza could have been used to raise a wide variety of fish. In recent tradition, the complex is referred to as the "murenario" due to the habitual presence of eels in the grottoes.[204]

The ponds below the Punta della Madonna are associated with the villa above. The villa, which covered nearly 40,000 square meters, made ample use of concrete faced with *opus reticulatum* and has been dated to the reign of Augustus and his immediate successors.[205] This chronology is supported by the ancient literature, which names Pontia as an island of exile under the emperors Tiberius and Caligula.[206] The remains of reticulate facing (pyramids) have been recently noted in the grottoes[207] and help place the construction of the ponds at the end of the first century B.C. or early first century A.D. The villas on the island were probably abandoned by the late second century A.D.[208]

Ventotene (Figs. 79 – 81)

The island of Ventotene (ancient Pandataria) lies 40 kilometers southeast of Ponza and 36 kilometers west of the island of Ischia. Located between the ancient port (to the north) and the Cala Nave (to the south) on the east end of Ventotene is a rock shelf that extends east from the tufaceous cliffs to the sea. Excavated into the shelf and the east face of the cliff are rock-cut enclosures that were designed to raise fish. Known since the late seventeenth century, the *piscina* on Ventotene was seriously studied first by Giulio Schmiedt.[209]

The complex consists of four major tanks: two tanks (Figs. 79, 81 : A, B) housed in artificial grottoes and two tanks (C, D) open to the sky. The construction of the fishpond involved the excavation of the grottoes, tanks, walkways, and conduits from the living rock. Basalt and concrete were added to complete the enclosures and to effect repairs.

The covered portions of the pond were housed in artificial grottoes fashioned into semicylindrical vaults 6 meters high and open to the east. Grotto A is rectangular, measuring 6.4 meters wide and 7.2 meters long. The interior of the grotto was lined with a walkway (1.1 to 1.5 meters in width), which enclosed a tank measuring 4.3 meters by 5.5 meters and is

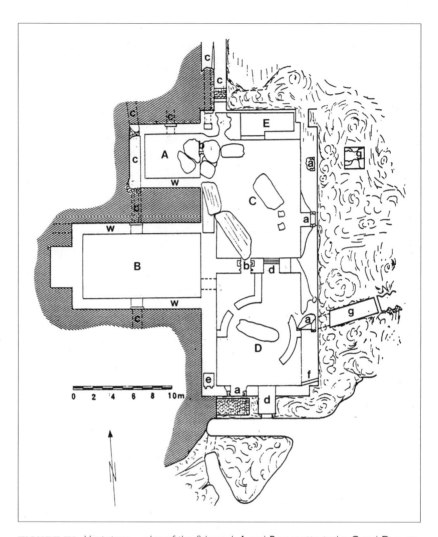

FIGURE 79. Ventotene—plan of the fishpond. A and B = grotto tanks; C and D = un-covered tanks; E = small tank; **a** = openings in the pond's perimeter with vertical runners for gates; **c** = channels to the port; **g** = channels to the open sea; **q** = channel leading inland; **d** = small tank; **e** = small tanks cut into the perimeter walkway; **f** = canal(?); **b, d** = openings between tanks with vertical runners for gates; **s** = freshwater conduit(?); **w** = walkways inside the grottoes. (Adapted from G. Schmiedt, ed., *Il livello antico del Mar Tirreno* [Florence 1972] pl. 190)

at least 2.5 meters deep. Traces of a decorative cornice can be noted run-ning around the inside of the grotto marking the point where the vault springs from the side walls. Grotto A is linked to the open portion of the pond (tank C) by a small opening in the walkway at the pond's east end. Remains of a basalt block carrying a vertical runner for a gate can be

FIGURE 80. Ventotene—main grotto tank (B). (Photo by J. Higginbotham)

made out in the water (Fig. 79:r). This portion of the pond has suffered due to the collapse of parts of the vault, chunks of which obscure many of the architectural details. Grotto A is connected directly to the port by a channel (p) that empties into the north side of the pond from beneath the walkway. This channel was designed to be closed by the insertion of a gate through a slot (1 meter by 25 centimeters) in the floor of the walkway along the wall of the grotto.

Grotto B, also rectangular, measures 8.6 meters wide and 13 meters long. The inside of the grotto is lined with a walkway (about 1 meter wide), which delimited a tank measuring 6.5 by 12 meters and at least 2 meters deep. A niche (4.2 meters wide, 2 meters deep, and 4 meters high), which was surmounted by an arch, was cut into the back wall of grotto B (Fig. 80). Traces of a decorative cornice, which is at the same height as the cornice around grotto A, can be made out running around the inside of the grotto B.

A small arched portal 80 centimeters wide and 1.6 meters tall (Fig. 79:3) was cut through the back wall in the northwest corner of the grotto. This opening leads to a channel of unknown origin, which is large enough to have served as a corridor, permitting access to the grotto, or as a conduit for fresh water stored in cisterns west of the fishpond. Seawater was supplied by a long channel—80 centimeters wide, 1.3 meters high, and 18 meters long—that originates inside the ancient port and continues behind grotto A and into the northern side of grotto B (c).[210] An analogous channel opens on the southern side of the grotto and continues to an unknown location inland (q). This channel is probably another connection (along with channel s) to freshwater reservoirs on the island. Both channels (c and q) were surmounted by arched portals and were closable by gates that could be inserted into slots (1.4 meters long and 25 centimeters wide) cut through the walkway above each channel inlet. The tank in grotto B is linked to the open portions of the fishpond (tank D) by an opening (1 meter high, 1 meter wide, and 1.6 meters long) that runs under the walkway at the east end of the grotto. The prominent niche, larger size, and central position of grotto B make it the focus of the complex.

Situated on the rock shelf east of the grottoes are the open tanks of the pond. This portion was excavated so as to create a leveled walkway (1.5 to 1.65 meters wide on the long sides and slightly narrower on the short sides) around the tanks. A wall of rock (1.5 meters wide) was fashioned that divided the open portion of the pond into two tanks (C, 8.7 by 11.8 meters; D, 8.7 by 11.2 meters).

Two openings in this wall allowed the circulation of water between these tanks (b, d). The westernmost opening (b) was equipped with two sets of vertical runners for the placement of two movable gates[211] and, with both gates in place, an area (1 meter by 95 centimeters) could be enclosed. A double-gate arrangement, such as this, could have been used to trap fish trying to travel between tanks. The easternmost opening (d), which was 1.5 meters wide, was closable by a single gate which was held by a groove in a block placed at the bottom of the opening.

Tank D was subdivided by the insertion of a circular tank (6.4 meters in diameter) that was constructed of concrete walls (70 centimeters wide). The walls of the circular tank, which do not abut the walls of tank D, were connected to the rectangular tank by spur walls (two 40 centimeters long, one 2.25 meters long, and one not preserved). The result was to create five tanks from one. An opening in the circular tank (75 centimeters wide) links the circular tank to the corner. Three other openings probably connected the circular tank to the respective corner areas within the rectangular tank.[212]

The northwestern end of tank C was leveled to form a small platform (measuring 4.1 by 2.5 meters). Immediately east of the platform was a small tank (1.9 meters wide and 5.4 meters long), which may have served as a holding area for fish (E). Two smaller holding tanks (e) were cut into the perimeter walkway on the western side of the open tanks: one between the entrances to the grottoes (measuring 1.1 by 3.8 meters) and another at the southwest corner of tank D (measuring 1 by 1.3 meters).

Several openings through the perimeter of the pond permitted the circulation of seawater within the enclosure. The pond's southern side was serviced by two openings (a, f). The westernmost opening (a) was cut through the perimeter walkway and was equipped with a sliding gate. Two basalt blocks, which were provided with vertical grooves, were inserted in the sides of the opening (1.2 meters apart). The easternmost opening (f) was through a small enclosure (1.7 meters wide and 2.7 meters long) that protruded beyond the limits of the pond. At its southern end a small parapet wall (35 centimeters to a side) created an opening (1 meter wide) to an artificial inlet south of the pond. This same inlet also supplied water to a channel connected to opening a.

In addition to channels c and p, the northern side of the pond was supplied by two conduits (m and n) that linked the enclosure to the salt water in the ancient port. These channels (m and n) ran on parallel courses separated by a small sliver of rock. Channel m passed beneath the small platform (now collapsed) and emptied into the northwest corner of tank C. Channel n moves under the rock 4 meters from the pond and empties into the same corner as channel m.

The eastern side of the fishpond was supplied by three channels that cut through the rock shelf east of the complex with the open sea (Fig. 81:g). These channels enter the pond through three openings (Fig. 79:h, i, j). Each of these apertures was equipped with vertical runners designed to hold sliding gates. The southernmost channel (g) was 1.6 meters wide, 6.7 meters long, and cut so that most of its course was open to the sky. Concrete, with small pyramidal blocks of tufo, was used to line parts of the channel. A narrow bridge of stone (20 centimeters wide) spans the channel and probably was part of some sort of a gate.

The channel, which fed the center of the pond (i), was tunneled beneath the rock shelf and its exact course is unknown. The northernmost channel connects the pond (j) with the sea over 30 meters to the east and runs mostly below the shelf. Three square access holes (measuring 2 meters square) were cut through the shelf to the channel below (Fig. 81). Each hole (Fig. 79:k) exposed the location of five sliding gates: two in the center hole, one in the other two. A slot above the channel, at the seaward end of the shelf, permitted the insertion of a sixth gate.

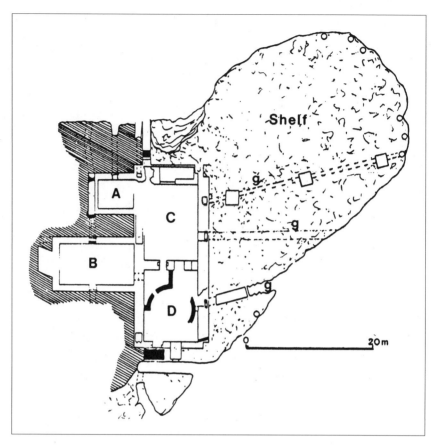

FIGURE 81. Ventotene—plan of the fishpond. **A** and **B** = tanks in grottoes; **C** and **D** = uncovered tanks; **g** = rock-cut channels to the sea. (Adapted from C. Bon, R. Buitoni, G. M. De Rossi, and M. Liverani, *Le Isole Pontine I. Ventotene: immagini di un'isola* [Rome 1984] fig. 2)

This complex system of water supply appears to have been designed to direct the flow of water into chosen parts of the fishpond. The gates, if solid, would interrupt the flow of water and restrict the movement of fish while perforated barriers would permit water to circulate. The placement of gates in series (i.e., between tanks C and D, and in the long seaward channel) facilitated the capture of fish attempting to enter or leave the pond. Fresh water, stored in cisterns near the pond, was probably used to supplement the water supply. The resulting brackish conditions within the fishpond would have helped to lure the fish into the enclosure or incite the migratory exodus.

On the hill above the ponds, in the località Polveriera, are the remains of concrete terraces and cisterns of a Roman villa. The use of concrete faced in *opus reticulatum* with stone quoins supports an Augustan date for the initial construction. It is reasonable to date the construction of the pond with the building of the villa above and other villas on the island. Like Ponza, Ventotene was a favored spot for exiles during the Roman Empire.[213] The island was the site of several villas, the largest of which is located on the Punta Eolo (the so-called Villa di Giulia).[214] The island probably became imperial property under Augustus and continued as the emperor's possession until Pandataria was abandoned in the late second century A.D.[215]

Santa Maria Capua Vetere

Excavations in the city of Santa Maria Capua Vetere during the 1970s unearthed a small rectangular fishpond. This pond, located in the Piazza Mercato, measures 5 by 9.8 meters in plan and was designed with five pots incorporated into the fabric of its concrete walls. The pots allowed fish, particularly eels, to find refuge from other fish and the heat.[216] Its location inland indicates that fresh water was used to fill this pond.

Baiae—Terme di Baia (Figs. 82, 83)

The existence of fishponds along the coast of the Bay of Naples is well attested in Latin literature. Ancient writers record fishponds belonging to Q. Hortensius in his villa at Bauli, those belonging to L. Licinius Lucullus in his villas at Misenum and Neapolis, those of C. Hirrius near Baia, those of Servilius Vatia at his villa on an effluence of Lago del Fusaro, and those of L. Marcius Philippus. Hortensius, as is recounted by Varro, relied on the rich fishing and fish-raising tradition in the Bay of Naples to stock and maintain his ponds.[217] However, the archaeological remains along the submerged stretches of shoreline do not provide many recognizable and hence describable examples of *piscinae*.[218] What follows is admittedly a small sample of the fishponds that once adorned the coast of this bay.

Archaeology provides evidence for two monuments in the vicinity of Baiae that were used to confine fish: one located in the complex known as the Terme di Baia, and the other the only solid evidence of which is depicted on the surfaces of three glass flasks of the later Empire.

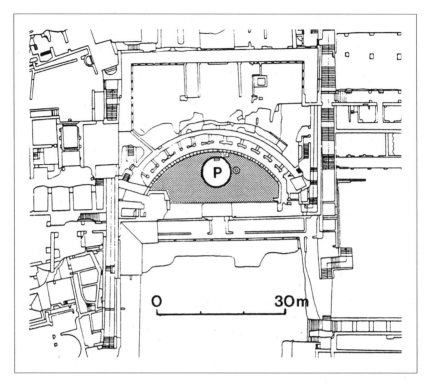

FIGURE 82. Baiae, Terme della Sosandra—plan of terraces and circular fishpond (**P**). (Adapted from M. Borriello and A. D'Ambrosio, *Baiae-Misenum* — *Forma Italiae* I.14 [Florence 1979] pl. I)

The ruins of Baiae with its sulfurous waters have long been associated with bathing. It comes as no surprise that, when the area was designated as an archaeological park before the Second World War, the principal buildings were identified as baths.[219] The buildings, unearthed in the excavations that began in 1941, stand not as a single complex but as just a section of the dense array of architecture that lined the shore of the *Sinus Puteolanus*.[220] The buildings probably form part of a large palatial villa that grew during several phases from the first half of the first century B.C. through at least the third century A.D. The southern portion of this complex is dominated by the so-called Terme della Sosandra. This orthogonally planned section was built on several terraces that step down the hill toward the sea. The second terrace from the top is framed by a semicircular portico and is the site of a circular fishpond (Fig. 82:P).[221]

The pond is 6.9 meters in diameter, 1.5 meters deep, and positioned so that the top of the pond is flush with the floor of the terrace (Fig. 83).

FIGURE 83. Baiae, Terme della Sosandra—circular fishpond on the semicircular terrace. (Photo by J. Higginbotham)

Water was supplied from an aqueduct, which filled a square-topped cistern adjacent to the pond. Concrete faced in *opus reticulatum* was used to construct the fishpond. This surface was coated with a layer of plaster. Arrayed around the bottom of the pond are nine arched recesses (50 centimeters high, 40 centimeters wide, and 30 centimeters deep). A small stairway leads down into the pond from its west or porticoed side.

The Terme della Sosandra appears to have been added to the complex in the first century A.D.[222] Dio Cassius (61.17) notes that Nero came into the possession of a Baian villa belonging to the emperor's aunt Domitia in A.D. 59. It is possible that the villa referred to by Dio Cassius should be associated with the hillside ruins at Baiae and that the Terme della Sosandra may be an addition by the new imperial owner.

Baiae — The Glass Flasks (Figs. 84, 85)

The three glass flasks that show the Baian coast are known by their findspots: the Populonia, Ampurias (Spain), and Warsaw flasks.[223] The schematic images on these vases have attracted much attention from those interested in the topography of the area.[224] They cover monuments on the coast from the Castello di Baia to the Punta del Fortino Vecchio as they existed in the late third or early fourth century A.D. (Fig. 84).

The three flasks show an oyster bed seen from a slightly elevated or bird's-eye perspective as a lattice of thin barriers (Fig. 85). On all three bottles the structure is labeled as *OSTRIARIA*. The two *piscinae*, which flank the oyster bed, are also rendered from a bird's-eye perspective. The ponds are divided into two main sections: one rectangular, the other semicircular.[225] These sections are subdivided further into separate tanks forming *piscinae loculatae*.[226] At first glance, these ponds appear as building fronts.[227] However, the crosshatched bands, which separate the rectangular and semicircular sections, are consistently employed on these flasks to suggest three dimensions. This is best exemplified on the Ampurias flask where the right side of the *ostriaria* is crosshatched to show the oyster bed's depth. Likewise, the hatched zones, which separate the main sections of the fishponds, are probably vertical walls and suggest the pond's depth.

On all three flasks each fishpond is labeled as a *stagnum*.[228] On the Populonia flask both fishponds are connected by what appears to be a balustraded walkway that spans the oyster bed. The Ampurias flask shows an elaborate portico behind the *ostriaria*, while the Warsaw bottle has no connection between the ponds.

Given the rather schematic rendering, an exact plan or location is difficult to reconstruct. The location of this fishpond – oyster bed complex depends largely on the placement of the imperial palace (*PALATIUM*), etched on the Populonia bottle, and the harbor mole (*PILAE*) depicted on the Ampurias and Populonia flasks.[229]

GAZETTEER OF FISHPONDS

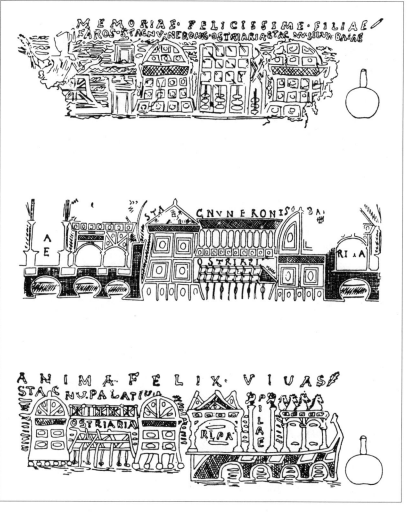

FIGURE 84. The shore of Baiae as depicted on three glass flasks. **Top** = Warsaw flask; **middle** = Ampurias flask; **bottom** = Populonia flask. (From J. Kolendo, "Parcs a huîtres et viviers a Baiae sur un flacon en verre du Musée National de Varsovie," *Puteoli. Studi di storia antica* I [1977] fig. I)

It is difficult to link, with certainty, any remains in the sea to the ponds depicted on the glass flasks. Some remains below the Castello di Pedro da Toledo (Castello di Baia) might be the ruins of a *piscina*.[230]

Puteoli (Fig. 86)

In the sea south of the acropolis (A) and east of the harbor mole of Puteoli are concrete remains that form a series of rectangular enclosures.

FIGURE 85. Detail of the fishponds and oyster beds (center) depicted on the Warsaw flask. (From J. Kolendo, "Parcs a huîtres et viviers a Baiae sur un flacon en verre du Musée National de Varsovie," *Puteoli. Studi di storia antica* 1 [1977] fig. 7)

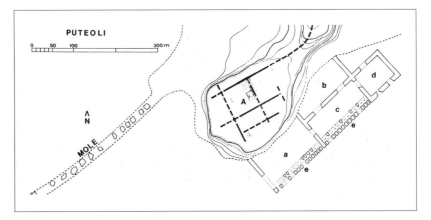

FIGURE 86. Port of Puteoli. **A** = arx of the city; **a – d** = separate tanks of the enclosure; **e** = rows of concrete piers. (From P. Sommella, "Forma e urbanistica di Pozzuoli romana," *Puteoli. Studi di storia antica* 2 [1978] fig. 167)

Noted on maps from at least the seventeenth century, these ruins were commonly referred to as the *"Piscina Veteres"* (*sic*).[231] The remains were plotted by Charles Du Bois at the beginning of this century but today are difficult to examine.[232] The concrete walls, as recorded by Du Bois, enclose a large rectangular area which measured 400 by 140 meters. At least four separate tanks were partitioned: one large rectangle (160 by 100 meters — a), two smaller rectangles (160 by 60 meters — b, c), and one square tank (80 by 80 meters — d). Concrete walls, 8 to 9 meters wide, delimit the tanks on all sides except for the seaward side of the enclosure. This side was formed by a double row of piers that stretch for about 320 meters of the pond's length (e). The outer row was composed of almost 30 rectangular piers, which measure 9 by 5 meters. The piers of the second line were roughly wedge-shaped and were positioned to line up with each interstice. This arrangement was designed to break the force of the waves while still allowing seawater to circulate within.

The plan of this enclosure possessed several features that compare favorably with the fishpond – oyster bed complex depicted on the Ampurias, Populonia, and Warsaw bottles. The central portion of the enclosure at Puteoli, which lacks internal subdivisions, was equipped with a breakwater that could not confine fish but was well suited to protect the temporary enclosures typical of oyster beds.[233] The tanks enclosed by solid walls were better adapted to the confining of fish. In addition, the double line of piers could have supported a wooden walkway that would connect the various parts of the complex and appear to span the central oyster bed. It is then possible to reconstruct a fishpond – oyster bed complex from the ruins at Puteoli reminiscent of the structures depicted on the glass bottles.

Pausilypon (Fig. 87)

In the area called Gaiola on the north shore of the Bay of Naples are the remains of a *villa maritima*, which is positioned on a rocky promontory with a good view of the bay. Based on building style, the ruins date from the last decades of the first century B.C. In addition to living quarters, an odeon, and a theater, the villa was equipped with fishponds, constructed on the shelf of volcanic rock that extends beyond the promontory. The villa was first studied in earnest by R. T. Gunther, at the beginning of this century, and published as a monograph.[234] Gunther consistently overestimated the rise in sea level since antiquity believing that most architecture that he observed underwater would have been above in the first century B.C.[235] Subsequent study has presented a more plausible reconstruction of the topography of the villa.[236]

The ponds were built around the small islands (Isole e Isolotti di Gaiola) which stand just offshore.[237] The larger of the two enclosures was built around the Isolotti di Gaiola (Fig. 87:XXVII), the very small islands east of the promontory. The precise dimensions of these remains were unclear in Gunther's day and are impossible to verify today. From

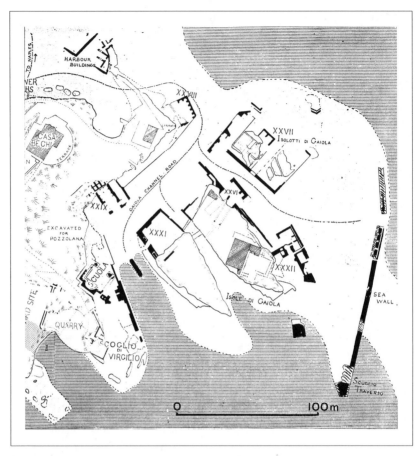

FIGURE 87. Pausilypon—plan of the ruins of the Villa of Vedius Pollio. **XXVI, XXVII, XXXII** = fishponds. (From R. T. Gunther, *Pausilypon: The Imperial Villa near Naples* [Oxford 1913] fig 1)

his plan it is possible to make out a rectangular enclosure which measures 54 by 38 meters in plan. The perimeter wall is nearly 2 meters wide and the scattered remains of architecture within the enclosure may be the vestiges of some sort of internal subdivisions or tanks. The two isolotti, inside the rectangle, are pierced with rock-cut channels, which ease the circulation of water inside the enclosure. One of these channels, located on the larger isolotto, is cut at an elevation (corrected for the change in sea level in the past two millennia) that would have precluded its use in the circulation of seawater and probably was employed in the conveyance of fresh water brought in from the mainland or cisterns on the islands themselves. The channels associated with the circulation of seawater (those which were submerged in antiquity) are between 1 and 2 meters wide and a little over 1 meter high. Concrete was used to line the inside of the channels.[238] Today, the channels and crevasses are popular fishing grounds for octopodes and gray mullets (*mugiles*).[239]

A second group of remains, which resemble fishponds, lies just off the southeast corner of the large Isole di Gaiola (XXXII). This area is protected by a long concrete sea wall—at least 160 meters long and about 4 meters wide—which is divided into two parts. Filled in at a later date, the sea wall in its original phase was formed by a series of piers with narrow openings between each (*opus pilarum*).[240] The openings in this wall allowed seawater to circulate while protecting the area near the islands from the full force of the sea.

The pond has a rectangular plan, measuring 38 by 12 meters, is anchored to a trapezoidal pier at its south end, and is connected to the island by a concrete wall or causeway approximately 3 meters wide. The remains of interior walls clearly suggest the partition of the pond into at least five tanks. Two small rectangular tanks can be observed on a projection between the pond and the connecting causeway. Immediately east of this projection and west of the pond is a narrow channel (3 meters wide and 7 meters long), which is closed off at one end by a semicircular wall and open to the sea on the leeward side of the pond. This inlet could have functioned as a slipway for the docking of boats servicing the fishpond. The east or seaward wall of the pond carries a small canal, which runs along the top of the mole. Conduits of this sort are usually associated with water from sources other than the sea.

The third area, given over to the raising of fish, lies at the northeast corner of the island and is centered around two rock-cut grottoes (XXVI). This side of the island is protected by a concrete wall which runs from the ponds (XXXII) at the southeast corner of the island to align with the wall which defines the northwestern edge of the enclosure around the Isolotti di Gaiola (XXVII). The long wall is broken in front of the grottoes (XXVI) where a barrier, over 10 meters beyond the entrances to the caves, defines an area roughly 10 meters square.

Both grottoes lie on slightly different axes, a fact that probably was dictated by the original orientation of the natural caves from which they were carved. The northernmost grotto is 15 meters long, 6.5 meters wide, and measures at least 5 meters to the top of the arched ceiling. The second grotto is 18 meters long, over 5 meters wide, and measures at least 5 meters to the top of its arched ceiling. There are the vestiges of concrete walls inside this grotto, which may have carried freshwater conduits. In addition, the back of this grotto was connected to the sea by a channel 10 meters long. The circulation of water within these grottoes led Gunther to suggest that these were *nymphaea* but the absence of niches and the careful combination of fresh and salt water support the association of these caves with the raising of fish. It is possible to visualize the entire area, northeast of the Isole di Gaiola, protected by the sea wall to the east, and comprising structures XXVI, XXVII, and XXXII, as a complex of *piscinae*. The remains of architecture on the islands suggest that rooms were constructed for the maintenance, dining, and enjoyment of the fishponds.

The villa at Pausilypon has been associated with the Roman *eques* Vedius Pollio. Pollio is recorded in several sources as having fishponds and to have used his voracious eels to punish clumsy or disobedient slaves.[241] The complex of fishponds with their accompanying buildings justify the attention of ancient authors. The proximity of the ponds to rooms, which could be used for dining, mesh well with the accounts of Pollio's banquet for Augustus, who saved a slave from being thrown to the *murenae*. This villa with its ponds came into the hands of the imperial family after Pollio's death in 15 B.C.[242] Thereafter, repairs or additions are attested well into the second century A.D.[243]

Herculaneum—Villa dei Papiri (Fig. 88)

At Herculaneum, there are several enclosures or pools which could have been used to hold fish. All possess sufficient depth (about 50 centimeters) and adequate circulation to function as *piscinae*.[244] Most are situated in domestic contexts. The pools from Herculaneum described here exhibit design characteristics unmistakably linked to Roman fishponds.

Located immediately northwest of the site of Herculaneum, the Villa dei Papiri was buried by 20 to 25 meters of pyroclastic matter as a result of eruptions of Vesuvius in A.D. 79 and again in 1631. This suburban villa, which was discovered accidentally in 1750, was explored by an extensive system of tunnels. Plans drawn by Charles Weber, soon after, reveal a design that included two long narrow ponds (*euripi*), which could have been used to raise fish.[245] Both ponds were built flush to the ground, fed by fresh water, and enclosed within peristyle courts.[246]

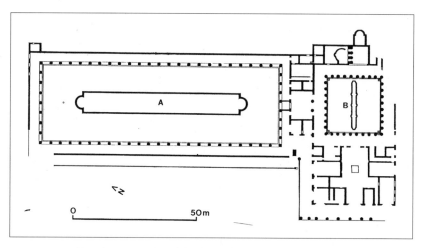

FIGURE 88. Herculaneum—plan of the Villa dei Papiri. **A** = pond in the Grand Peristyle; **B** = pond in the small peristyle court. (Plan drawn from C. Weber in D. Comparetti and G. de Pietra, *La villa ercolanese dei Pisoni* [Turin 1883] pl. 24)

A major portion of the villa was occupied by a grand rectangular peristyle, which measured 100 by 37 meters. The peristyle enclosed a long rectangular pond (A), rounded on its short ends, which was richly appointed with fountains and sculpture. The pond was constructed on a north-south axis and measured 66 meters long, 7 meters wide, and was just over 1 meter deep. The walls at each short end of the *piscina* were rounded to form semicircular appendages based on a circle 4.3 meters in diameter. A pond of this size certainly could have held fish though there were no recesses or sheltered areas provided for them.

The second pond (B) was situated in a square portico (21 meters square) which was located at the rear of the atrium. Oriented on an east-west axis, the *piscina* was 19 meters long and approximately 2 meters wide. The short sides of the pond were faceted; three short walls formed roughly semicircular ends. The perimeter was broken by six semicircular recesses (three on each long side), which measured less than 1 meter wide and 50 centimeters deep. These recesses provided spots where fish could escape direct sunlight and predacious neighbors. The pond was supplied by water from four conch shell fountains located at each corner of the peristyle.

The Villa dei Papiri is commonly associated with Calpurnii Pisones. This connection is based on the collection of papyri that were found in the villa, which contains many works of Philodemus of Gadara. This Epicurean philosopher was a favorite of L. Calpurnius Piso Caesoninus, who was Caesar's father-in-law and consul in 58 B.C.[247] Frescoes in Pompeian Second Style support an original construction phase in the first century B.C. It is not clear exactly when the *piscinae* were constructed. Like most of the residences in this vicinity the villa was undergoing restoration, after the earthquake of A.D. 62, when Vesuvius erupted in A.D. 79.

Herculaneum — The Palestra (Fig. 89)

The Palestra at Herculaneum is located in the eastern side of the city called by the excavators the Insula Orientalis (II, 4).[248] Three sides of the palestra have been excavated and reveal an open rectangular court surrounded by colonnades (Fig. 89). The center of the palestra is dominated by a large cruciform pool.[249] The north-south axis of the pool is 55 meters long while the east-west axis measures 31.5 meters and the arms of the cruciform plan are 5.8 meters wide. The pool was 1 meter deep at the edges and gradually sloped to 1.1 meters in the center of the enclosure.

196 The enclosure was built so that its margins were flush with the ground and concrete faced in *opus reticulatum* was used to form the walls of the pool. The interior of the enclosure was lined with a coat of *opus signinum*. The pool could be entered by way of four semicircular steps positioned in the northwest corner of the long northern arm. Water was supplied from fountains situated at the ends and center of the cruciform plan.[250]

Separate from the central cruciform pool and running along the north side of the Palestra is a second pool which was designed to raise fish. This pond was rectangular (measuring 30 by 3 meters and 2.35 meters in depth) and was constructed with the tops of its walls even with the level of the ground. The concrete walls of the pond, which were faced with *opus reticulatum*, were coated with plaster or *opus signinum*. Thirty-five *amphorae* were incorporated into the fabric of the walls so that the open ends of the vessels were flush with the vertical face of the walls. These *amphorae* were arranged in a single line midway up the height of the walls.[251] The resulting recesses presented openings which ranged from 20 to 30 centimeters in diameter. The added depth of this pond and the *amphorae* placed in its walls are in contrast with the design of the large cruciform pool. While the central pool of the Palestra could have been used for decoration and wading the smaller pond was better suited for raising fish.[252]

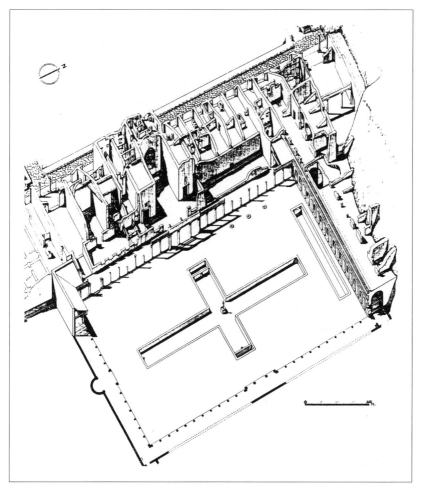

FIGURE 89. Herculaneum — axonometric view of the Palestra, with cruciform and rectangular ponds. (Drawing by R. Oliva in A. Maiuri, *Ercolano: I nuovi scavi (1927–1958)* I [Rome 1958] 141, fig. 111)

Maiuri postulated that the Palestra was built as a result of the reorganization of the *iuventutes* by Augustus.[253] The use of concrete faced in *opus reticulatum* supports an initial date of construction late in the reign of Augustus or during the tenure of the emperor Tiberius. When excavated, both ponds contained debris which predated the eruption of Vesuvius in A.D. 79, indicating that these hydraulic installations were out of use or under repair (as a result of the earthquake in A.D. 62) when the volcano erupted.

GAZETTEER OF FISHPONDS

Fresh water had been stored in cisterns since Pompeii's earliest periods and collected rainwater continued to serve as a supply for Pompeii's ponds. This supply was dramatically enhanced by the construction of an aqueduct during the reign of Augustus. From springs near Serino, 30 kilometers east of Pompeii, the aqueduct carried copious supplies of fresh water to Pompeii, Neapolis (Naples), and the north shore of the Bay of Naples.[254] The aqueduct entered the city immediately west of the Porta del Vesuvio (the highest point in the city). From here, through a system of towers and conduits, water was made available for a wide variety of uses, which included supplying the pools and ponds in the gardens of the city.[255] Most of these ponds appear to have been built for the private use and enjoyment of their owners, though some commercial motivation is possible.[256]

Many of the houses and villas at Pompeii were designed with pools and ponds which could have been used to hold fish. Reliable circulation and sufficient depth of water were essential to any fishpond and nearly seventy enclosures possessed these characteristics.[257] Many of these enclosures were even decorated with blue fresco interiors to enhance the semblance of deep ocean.[258] Criteria such as these make it probable that fish were kept in these enclosures. Ironically, the most direct and incontrovertible evidence, the remains of fish, is virtually absent.[259]

Among those ponds which best exhibit specific details or designs that facilitated the keeping and raising of fish is the one from the house in Regio VIII 2, 14. This house is located directly behind the civic buildings located at the south end of the Forum. Situated in the southeast corner of the house's peristyle is a small rectangular fishpond, measuring 1.6 meters wide, 3.5 meters long, and just over 1 meter deep.[260] The pond was placed so that it would not encroach on the open area of the peristyle, with the pond's east side abutting the stylobate of the peristyle.

The pond was built so that its upper margins were flush with the surrounding ground level. Concrete with an irregular facing was used to construct the walls of this enclosure and plaster was added to the interior of the pond to insure that it was watertight. The short walls of the pond were stepped toward the bottom to accommodate horizontal rows of *amphorae* and to facilitate entrance into the pond for harvesting or maintenance. The eastern side of the pond (Figs. 90, 91) was formed by three steps (30 centimeters high and 10 centimeter wide) that extended

FIGURE 90. Pompeii, House VIII 2, 14—eastern end of the fishpond, with rows of *amphorae* (one visible, the other obscured by debris). (Photo courtesy of the Fototeca Unione)

FIGURE 91. Pompeii, House VIII 2, 14—detail of eastern end of fishpond, with the visible row of *amphorae*. (Photo courtesy of the Fototeca Unione)

FIGURE 92. Pompeii, House VIII 2, 14—western end of the fishpond, with two rows of *amphorae*. (Photo courtesy of the Fototeca Unione)

for the entire width of the wall. Eleven *amphorae* (in two rows of six vessels over five) were inserted into the fabric of the lowest step so that the rims presented open recesses in the walls of the enclosure.[261] The western side of the pond was designed with a single broad step (50 centimeters high and 15 centimeters wide) that extended for the entire width of the wall. Seventeen *amphorae* were inserted into the interior face of the bottom step forming two superimposed rows of eight vessels over nine (Fig. 92). Thus, a total of twenty-eight vessels provided the fish with places of refuge from the sun and other fish.

The pond was built of irregularly faced concrete (*opus incertum*?) with the *amphorae* placed in the fabric of this construction. The rows of vessels were covered by flat roof tiles (Fig. 90) which formed the stepped sides of the pond. The interior of the pond was lined with a layer of plaster in order to waterproof the enclosure. Water probably was circulated within the pond by means of lead pipes though no traces of this system were noted. Damage to the upper margins of this pond have obscured details that might have clarified the configuration of the circulating system. The style of construction suggests a date in the late first century B.C., with repairs to the peristyle in the first century A.D.[262]

GAZETTEER OF FISHPONDS

Pompeii — Casa dei Capitelli Colorati, VII 4, 35/51

This large house is located north of the Forum between the Via degli Augustali and the Via della Fortuna (Via di Nola). Behind the *atrium* in the center of a large peristyle was a rectangular pond that measured 2 by 5.9 meters, with a depth of just over 1 meter.[263] The inside of the pond was lined with 2 to 3 centimeters of *opus signinum* and finished with a coat of plaster that was painted blue. A single *amphora* was inserted into the west side of the pond 94 centimeters from the south wall and 41 centimeters from the bottom of the enclosure. A small columnar fountain stood in the center of the pond. Other details of the circulating system are not known.

The Casa dei Capitelli Colorati was constructed in the second century B.C. The columns of the peristyle, which surrounds the pond, were refurbished in the first century B.C. when the capitals were decorated with painted stucco. It is possible to place the construction of the pond with the redecoration and ornamentation of this peristyle during the late Republic.[264] After the earthquake in A.D. 62 the columnar fountain was added to the center of the pond.[265]

Pompeii — Casa di Gavius Rufus, VII 2, 16 (Fig. 93)

The Casa di Gavius Rufus is located on the Vicolo del Panettiere northeast of the Forum. The focus of the house is a large peristyle, which occupies nearly two-thirds of the plan.[266] The peristyle enclosed a garden area with a small fishpond positioned at the south side along the stylobate of the colonnade.

The pond was formed by four concrete walls (20 centimeters wide) and designed so that its upper margins stood 15 centimeters above the ground level of the garden. The small enclosure was rectangular in plan (measuring 2.17 by 1.06 meters, with a depth of 52 centimeters), with its long sides parallel to the south side of the peristyle. Three small pots were placed into the fabric of the long north wall of the pond (Fig. 93). Arranged in a single line barely 20 centimeters from the bottom of the pond, these vessels created circular recesses (30 centimeters in diameter) in which fish could take refuge. The inside of the pond was lined with 2 to 3 centimeters of *opus signinum* and finished with a coat of blue-painted plaster, small traces of which still are visible. The upper margins of the pond are capped with a decorative border made of white marble plates.

GAZETTEER OF FISHPONDS

FIGURE 93. Pompeii, Casa di Gavius Rufus (VII 2, 16)—small fishpond, with three pots inserted into the north wall. (Photo by J. Higginbotham)

At least two phases of construction can be identified in the Casa di Gavius Rufus. The earliest fresco decoration in the house is painted in the Pompeian Second Style. Extensive remodeling was carried out after the earthquake of A.D. 62 with much of the walls around the peristyle garden decorated in the Pompeian Fourth Style.[267]

Pompeii — Casa di Meleagro, VI 9, 2 (Figs. 94, 95)

The Casa di Meleagro is located at the northern end of the Via di Mecurio northeast of the forum. The house was excavated between June 1829 and September 1830, when many of the frescoes were taken to the Museo Nazionale in Napoli.[268] Beside the *atrium* of the house is a large peristyle, which was the focus of this residence (Fig. 94). In the center of the peristyle, a decorative fishpond was built into the ground so that its upper margins stood just above (approximately 15 centimeters) the level of the ground (Fig. 95). The pond is generally rectangular in plan (3.55 by 5.73 meters, with a depth of 1.2 meters) with its perimeter broken by eight alternating rectangular and semicircular niches — one semicircular niche (1.6 meters wide and 40 centimeters deep) on each short side, and two rectangular niches (78 centimeters wide and 40 centimeters deep)

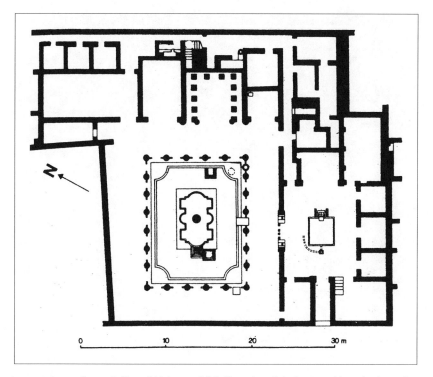

FIGURE 94. Pompeii, Casa di Meleagro (VI 9, 2)—plan of the house, with peristyle garden and fishpond. (From A. de Vos and M. de Vos, *Pompei, Ercolano, Stabia. Guide archeologiche Laterza* [Bari 1982] 187)

flanking a single semicircular niche (91 centimeters wide and 40 centimeters deep) on each long side. These recesses provided shade for the fish and protection for the smaller fry.

The walls and floor of the pond were constructed of concrete. The upper rim of the pond was revetted with white marble plate and the interior was lined with *opus signinum* finished by a coat of blue-painted plaster. A small cascade (1.43 meters wide and 57 centimeters high) with six small stairs was positioned at the west side of the pond. The top of the stairs was fitted with a water jet, which spewed water down the stairs of the cascade and into the pond. The fountain and cascade supplied the pond with an aerated supply of water. Water also issued forth from a columnar fountain standing in the center of the pond. This column (1.27 meters high and 25 centimeters in diameter) was constructed of masonry coated with blue-painted plaster and was crowned with a marble fountainhead that resembles a column base. A single overflow

FIGURE 95. Pompeii, Casa di Meleagro (VI 9, 2)—fishpond from the west. (Photo by J. Higginbotham)

(11 centimeters in diameter) pierced the north wall of the northeastern niche below the rim of the pond. This configuration would have maintained the water level nearly 30 centimeters below the top of the pond.

Immediately south of the cascade and west of the fishpond was a small square tank (measuring 58 by 59 centimeters in plan and 59 centimeters deep). This tank, which was topped with marble revetment and painted blue, was linked to the larger pond by a single pipe and probably served as an enclosure for special fish or to hold the fish while the larger pond was being cleaned.[269]

The peristyle was not part of the original design of house. Decoration of the walls and columns of the peristyle correspond to the Pompeian Fourth Style. It is probable that the garden peristyle with its pond was constructed after the earthquake of A.D. 62.[270]

Pompeii—Villa di Diomede (Figs. 96, 97)

The Villa of Diomedes is located 200 meters northwest of Pompeii outside the Porta di Ercolano on the Via dei Sepolcri. Excavation of the villa was carried out between 1771 and 1774, when most of the frescoes were removed for display in the Museo Nazionale di Napoli. The residence was arbitrarily assigned to M. Arrius Diomedes, a freedman whose tomb was located opposite the entrance to the villa.[271]

FIGURE 96. Pompeii, Villa di Diomede—lower peristyle. (From A. Maiuri, *Pompei* [Rome 1978] pl. 59, no. 99)

The villa was built on two artificial terraces that were positioned on the slope of a hill. This design made it possible to enjoy a panoramic view of the Bay of Naples. On the upper terrace a triangular courtyard, south of the main entrance, enclosed a rectangular pool 2.17 meters by 2.85 meters with a depth of 1.1 meters. A fresco depicting an aquatic scene was painted on the wall above the north side of the pool.[272]

The lower terrace was dominated by a large peristyle garden (Fig. 96) which was surrounded by a portico of stout square pillars connected by flat arches. In the center of this sunken garden was a fishpond (Fig. 97:P) with a dining pavilion (D) nearby.[273] The pond was basically rectangular in plan measuring 7.1 by 6.2 meters, with a depth of approximately 1.75 meters. The eastern side of the pond, on the side toward the villa, was curved to form an apse which was 4.4 meters wide and 1.75 meters deep. The entire structure was built into the ground so that its upper margins stood just above the level of the surrounding garden.

The long sides of the fishpond were punctuated by alternating rectangular and semicircular niches: three rectangular and two semicircular niches to a side. The rectangular niches were 80 centimeters wide and 59 centimeters deep, while the semicircular niches were formed on a diameter of 1.18 meters (59 centimeters deep). The resulting recesses provided refuge and shade for the fish in the pond.

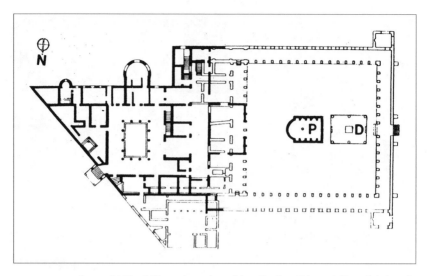

FIGURE 97. Pompeii, Villa di Diomede—plan of the villa. **P** = fishpond; **D** = dining pavilion. (From A. Maiuri and R. Pane, *La Casa di Loreio Tiburtino e la Villa di Diomede in Pompei* [Rome 1947] pl. 9)

The fishpond was built of concrete walls (approximately 45 centimeters wide) faced with brick, tufo blocks, and *opus reticulatum*. The interior of the pond was lined with 2 to 3 centimeters of *opus signinum* and finished with a layer of blue-painted plaster, traces of which are preserved inside the apsidal end of the enclosure. Water jets, which supplied fresh water to the pond, were arranged around the perimeter and atop a brick column positioned in the pond's center.[274]

A raised concrete platform, which supported an open dining area, was positioned on axis with the pond between the *piscina* and the west colonnade of the peristyle. The platform was constructed of concrete faced with brick, tufo blocks, and *opus reticulatum* in a fashion identical to the fishpond. Rectangular in plan (measuring 9.3 by 7.5 meters), the platform was 50 centimeters high and approachable by stairways at both its east and west ends. Small brick parapet walls (35 to 40 centimeters in height) were set around the edges of the platform. The lower courses of six brick columns were arranged around this perimeter and probably supported a wooden arbor, or *pergula*, which provided shade for an outdoor dining pavilion. The connection between dining facilities and *piscinae* recall the larger and earlier seaside ponds of the *piscinarii*.

The Villa di Diomede was first constructed during the late Republic and remodeled during the Empire.[275] Wall decoration throughout was of the Pompeian Fourth Style and reflects the major renovations after the earthquake in A.D. 62. Construction of the peristyle and its *piscina-pergula* was initiated after the earthquake.[276]

Pompeii — Praedia di Iulia Felix, II 4 (Figs. 98 – 100)

The *praedia* or property belonging to Iulia Felix is located on the Via Abbondanza in the eastern part of the city. The site was excavated first in 1755 – 57, reburied, and then reexcavated in 1936 and between 1951 and 1952.[277] No published reports exist of the recent excavations of this villa but other studies have presented information about the site.[278]

The property occupied an entire insula block with nearly one-half of the area given over to the buildings of the villa.[279] A major focus of the villa was a large peristyle garden, which was equipped with an adjoining dining room and a long fishpond or *euripus* (Fig. 98:E). The *euripus* extended for nearly the entire length of the garden (measuring just over 20 meters long and 2.5 meters wide) and was built into the garden so that the upper margins of the enclosure stood approximately 15 centimeters above ground level (Fig. 99). Three small bridges (the central bridge is 1.2 meters wide while the other two are 75 centimeters wide), which are supported by low brick arches, span the fishpond at roughly equal intervals and permit easy movement across the *euripus*. The long sides of the pond were broken by alternating semicircular and rectangular niches — four to a side — which were arranged in opposing pairs. The semicircular niches measured 78.5 centimeters wide and 59 centimeters deep, while the rectangular niches measured 49 centimeters wide and 59 centimeters deep. Each niche was divided by a single large brick (*bipedalis*) which was placed horizontally across the niche (50 centimeters from the bottom), creating a small recess at the bottom of the pond (Fig. 100). The niches and the accompanying recesses provided refuge and shade for the fish in the pond.

The distance from the top to the bottom of the fishpond is 1.35 meters, but the water level was maintained well below (approximately 40 centimeters) the top of the pond. Water was supplied from at least two positions: a lead pipe, which enters the pond through the top of the north wall, and a clay conduit, which enters near the center of the western side of the *euripus*. Overflow was carried from the pond by two clay conduits, through both of its long sides, at the southern end of the enclosure. The position of these clay pipes indicates that water was maintained at a depth of about 90 centimeters. Water level just would have

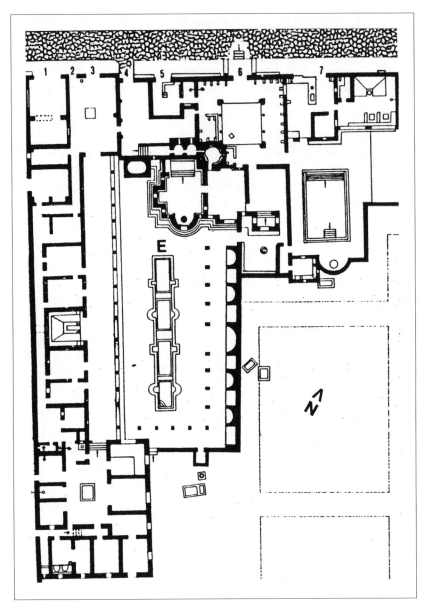

FIGURE 98. Pompeii, Praedia di Iuliae Felicis (II 4)—plan of the villa. **E** = long fishpond or *euripus*. (From H. B. Van der Poel, L. Garcia y Garcia, and J. McConnell, *Corpus Topographicum Pompeianum: The Insulae of Regions I–IV* [Rome 1986] 47)

FIGURE 99. Pompeii, Praedia di Iuliae Felicis (II 4)—long fishpond or *euripus* from the south. (Photo by J. Higginbotham)

FIGURE 100. Pompeii, Praedia di Iuliae Felicis (II 4)—detail of semicircular niche, with small recess at the bottom. (Photo by J. Higginbotham)

reached the undersides of the three footbridges and have left a freeboard of sufficient height to prevent jumping fish from escaping the pond. An access to a major drain was positioned at the bottom of the southern end of the *euripus*. This opening was used during the periodic cleaning of the pond when water and accumulated sediment could be flushed into the sewer. The cleanout was closed by a lead panel during normal operation of the pond.

The walls of the *euripus* were constructed of concrete with irregular stones used in the aggregate and facing. Bricks were employed to form the arches of the footbridges and the recesses at the bottom of the niches. The upper margins of the pond were topped by marble slabs, which form a decorative border (approximately 27.5 centimeters wide) for the fishpond. This upper border overhangs the interior of the pond (nearly 5 centimeters), enough to cover the layers of *opus signinum* and blue-painted stucco that lined the walls. Seven statuettes were recorded as having been found near the perimeter of the pond and were probably used to decorate the edge of the *euripus*.[280]

Running parallel to the pond was a long colonnade that formed the western side of the garden. Behind the pillars of this colonnade was a dining room (*triclinium*) positioned so revelers could look out upon the garden and the *euripus*. A cascade at the back of the dining room poured water into the room, where it ran beneath the dining couches and, by way of a subterranean conduit, into the pond.[281] The Praedia, with its baths, dining facilities, and gardens, probably was designed as a sort of club where members could relax and revel. The property assumed this final form after the earthquake of A.D. 62 as a result of the efforts of the enterprising owner, Julia Felix.[282]

Pompeii — Casa di D. Octavius Quartio, II 2, 2

The House of D. Octavius Quartio (or M. Loreius Tiburtinus) is located between Via Abbondanza and the Great Palaestra in the eastern part of the city. The site was excavated between 1918 and 1921 and its gardens have recently undergone restoration.[283]

The house occupied the greater part of an insula block with its main entrance on the Via dell'Abbondanza. After the earthquake of A.D. 62, much of the house had been turned into a series of garden spaces, the largest of which consisted of a porticoed terrace at the back of the house overlooking a large lower garden beyond. The primary focus of this large garden area was an elaborate hydraulic installation consisting of two long, narrow ponds, or *euripi*. In plan, the ponds were arranged perpendicular to one another resembling the letter T. Though located on different levels, both ponds were connected by means of an intervening fountain with a stepped cascade.

The smaller *euripus* (measuring just over 20 meters long, 1 meter wide, and 1.4 meters deep) was positioned in the center of the upper terrace which runs across the back of the house. An *oecus,* or reception hall, on the north central side of the *euripus* provided a comfortable point of vantage from which to view the pond and the garden beyond. An outdoor masonry *biclinium* was built against the wall at the east end of the terrace. Between the couches and against the wall stands an *aedicula* niche flanked by two columns.[284] The pond runs between the couches of the *biclinium* and right up to the niche. Two small bridges, which are supported by low masonry arches, cross the fishpond—one opposite the large *oecus* and the other in front of the *biclinium*. The bridges create secluded and shaded areas, which were important for keeping fish. Ten marble statuettes, used to decorate the edge of the *euripus*, were found near the perimeter of the pond.[285] The *euripus, biclinium,* and *aedicula* niche were covered by a wooden arbor supported by the house wall and eight masonry piers. This arrangement provided shade not only for the guests but for the fish kept in the pond.

A tetrastyle pavilion housing a fountain was placed near the center of the upper *euripus*, opposite the large *triclinium* (approximately 12 meters from the western end of the pond). Accessible by one of the footbridges, the marble-clad fountain fed the upper pond through several jets in a semicircular array. The pavilion marked the point of axis and connection between the two *euripi*. Water from the upper fountain then was piped into a *nymphaeum*, located directly beneath the tetrastyle pavilion, which fed the large pond in the lower garden.

The *nymphaeum* is flanked by two short columns and decorated with a fresco illustrating marine life. Water poured forth from the mouth of a marble mask, depicting a water god, and into a small settling basin. From here, water was conveyed through a second marble sculptural fountain (an *amorino* holding a mask), down a two-step cascade, and finally into the northern end of the large *euripus*.[286]

The large *euripus* bisected the lower garden, or *hortus,* which occupied nearly two-thirds of the insula. Coursing for nearly 50 meters, this long fishpond, in reality, consists of six interconnected tanks punctuated by three ornamental structures. In plan, the large *euripus* is slightly off a straight line. Conduits located in the upper margins of the pond ensure proper circulation along the entire length of the *euripus*.

Water from the *nymphaeum* fed directly into a long rectangular tank approximately 24 meters long, 1.2 meters wide, and 1 meter deep. Three fountain jets (two on columns, one a square pier) were placed down the center of the tank at regular intervals (6 meters apart). This segment was followed by a rectangular pool (about 4 by 3 meters and 1.4 meters deep), covered by a vine arbor supported on four masonry columns. In the center of the pool was a marble-clad fountain founded on a low masonry vault. The fountain is pyramidal in design with stepped cascades running down each of the four sides. Water spouted from a fountain jet at the top of the pyramid and from statuettes placed on twelve little bases around the perimeter of the pool. Shade from the arbored *pergula* and supporting vault would have provided ample protection for the fish. Diners could enjoy the garden and its *euripus* from a masonry *triclinium*, which was located directly east of the fountain and *pergula*.

Moving south, the fountain pool was followed by a small rectangular tank (approximately 2 meters long, 1.2 meters wide, and 1.4 meters deep). The increase in depth led Spinazzola to suggest that the change was required to meet the needs of different species of fish.[287] This could also facilitate flow north to south, particularly when the *euripus* was drained for cleaning or maintenance. With the next segment the plan of the *euripus* deviates slightly to the east aligning with the rear entrance to the garden. The following tank measures nearly 6 meters in length, 1 meter wide, and 1.4 meters in depth. Built over the northern end and masking the change in axis is a small tetrastyle *aedicula* supporting a masonry roof. The *aedicula* sits atop a small vault, roughly a meter square, which provides yet another shaded recess for the fish.

The third ornamental structure along the course of the *euripus* was a rectangular pool (4 meters long, 1.7 meters wide, and 1.4 meters deep), covered by an arbored *pergula* supported by four columns. A square pillar of *opus vittatum* in the pool's center held a fountain jet. The course of the *euripus* ended with a rectangular tank (6 meters long, 1.2 meters wide, and 1.4 meters deep), which stops just short of the rear door of the garden. Arbored walkways lined both sides of the large *euripus*, permitting convenient enjoyment of the entire course of the fishpond.

The walls of both *euripi* and the arches of the footbridges were constructed of concrete with irregular stones used in the aggregate. The upper margins of the pond were topped by marble slabs which form a decorative border (approximately 20 to 24 centimeters wide) for the fishponds. This upper border overhangs the interior of the pond (nearly 5 centimeters), enough to cover the layers of *opus signinum* and blue-painted stucco that lined the walls.

Sorrento—Villa del Convento dei Cappuccini (Fig. 101)

The coast near the city of Sorrento, ancient Surrentum, is the site of three rock-cut *piscinae*: one at the Villa del Convento dei Cappuccini, sometimes called the Villa Nicolini, and two ponds associated with the so-called Villa of Agrippa Postumus below the Albergo delle Sirene on the Piazza Vittoria. All three ponds were excavated primarily from the tufo cliffs which rise precipitously from the sea.

The Villa del Convento dei Cappuccini is built on the ruins of an ancient *villa maritima*. Parts of the ancient villa were built on terraces that were cut into the cliffs and finished with concrete walls faced in *opus reticulatum*.[288] Stairs and covered corridors linked the uppermost portions of the villa to the lower terraces. The lowest terrace runs just above the sea and behind a small promontory into which was built a covered fishpond.

The pond was enclosed completely within a rock-cut barrel vault. The main room of this enclosure was rectangular in plan (11.8 by 6.5 meters) and measured nearly 9 meters from the bottom of the chamber to the top of the vault. The northern and southern sides of the pond were lined with a concrete walkway (Fig. 101:W) approximately 80 centimeters wide. The walkway crosses the pond just short of the seaward or western wall of the grotto, creating a narrow rectangular tank approximately 85 centimeters wide and 6.5 meters long. The vault rises nearly 6 meters above the level of the walkway. Along the eastern end of the grotto, the walkway widens to form a broad platform (P), 4.7 by 3.5 meters, which was covered by an arched vault standing 2.5 meters above the platform. The remainder of the pond is divided into two tanks separated by a concrete partition wall (60 centimeters wide), which projects nearly a meter above the level of the walkways. Both tanks are linked by an opening (2.4 meters wide) in the center of the partition wall. This opening probably was equipped with a gate, though no evidence of any barrier remains.

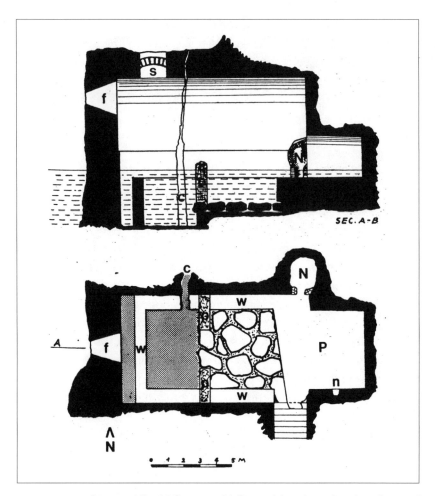

FIGURE 101. Sorrento, Villa del Convento dei Cappuccini — plan and section of covered fishpond. **P** = platform; **W** = walkway; **N** = niche tank(?); **c** = fissure in wall of grotto; **f** and **s** = lightwells; **n** = small niche (for lamp?); **p** = partition wall. (From P. Mingazzini and F. Pfister, *Surrentum — Forma Italiae* I.2 [Florence 1946] 103, fig. 14)

The seaward tank was excavated to a depth of 3 meters below the walkways. The floor of the landward or eastern tank steps up 70 centimeters toward the shore and is lined with a single course of irregular boulders making this tank much shallower (1.4 meters deep). The boulders were placed in such a way as to leave sizable spaces between each stone. The resulting crevices would have made perfect hiding places for rock-loving fish.[289]

Rock-cut stairs linked the fishpond to the terrace above and entered the grotto through a doorway on the southern side of the enclosure. The doorway opens onto the concrete platform at the pond's eastern end. A small niche (n) in the southern wall of the platform probably was used to hold a lamp to help light this end of the grotto. In addition, the western end of the vault was pierced by two openings (f, s), which helped light and ventilate the interior of the grotto. The wall at the northern end of the platform was cut to form a roughly oval recess (1.6 by 2 meters). This recess (N) was closed off by a low wall and may have functioned as a little tank for special fish.

Seawater entered the enclosure through a fissure in the northern side of the grotto (c). This natural opening has widened since antiquity and the movement probably has destroyed any evidence of a closable barrier.[290] The villa was supplied with fresh water from a branch of an ancient aqueduct originating near Formiello.[291] It is conceivable that some sort of water conveyance system could have carried fresh water down to the lower levels of the villa and the fishpond. Concrete walls, faced in *opus reticulatum* without the use of brick, are the only indicators of the date of the villa and these provide a terminus post quem for their construction of the mid first century B.C.

Sorrento — Villa of Agrippa Postumus (Figs. 102, 103)

The villa commonly attributed to Agrippa Postumus is located along the shore below the Albergo della Sirena. This area corresponds to almost the total length of the ancient city of Surrentum. The villa was constructed on terraces that stepped down to the sea. The coastal structures of the villa included *nymphaea*, pavilions, baths, and two rock-cut fishponds (Fig. 102:A, C).[292]

The ponds were cut into the rock of the shore and appear to have been accessible primarily from the sea. Submerged structures in front of the ponds probably supported wooden walkways and platforms. It would have been possible to reach these shorefront structures by boat or from the villa by way of stairs located in the eastern portion of the complex away from the ponds.[293] The entrance to the complex was through a structure that was covered by a rock-cut semicylindrical vault (approximately 7 meters high) and was known as the Basilica di San Giorgio on account of the grotto's similarity to a vaulted nave (A). The so-called Basilica was rectangular in plan (measuring 19 meters long and 8.5 me-

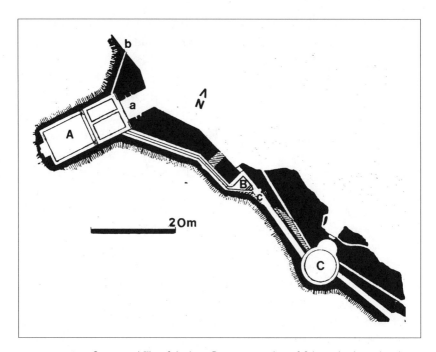

FIGURE 102. Sorrento, Villa of Agrippa Postumus — plan of fishponds along the shore. **A** = rectangular fishpond; **a** = entrance / landing; **b** = circulation channel; **B** = triangular chamber; **c** = stairway; **C** = circular fishpond ("Bagno dei Frati"). (From P. Mingazzini and F. Pfister, *Surrentum — Forma Italiae* 1.2 [Florence 1946] 114, fig. 21)

ters wide) and open toward the sea. The entrance to the grotto was preceded by a rectangular vestibule (a), which served as the principal connection to the sea and a sheltered landing for boats. This rock-cut opening was 6.2 meters long, 4.4 meters wide, and was fitted with two sets of vertical runners which could hold movable gates. A single channel (b) enters the pond from the north. This connection to the sea, which is 9 meters long and approximately 50 centimeters wide, enters the grotto through the northern corner of the enclosure.

The interior of the grotto was designed with rock-cut walkways (70 centimeters wide) that lined the perimeter of the enclosure. Rock-cut partitions within the grotto divided the pond into three rectangular tanks: two small seaward tanks and a large main tank at the back of the grotto. The small seaward tanks were of different dimensions, both being 6.2 meters long with the northernmost tank measuring 2.7 meters in width and the southernmost measuring 3.5 meters in width. The main tank was 6.7 meters wide and 9 meters long. Blocks, inserted into the wall dividing the main tank from the smaller ones, were fitted with vertical runners that would have held movable gates. The back wall of the grotto was cut to form a niche 3.2 meters wide, 1 meter deep, and 4 meters high. Remains of plaster on the walls of the niche indicate that this recess was decorated. This niche stood at the level of the walkway and was probably designed to hold a statue.[294]

Nearly 50 meters separates the rectangular pond (A) from the second fishpond in this complex. Both ponds are linked by a broad corridor (approximately 1.7 meters wide), which exits from the eastern corner of the rectangular pond (A). Narrow walkways (approximately 50 centimeters wide) line both sides of this corridor leaving a channel (approximately 70 centimeters wide) running down the center. Following an indirect route, the corridor opens on to a rock-cut chamber (B), triangular in plan, which measures approximately 5.5 meters to a side. The walkways continue around the sides of the chamber, leaving a triangular tank in the middle. This chamber was connected directly to the sea by a short conduit (1.25 meters long and 75 centimeters wide).

A second corridor exits from the eastern side of the chamber and leads to the eastern side of the circular fishpond (C). There is no central channel in the floor of this corridor as was noted in the link between the rectangular fishpond (A) and the triangular chamber (B). The circular fishpond is commonly called the Bagno dei Frati due to the fact that monks, who resided in the nearby Convento degli Agostiniani, used to bathe in this rock-cut room.

The Bagno is circular in plan, measuring 6.7 meters in diameter, and is surrounded by a walkway 60 centimeters wide (Fig. 103). The fishpond is covered by a rock-cut dome, which stands 4.6 meters above the level of the circular walkway. The interior of the pond was slightly less than 1 meter deep.[295] The northern side of the enclosure was cut to form a semicircular niche. The niche is 1.5 meters wide, 75 centimeters deep, and is covered by a rock-cut hemispherical dome, which stands 1.85 meters above the level of the walkway. Roughly circular apertures were cut in the northern sides of both the main dome (approximately 1 meter in diameter) and the hemispherical dome (approximately 40 centimeters in diameter) of the small niche (Fig. 103 . V, W). These openings functioned as lightwells for the pond and permitted the free circulation of air within the confines of the circular room.[296]

Long channels were excavated in the rock in order to facilitate the circulation of seawater and to permit the entry of fish into the enclosure. The eastern side of the pond was linked to the sea by two parallel chan-

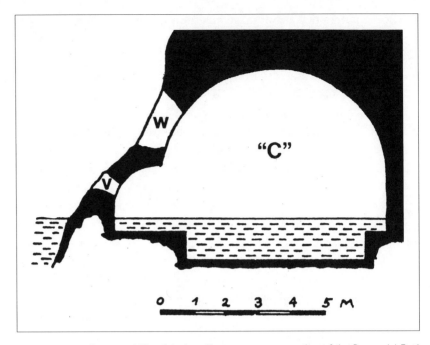

FIGURE 103. Sorrento, Villa of Agrippa Postumus—cross-section of the Bagno dei Frati (circular fishpond C). **V** and **W** = lightwells. (From P. Mingazzini and F. Pfister, *Surrentum—Forma Italiae* 1.2 [Florence 1946] 116, fig. 22)

nels. Both conduits are approximately 15 meters long; the northern channel is about 40 centimeters wide, while the southern channel is over a meter wide. The western side of the pond was linked directly to the sea by a single channel 20 meters long and approximately 40 centimeters wide. All channels probably figured into the circulation system of this pond. The wider channel to the east may have been equipped with closable gates and could have served as an entrance for fish seeking the shade and shelter of the cavelike fishpond. Fresh water, which emanated from the hill above and supplied the *nymphaea* along the shore, fed the fishponds as well.[297] The resulting brackish conditions inside the ponds would have provided additional inducement for fish to enter these confines.

It is probable that the ruins below the Albergo delle Sirene belong to the villa occupied by Postumus during his initial exile to Surrentum.[298] The villa was constructed during the first century B.C. and perhaps should be associated with the activities of M. Vipsanius Agrippa, friend and cohort of the emperor Augustus.[299] Upon the death of Agrippa the villa probably was left to the emperor and was a logical spot to send the fish-loving son of the elder Agrippa.[300] Examination of the architecture of the villa suggests three major building phases. The first, which is typified by concrete walls faced in *opus incertum*, probably dates to the late second or early first century B.C. The second phase, characterized by concrete walls faced in an irregular *opus reticulatum* with squared tufo blocks at the corners, must be placed in the last half of the first century B.C. The final phase saw the extensive use of fired bricks and tufo blocks to face concrete cores. It is likely that these facings represent repairs to the villa after the eruption of Vesuvius in A.D. 79.[301]

It is probable that natural grottoes and inlets, which were fed by both salt and fresh water, were hewn and enlarged into the *nymphaea* and *piscinae* along this shore. Attempts to date rock-cut structures are problematic. The walls of the corridor, which linked both fishponds, were largely cut from the tufo of the cliffs. At scattered points along this corridor, concrete faced in an irregular *opus reticulatum* was used to straighten the line of the walls.[302] This type of facing is consistent with the building technique used in the villa's second phase and fits conveniently with the hypothesis of an Agrippan/Augustan date.

LUCANIA

Paestum — Santa Venera (Figs. 104, 105)

The sanctuary in the località Santa Venera is located outside the walls, just south of the city of Paestum. Evidence gleaned from epigraphic finds and statuary point to Venus as the divinity that was worshiped at Santa Venera.[303] Buildings associated with this sanctuary first appeared in the early fifth century B.C. Later, during the early years of the Empire, the Roman benefactors of the sanctuary added a fishpond to the site. The *piscina* in the località Santa Venera is situated south of the large rectangular hall belonging to an extramural sanctuary.[304] The pond is roughly rectangular in plan (measuring 6 by 3 meters) with its northern short wall running parallel to the portico of the rectangular hall.[305] The pond was constructed so that the upper margins would stand just above the surrounding ground level. The measured depth of the enclosure was between 1.2 and 1.3 meters (Figs. 104, 105).

Construction of the pond began with the excavation of a rectangular pit, slightly larger than the intended dimensions of the enclosure, and ended on a layer of travertine (crosta), which served as the bottom of the

FIGURE 104. Paestum, Santa Venera—the fishpond from the south. (Photo by J. Higginbotham)

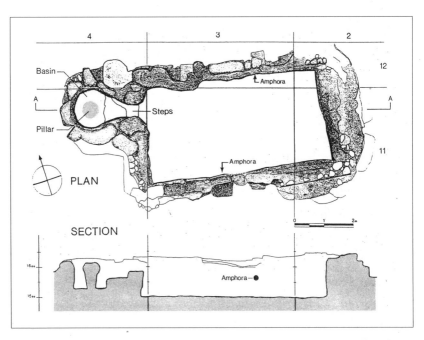

FIGURE 105. Paestum, Santa Venera—plan and section of the fishpond. (Drawing by David Myers)

tank. The walls of the *piscina* were built of limestone ashlars, which lined the pit and were buttressed on the exterior by stones and earth. The upper rim of the pond was topped by limestone slabs laid horizontally about the perimeter. The interior of the fishpond was sealed by a coat of *opus signinum*, which was applied in thicker layers at the corners of the structure.[306]

The centers of the eastern and western walls of the pond were pierced by a single circular hole. *Amphorae* were placed in these holes from outside so that their open ends would be flush with the interior faces of the walls. The resulting recesses (approximately 15 centimeters in diameter and 40 centimeters deep) provided the fish with places of refuge from the sun and predacious relatives.

A circular basin, the walls of which were constructed in a manner identical to that of the pond, was attached to the eastern end of the north wall of the *piscina*. The basin and fishpond are linked by a narrow passage which would have allowed water to circulate between both. The floor of the passage is stepped so that it would be possible to descend into the basin from the upper edge of the *piscina*. The basin has an interior diameter of 1.2 meters and a depth of 1 meter. In the middle of the basin stands a mushroom-shaped pillar that measured 90 centimeters in height, with a diameter at its base of 30 centimeters increasing to 50 centimeters. The top of the pillar, which would have stood approximately even with the level of water in the basin, was fitted with a small rectangular cutting. This cutting, which was lined with lead, may have held a tenon for a statuette or decorative basin (*labrum*).

Two conduits were used to circulate fresh water through the fishpond — one made of collared terra cotta pipes and the other an open canal fashioned of tiles and mortar. The remains of these water-carrying structures were unearthed northeast of the pond running on a diagonal course northeast-southwest. Fresh water was conveyed from the Capodifiume to the fishpond in the open brick and mortar canal. This canal emptied into a small catch basin situated atop the eastern wall of the *piscina*. The basin collected sediment from the water before cascading into the pond. Overflow was carried from the pond through collared pipes, which exited the northeast corner of the pond, and conveyed to a drain that ran in front of the rectangular hall of the sanctuary. This simple circulating system was positioned near the attached basin where the constricted space would directly benefit from the force of the water.

GAZETTEER OF FISHPONDS

All joints between blocks, pipes, and tiles were sealed with the same *opus signinum* that was used to line the inside of the pond.

Pottery, retrieved in the fills used to buttress the exterior of the *piscina*, dates the construction of the fishpond to the early years of the first century A.D. The amount of incrustation inside the *piscina* and the conduits points to periods of stagnation when water supply was interrupted for lengthy periods of time. Despite these apparent problems, the pond continued in use until the eruption of Vesuvius in A.D. 79. Ash from this catastrophe was found in copious quantities on the inside of the pond and its conduits.

A complex similar to the *piscina* at Santa Venera can be found in the sanctuary of Hera within the city walls (Fig. 106).[307] Located approximately 20 meters north of the east facade of the Temple of Hera II, the complex consists of two connected pools, one of which was fitted with steps and a basin/pillar arrangement similar to the one attached to the *piscina* at Santa Venera. Like the pond at Santa Venera, this pool was meant to be entered, though it is not certain whether the complex in the Hera sanctuary contained fish. In its location south of the sanctuary, the *piscina* was the focus of a large open area framed by the portico of the complex's rectangular hall. The pond with its attached circular basin and portico is similar to decorative arrangements found in many Roman gardens. The fishpond at Santa Venera certainly functioned as an aesthetic centerpiece for this part of the sanctuary. It may have even confined fish held sacred in the rites of this cult. While it may be tempting to visualize cult adherents entering the basin performing some sort of ritual bathing, the steps probably just eased the cleaning and general maintenance of the pond.

The city of Paestum boasted other *piscinae* that could have held fish. Inside the city are the remains of two large *piscinae*: one within the peristyle of the so-called Gymnasium (Fig. 107) and the other in a residential quarter west of the temples of Hera (Figs. 108, 109). Both ponds were equipped with structures that probably supported platforms. From these platforms spectators could enjoy the amenities of the *piscinae* while perched above the water. This design could also have provided shaded waters for fish. The exact purpose of these ponds is uncertain. The *piscina* in the Gymnasium was designed with a ramp that permitted easy entry into the pond. Though the area has long been known as the Gymnasium, a recent study has suggested that this *piscina* was used for

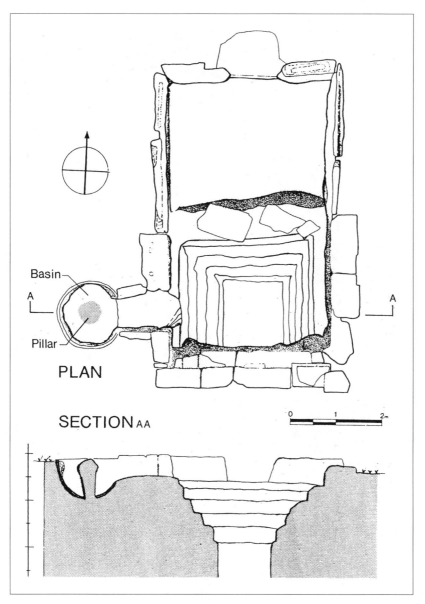

FIGURE 106. Paestum, Sanctuary of Hera—plan and section of ritual complex. (Drawing by David Myers)

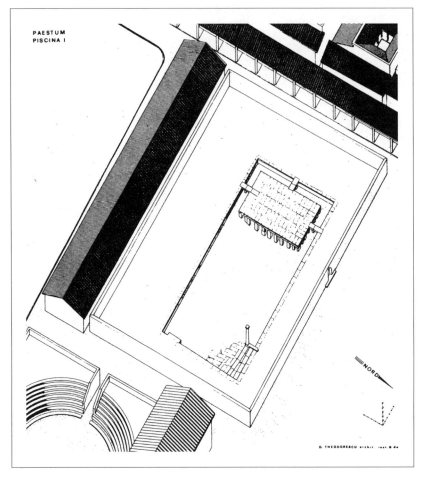

224

FIGURE 107. Paestum, Gymnasium — axonometric drawing of pool and surrounding buildings. (From E. Greco and D. Theodorescu, *Poseidonia-Paestum* 3 [Rome 1985] fig. 71)

ritual purification associated with the cults of Venus Verticordia and Fortuna Virilis.[308] Given that there are no traces of a temple or shrine, another plausible suggestion is that this pond served as the centerpiece of a large public garden. In this context the presence of fish in the *piscina* would not be unusual. The structures at the western end of the pond would have allowed the casual enjoyment of the pool while providing an area of refuge and shade for the fish.

The same uncertainty surrounds the interpretation of the *piscina* located in the residential zone west of the temples of Hera. This *piscina*

FIGURE 108. Paestum, residential area—large pool and surrounding portico. (Photo by J. Higginbotham)

FIGURE 109. Paestum, residential area—north end of pool, with supporting walls for platform. (Photo by J. Higginbotham)

takes up almost an entire insular block and probably was built during the early years of the Empire. The purpose of such a complex is difficult to explain. The structures in the northern end of the pond supported flooring that would have served as a convenient point of vantage and may have provided shade for fish.[309]

GLOSSARY

Aedicula: A small building or niche framed by columns, which support an entablature and pediment.

Aestuarium: A channel extending inland from the sea.

Amphora: A ceramic storage vessel with two vertical handles.

Ashlar: Rectangular block of cut stone.

Atrium: The central hall of a traditional Roman house.

Biclinium: Dining structure with two couches (*klinai* in Greek) arranged opposite or at right angles to one another.

Cancelli: Latticed or perforated gate used to close channels or confine fish.

Cuniculus: An underground passage or canal.

Euripus: A long, narrow pond (literally a "channel" or "strait").

Exedra: An architectural recess, often semicircular or rectangular in shape.

Hortus: A garden or open area at the rear or at the side of a house.

Insula: A residential block (literally an "island") often in the hands of a single owner.

Iter (pl. itinera): A channel or passage (literally a "path" or "way").

Labrum: A circular basin frequently found in baths or as part of a fountain.

Nymphaeum: A fountain house often decorated to resemble a cave or grotto.

Oecus: Reception room usually attached to a peristyle and often used for dining.

Opus incertum: Concrete facing fashioned of irregularly shaped stones and fitted tightly together by mortar. It is probable that this facing first appeared in Rome at the end of the third century B.C. and continued in use into the first century B.C.

Opus quasi-reticulatum: Concrete facing of roughly squared stones placed in courses of irregular line. This facing dates generally to the first half of the first century B.C. and represents a transition to *opus reticulatum*.

Opus reticulatum: Concrete facing made of small squared stones carefully cut into pyramidal shapes of uniform dimensions. The resultant pattern resembles a net (*rete* in Latin), hence *reticulatum*. This facing first appeared in Rome in the middle of the first century B.C. and continued into the imperial period.

Opus signinum: Waterproof mortar of lime with crushed terracotta as aggregate.

Opus testaceum: Concrete facing of fired brick laid in horizontal courses. This facing was employed as early as the first century B.C. and gradually replaces *opus reticulatum* during the first century A.D.

Opus vittatum: Concrete facing formed of small squared stone blocks with alternating courses of fire brick. At Pompeii, this facing is characteristic of building after the earthquake of A.D. 62.

Pergula (pergola): A vine arbor supported by columns.

Peristyle: A colonnade that surrounds a building or lines an open courtyard or garden.

Specus: An enclosed recess where fish may lurk (literally a "cave" or "hollow").

Tablinum: The principal reception room situated off the atrium where the owner met clients and guests.

Triclinium: Dining structure with three couches (*klinai* in Greek) arranged in a U-shaped configuration.

NOTES

ABBREVIATIONS

Aelian *NA*	Aelian, *De Natura Animalium*
AJA	*American Journal of Archaeology*
AJP	*American Journal of Philology*
AnalRom	*Analecta romana Instituti Danici*
AnnInst	*Annales Institutorum*
ANRW	*Aufstieg und Niedergang der römischen Welt*
ArchCl	*Archeologia classica*
ArchDelt	Ἀρχαιλογικὸν Δελτίον
ArchSocRomSt	*Archivio della Società Romana di Storia Patria*
Aristotle *HA*	Aristotle, *Historia Animalium*
AttiCStR	*Atti del . . . Congresso Nazionale di Studi Romani*
AttiPontAcc	*Atti della Pontificia Accademia Romana di Archeologia*
BAR	*British Archaeological Reports*
BdA	*Bollettino d'Arte*
BdI	*Bulletino dell'Instituto di Corrispondenza Archeologica*
BEFAR	*Bibliothèque des écoles françaises d'Athènes et de Rome*
BonnJb	*Bonner Jahrbücher des Rheinischen Landesmuseums in Bonn*
BSA	*Annual of the British School at Athens*
CIL	*Corpus Inscriptionum Latinarum*
CJ	*Classical Journal*
Columella *Rust.*	Columella, *De Re Rustica*
CW	*Classical World*

DarSag	C. Daremberg and E. Saglio, *Dictionnaire des antiquités grecques et romaines* (Paris 1877 – 1919)
EAA	*Enciclopedia dell'arte antica, classica e orientale*
Gellius *NA*	Aulus Gellius, *Noctes Atticae*
Horace *Sat.*	Horace, *Satirae* or *Sermones*
Isidorus *Orig.*	Isidorus, *Origines* or *Etymologiae*
JdI	*Jahrbuch des Deutschen Archäologischen Instituts*
JFA	*Journal of Field Archaeology*
JRA	*Journal of Roman Archaeology*
JRS	*Journal of Roman Studies*
MAAR	*Memoirs of the American Academy in Rome*
Macrobius *Sat.*	Macrobius, *Saturnalia*
Martial *Epigr.*	Martial, *Epigrammaton libri*
MEFRA	*Mélanges de l'école française de Rome, Antiquité*
MélRome	*Mélanges d'archéologie et d'histoire de l'école française de Rome*
MemLinc	*Memorie. Atti della Accademia Nazionale dei Lincei, Classe di scienze morali, storiche e filologiche*
MemPontAcc	*Memorie. Atti della Pontificia Accademia Romana di Archeologia*
MontAnt	*Monumenti antichi*
NSc	*Notizie degli scavi Antichità*
Oppian *Hal.*	Oppian, *Halieutica*
PBSR	*Papers of the British School of Archaeology at Rome*
Plato *Pol.*	Plato, *Politicus*
Pliny *Ep.*	Pliny the Younger, *Epistulae*
Pliny *HN*	Pliny the Elder, *Historia Naturalis*
RA	*Revue archéologique*
RE	A. Pauly and G. Wissowa, *Real-Encyclopädie der klassischen Altertumswissenschaft*
RendNap	*Rendiconti dell'Accademia di Archeologia, Lettere e Belle Arti, Napoli*
RendPontAcc	*Atti della Pontificia Accademia Romana di Archeologia, Rendiconti*
RivGeogrIt	*Rivista della Real Società di Geografia italiana*
RM	*Mitteilungen des Deutschen Archäologischen Instituts, Römische Abteilung*
RStLig	*Rivista di studi liguri*
SicArch	*Sicilia archeologia*
StEtr	*Studi etruschi*
StRom	*Studi romani*
TAPA	*Transactions of the American Philological Society*
Varro *Rust.*	Varro, *De Re Rustica*
ZPE	*Zeitschrift für Papyrologie und Epigraphik*

INTRODUCTION

1. The fishpond at Torre Astura measures 175 meters by 130 meters, which covers a little over five and a half acres, while the pond located in the garden of the House of Gavius Rufus (VII 2, 16) at Pompeii measures 2.56 meters by 1.46 meters.

2. G. M. Zappi (d. 1596) in *Annali e memorie di Tivoli di Giovanni Maria Zappi*, ed. V. Pacifici (Tivoli 1920) fols. 79 – 80. This interpretation was reiterated by Filippo Alessandro Sebastiani in the nineteenth century (*Viaggio a Tivoli. Antichissima città latinosabina fatto nel 1825* [Tipografia Tomassini di Foligno 1828] 89 – 93). Bibliographic references and abbreviations follow a format outlined in "Notes for Contributors and Abbreviations," *AJA* 90 (1986) 381 – 94.

3. R. Del Rosso, *Pesche e peschiere antiche e moderne nell'Etruria maritima* 1 (Florence 1905).

4. L. Jacono, "Note di archeologia marittima," *Neapolis* 1 (1913) 353 – 71; "Nettuno—*Piscinae in litore constructae*," *NSc* 21 (1924) 333 – 40; "Un porto duomillenario," *AttiCStR* 3 (1935) 318 – 24; and "Una singolare piscina marittima in Ponza," *Campania Romana* 1 (Naples 1938) 145 – 62.

5. M. Ponsich and M. Tarradell, *Garum et industries antiques de salaison dans la Méditerranée occidentale* (Paris 1965); O. Da Veiga Ferreira, "Algunas consideracoes sobre as fabricas de conservas de peixeda antiquidade encontradas em Portugal," *Archivo de Beja* 23 – 24 (1966 – 67) 123 – 34; R. Sanquer and P. Galliou, "Garum, sel et salaisons en Armorique gallo-romaine," *Gallia* 30 (1972) 199 – 223; R. I. Curtis, *Garum and Salsamenta: Production and Commerce in Materia Medica* (Leiden 1991); J. C. Edmondson, *Two Industries in Roman Lusitania: Mining and Garum Production*, BAR International Series, 362 (Oxford 1987); M. Ponsich, *Aceite de oliva y salazones de pescado: Factores geo-económicos de Bética y Tingitania* (Madrid 1988).

6. For evidence of Italian production, see R. I. Curtis, "A. Umbricius Scaurus of Pompeii," in *Studia Pompeiana et Classica in Honor of Wilhelmina F. Jashemski* 1 (New Rochelle, N.Y. 1988) 19 – 49, and *Garum and Salsamenta* 85 – 96. Fish sauce production is hypothesized at Cosa on the basis of rather tenuous evidence; see A. M. McCann, J. Bourgeois, E. K. Gazda, J. P. Oleson, and E. L. Will, *The Roman Port and Fishery of Cosa* (Princeton 1987) 340 – 41.

7. T. Corcoran, "The Roman Fishing Industry of the Late Republic and Early Empire" (Ph.D. diss. Northwestern University 1957) 85 – 144.

8. J. H. D'Arms, *Romans on the Bay of Naples* (Cambridge, Mass. 1970).

9. Cicero *Ad Atticum* 2.8.2.

10. Plato *Pol.* 264b – c.; M. C. Besta, "Pesca e pescatori nell'Egitto greco-romano," *Aegyptus* 2 (1921) 67 – 74. Pisciculture was practiced by the Egyptians in the "sacred lakes" such as those seen at Karnak or Denderah. Wall paintings dating from as early as the Middle Kingdom show fish-filled ponds in an architectural setting. Fishponds arranged in a centralized courtyard can be found in the northern palace at Tell el-Amarna.

11. Aristotle (*HA* 8.592a.2) mentions a pond built for eels with waterproof lining and provisions for circulation. The popularity of eels in the Strymon and Lake Kopais is mentioned by Athenaeus (*Deipnosophistae* 7.300b – c), Aristotle *HA* 8.592a.8, and Aristophanes *Acharnians* 880. Pliny the Elder (*HN* 8.44) mentions that Alexander the Great had artificial ponds for fish constructed to facilitate the research of Aristotle.

12. *RE* 9 (1914) 844 – 50, s.v. Ichthys (R. Cumont). The exact use to which fish were put in a religious context is nowhere very clear. At Labraunda in Caria, fish sacred to Zeus were kept in the *fons Jovis* (Aelian *NA* 12.30). This "fountain" has yet to be located with any certainty. Fish, whose movements were interpreted as

divinely inspired, functioned as oracles at the *fons Apollinis* (Pliny *HN* 32.17) and at the *fons Limyrae* (Pliny *HN* 31.22) in Lycia. At other temple ponds fish were also kept for decoration, like the sacred eel enclosed in the Spring of Arethusa in Sicily (Diodorus V.3.5; Silius Italicus *Punica* 14.53 – 54; Aelian *NA* 8.4).

13. Diodorus Siculus 11.25.4. Despite its scale, no physical evidence of this large structure remains.

14. Other sources include Aulus Gellius and Athenaeus. These sources are collected in *DarSag* 5 (1919) 959 – 62, s.v. Vivarium (Georges LaFaye); *RE* 20 (1950) 1783 – 85, s.v. Piscina (K. Schneider); Corcoran (supra n. 7).

15. Varro *Rust.* 3.17.1 – 10.

16. Varro (*Rust.* 3.3.5) refers to ponds set up in streams. Columella (*Rust.* 8.16.2) identifies the Veline, Sabatine, Volsinian, and Ciminian as lakes filled with fish from the sea. These lakes correspond to the Lago di Piedi di Luco, Lago di Bracciano, Lago di Bolseno, and the Lago di Vico respectively. Pliny (*HN* 9.75) says that in his day eels were being raised in Lacus Benacus in the territory of Verona.

17. Plautus *Truculentus* 35; *Poenulus* 293. A quotation from the fifth oration of Scipio (*Contra Claudium Asellum*), which mentions a fishpond, is recorded by Aulus Gellius (*NA* 2.20.6).

18. Corcoran (supra n. 7) 128 suggests that the existence of the large fishpond at Acragas in the fifth century B.C. supports the notion that the Romans got the idea for these structures from Magna Graecia or Sicily. Though unattested in the archaeological remains, it is probable that the Etruscans and other early Italian peoples practiced pisciculture and likewise may have passed on this practice to the Romans. The desire for *luxuria* coupled with a greater facility in the use of hydraulic concrete, which coalesced in the late second century B.C., led to the monumentalization of a practice long known in Italy.

19. Pliny *HN* 9.170. According to Corcoran (supra n. 7) 129, the invention, attributed to Licinius Murena, most probably refers to the construction of large seaside fishponds and not artificial enclosures in general.

20. Varro *Rust.* 3.3.10; Columella *Rust.* 8.16.5; Macrobius *Sat.* 3.15.2 (after Varro).

21. Pliny *HN* 9.62 – 63; Macrobius *Sat.* 3.16.10; H. Keller, *Die Antike Tierwelt* (Leipzig 1913); E. De Saint-Denis, *Le Vocabulaire des animaux marins en latin classique* (Paris 1947); J. André, *L'Alimentation et la cuisine à Rome* 2nd ed. (Paris 1981) 97 – 116.

22. Varro *Rust.* 3.3.9; Columella *Rust.* 8.16.2 – 3.

23. M. Porcius Cato fr. 174 preserved in Aulus Gellius *NA* 13.24.1; for additional sources and further discussion, see D'Arms (supra n. 8) 15 – 17.

24. G. Schmiedt, ed., *Il livello antico del Mar Tirreno. Testimonianze dei resti archeologici* (Florence 1972).

25. Coastal surveys, particularly on the island of Crete and in Italy, have been instrumental in identifying many fishponds. The study of changes in sea level since antiquity has found in the fishpond a useful measure. For a saltwater fishpond to function, the sea level has to be taken into account when the enclosure is constructed. Certain features were designed with the sea level (the tidal range) in mind and when these ancient levels are compared with modern levels the result is a good index of the change since the construction of the tank. See Schmiedt (supra n. 24) and esp. G. D. Conta in Schmiedt (supra n. 24) 215 – 21; J. Leatham and S. Hood,

"Sub-marine Exploration in Crete, 1955," *BSA* 53 – 54 (1958 – 59) 263 – 80; D. J. Blackman and K. Branigan, "An Archaeological Survey on the South Coast of Crete between the Ayiofarango and Chrisostomos," *BSA* 70 (1975) 17 – 36; E. Linder and O. Laenhardt, "Recherches d'archéologie sous marine sur la côte méditerranéenne d'Israel," *RA* (1964.1) 47 – 51; R. A. Yorke and M. F. Dallas, "Underwater Surveys of North Africa, Jugoslavia, and Italy," *Underwater Association Report* (1968) 21 – 34.

26. F. Castagnoli, "Astura," *StRom* 11 (1963) 637 – 44; F. Piccarreta, *Astura — Forma Italiae* 1.13 (Florence 1977); S. Picozzi, "La peschiera di Santa Marinella," *Il Subacqueo* 7 (1980) 64 – 65; McCann et al. (supra n. 6).

27. Along the coasts of Italy are scores of nondescript offshore ruins that may be the remains of *piscinae*. At inland sites the existence of small pools and basins are commonplace. The majority of these structures are not treated in this study due to their uncertain function or plan. The structures selected are all of those which exhibited some detail or feature that indicated that fish were held within.

28. For the usages of *piscina*, see *RE* 20 (1950) 1783 – 85, s.v. Piscina (K. Schneider).

29. Aulus Gellius (*NA* 2.20.6) voices a minority view when he says that the term *piscina* was synonymous with *lacus* or *stagnum* but should be distinct from *vivarium*, which was more appropriate for an enclosure for wild animals.

30. Pliny *HN* 9.49, 59, 91 – 92; 31.94; 37.66. Horace's usage (*Sat.* 2.5.44) is most often translated as "fishpond" but this is surely in error. Curtis (supra n. 5) 53 – 54, n. 43, cites a scholiast to this passage who clearly equates *cetaria* with salting vats.

31. Corcoran (supra n. 7) 126 – 27; Livy 23.34.4; Macrobius *Sat.* 2.12.

32. Aulus Gellius (*NA* 2.20.7), writing in the second century A.D., concluded that pools or ponds that confine live fish were given their own name—*piscinae* ("*lacus vero aut stagna quae piscibus vivis coercentur clausa suo atque proprio nomine piscinas nominaverunt*").

233

CHAPTER ONE

1. Columella *Rust.* 8.16.6 – 17.16.

2. Cane and wooden barriers may have been employed in these lagoonal fishponds. This material usually does not survive and leaves little evidence for the archaeologist.

3. Varro *Rust.* 3.17.1 – 2.

4. Varro *Rust.* 3.17.3.

5. Columella (*Rust.* 8.16.2) names four lakes located in Tuscany and Umbria: the Lacus Velinus (Lago di Piedi di Luco near Terni) in Umbria, the Lacus Sabatinus (Lago Bracciano), Lacus Volsiniensis (Lago di Bolseno), and Lacus Ciminius (Lago di Vico near Viturbo) in Tuscany.

6. Varro *Rust.* 3.17.2: "*Primum enim* [piscinae] *aedificantur magno secundo implentur magno tertio aluntur magno.*"

7. Thirty-nine of the fifty-six fishpond sites included in this study were located along the shore and were connected to the sea.

8. Columella *Rust.* 8.17.1: ". . . *nec intra consaeptum sinat remanere veterem.*"

9. Ibid.: "*Namque id simillimum est pelago quod agitatum ventis assidue renovatur nec concalescere potest quoniam gelidum ab imo fluctum revolvit in partem superiorem.*"

10. Varro *Rust.* 3.17.8 – 9: ". . . *in locis pestilentibus.*"

11. Columella *Rust.* 8.17.1–6.

12. Ibid. Varro (*Rust.* 3.17.8) uses the term *aestuaria* to describe the channels that connect fishponds to the sea.

13. Columella *Rust.* 8.17.6. Cuttings for such gates are included in the design of fishponds at Cosa, Torre Valdaliga, Punta della Vipera, Fosso Guardiole, Astura (La Saracca), Torre Astura, Circeo (Piscina di Lucullo), Sperlonga, Formia (Giardino Publico), Ponza, Ventotene, and Sorrento. A grate, fashioned from a stone slab, was recovered from a fishpond on the island of Crete at the site of Mochlos and is noted in J. Leatham and S. Hood, "Sub-marine Exploration in Crete, 1955," *BSA* 53–54 (1958–59) 275. A stone block, which is wedged into the vertical grooves of a channel in the rectangular pond at Fosso Guardiole, appears not to be an original gate (cf. B. Frau, "From the Etruscan Ports of Graviscae and Martanum: Elements for a New Methodology in the Field of Maritime Archaeological Research," in A. Raban, ed., "Harbour Archaeology: Proceedings of the First International Workshop on Ancient Mediterranean Harbours, Caesarea Maritima June 24–26, 1983," *BAR* 257 [1985] 99, fig. 4). Despite Columella's suggestion, metal gates must have suffered in the corrosive waters of the sea. Stone gates would have withstood this hostile environment without corroding and would not have swelled or warped as wooden barriers would. The fishpond on the island of Giglio (Fig. 7) was situated in a natural cove surrounded by rocky cliffs. Cuttings on either side of the large opening to the sea held long wooden beams, which probably supported a flexible barrier or net.

14. Rivers and springs supplied fresh water for several inland fishponds. At Tivoli, the *piscinae* in the so-called Villa of Vopiscus and the Villa of Quintilius Varus were supplied from the Anio. The fishpond at the so-called Villa of Horace near Licenza was fed from a nearby spring. The ponds at Grottarossa near Rome and in the località Santa Venera at Paestum drew water from local rivers (the Tiber and the Capodifiume respectively). Inland fishponds around the Bay of Naples were supplied primarily from the Serino springs near Avellino by way of an Augustan aqueduct.

15. Vitruvius 8.1–6; Frontinus *De Aquis Urbis Romae* 1.23–63; 2.77–130.

16. Vitruvius 8.6.

17. A brackish environment is characterized by salinity ranging from one to thirty parts per thousand.

18. It is alleged that eels raised in the Limni Pambotis, a lake near Ioannina in northwestern Greece (Epirus), are stimulated to breed by the dumping of salt in their enclosures. These eels normally migrate to the sea by way of a *katabothros* (καταβο´θρος), or underground river, at the west end of the lake. In addition, studies of Pacific or Japanese common eels have indicated that changes in salinity influence the migratory impulse and determine the location of spawning. For preliminary results of Katsumi Tsukamoto research on the Japanese common eel, see R. Mestel, "Quest for Eel Dorado," *Discover* 14.1 (January 1993) 38–40.

19. Pliny the Elder (*HN* 9.56) notes that fish are nourished by rainwater when it falls into the sea. Aelian (*NA* 9.64) concurs that some fresh water is good for sea fish.

20. Cicero *De Officiis* 3.58–59.

21. Varro *Rust.* 3.3.10; 3.17.9; Velleius Paterculus 2.33.4; Pliny *HN* 9.170; and Plutarch *Lucullus* 39.3, where the appellation is attributed to Tubero the Stoic.

22. Of the thirty-nine fishponds included in this study that were located along the seashore, twenty-six were designed to combine both salt and fresh water so as to create brackish conditions within the enclosures: Pianosa, Santa Liberata, Cosa, Or-

betello, Giglio, Pian di Spille, Martanum, Torre Valdaliga, La Mattonara, Punta della Vipera, Fosso Guardiole, Grottacce, Nettuno (Villino Nesi), Astura (La Saracca, La Banca, and Torre Astura), Circeo (Piscina di Lucullo and Torre del Fico), Sperlonga, Formia (Villa of Cicero, Giardino Publico, and Via Vitruvio), Ventotene, Ponza, Pausilypon, and Sorrento (Villa of Agrippa Postumus and Villa Nicolini). The remains of the other seaside ponds presented no definitive evidence of a brackish environment.

23. In addition to the Tagliata at Cosa, channels of this sort are found as part of the *piscinae* at Torre Valdaliga, La Mattonara, Ponza, Ventotene, and the so-called Villa of Agrippa Postumus at Sorrento.

24. Columella *Rust.* 8.17.1: "*Id autem stagnum vel exciditur in petra cuius rarissima est occasio vel in litore construitur opere signino*" (The pond is either cut into the rock, which happens rarely, or is constructed of mortar on the shore). Columella uses *opus signinum* here to describe hydraulic mortar but there is some ambiguity over the meaning of this term in ancient and modern usage. *Signinum* is used by the Elder Pliny (*HN* 35.165) to define a mixture of lime, sand, and broken or powdered potsherds. While Vitruvius (2.5.1) describes this pink colored mortar he does not call it *opus signinum*. Modern usage of the term is drawn from Pliny's definition and describes pavements and mortars with broken and pulverized pottery. See M. E. Blake, *Ancient Roman Construction in Italy from the Prehistoric Period to Augustus* (Washington, D.C. 1947) 322–23.

25. The only ponds that appear to have been cut completely from the rock are found on Ponza. The grotto fishponds on Ventotene and at Sorrento are almost entirely cut from the rock but have some details rendered in concrete.

26. See V. Scrinari, "Il porto di Claudio ed osservazioni sulla tecnica del conglomerato cementizio sotto i Romani," *Industria italiana del cemento* 7 (1963) 527–38. Questions remain as to how the components of the concrete could be placed in the forms so that they did not separate in the standing water. It is probable that a wet mixture of sand, lime, pozzolana, and aggregate was placed in between the walls of the forms. Dry ingredients would separate, when coming in contact with water, and loosen the mixture vital for hardening. For a discussion of Vitruvius's description of concrete construction and the use of a tube for "pouring" concrete, see C. Dubois, "Observations sur un passage de Vitruve," *MélRome* 22 (1902) 452–54.

27. Supplies were exported from the vicinity of Puteoli as far away as Caesarea in Palestine for projects using hydraulic concrete. Pozzolana, probably from Puteoli, was used in some of the walls in the port and fishery at Cosa. Submerged load-bearing walls were constructed of concrete composed of Volsinian tufo aggregate, lime, and pozzolana while other less vital walls substituted sand for the pozzolana and added limestone and ceramic fragments to the aggregate (A. M. McCann, J. Bourgeois, E. K. Gazda, J. P. Oleson, and E. L. Will, *The Roman Port and Fishery of Cosa* [Princeton 1987] 95).

28. Remains of the wooden forms and the horizontal lines left by these planks are preserved on many of the walls belonging to the lagoonal fishery at Cosa (McCann et al. [supra n. 27] 91–95). In this study I noted similar lines on the *piscinae* at Santa Liberata, Astura (La Saracca, La Banca, and Torre Astura), Circeo (Piscina di Lucullo), and Formia (Giardino Publico).

29. Vitruvius 5.12.1–3. For a discussion of the method used in the forming of concrete structures for the port at Side (southern Turkey), see H. Schlager, "Die Texte Vitruvius im Lichte der Untersuchungen am Hafen von Side," *BonnJb* 171

(1971) 150 – 61. Concrete units measuring ten to eleven meters to a side were used in the harbor mole and suggest the standardized construction of these elements.

30. Vitruvius suggested three methods of underwater concrete construction. The second method was employed when seas were too rough or too deep to anchor the cofferdams. The forms for the piers were built on shore atop a foundation of sand. After the concrete blocks had set, the sand from beneath was allowed to erode and the blocks tumbled into the sea. Successive blocks would be fashioned on the preceding ones thus permitting the extension of the mole onto the sea. The third manner of underwater concrete construction used double-walled cofferdams. Concrete was placed between the walls creating a waterproof shell, which, when settled on the sea floor, could be filled with mortar or rubble. Vitruvius suggests that this type of cofferdam would be useful when pozzolana was unavailable and the need for dry concrete construction was necessary. Here, water would be expelled from the spaces between the walls of the cofferdam allowing the concrete to set without any contact with seawater. J. P. Oleson, "Herod and Vitruvius: Preliminary Thoughts on Harbour Engineering at Sebastos, the Harbour of Caesarea Maritima," in Raban (supra n. 13) 165 – 72, notes the use of double-walled cofferdams at Caesarea Maritima in Palestine. Here, concrete, which included pozzolana, was used to fill the caissons. It is believed that the space between the doubled walls were filled first to secure the box on the bottom of the sea. The remainder of the caisson was filled when the caisson was in place. It does not appear that water was meant to be pumped from the double-walled caissons at Caesarea.

31. A double-walled cofferdam may have been used to form a rectangular tank in the *piscina* at Grottacce (Fig. 26:d). No seams were discernable at the corners of this tank, which suggests that the small enclosure is one mass of concrete.

32. Though most of these were laid in a single mass, the mole around the pond at La Banca near Astura was made by several parallel concrete walls placed side by side.

33. The use of this method was evident in the construction of the walls belonging to the ponds at Pianosa, Giglio, Torre Valdaliga, La Mattonara, and Scauri.

34. Columella *Rust.* 8.17.10 – 11. The circulation of water through the pond would tend to deposit waterborne sediment inside the enclosure. The accumulation of sand and other detritus at most of the sites today attests to this problem. Obstructions in the sea, such as fishponds, would slow down the flow of water allowing sediment to settle against the obstruction. Gaps and openings through the mole were designed to help carry away this accumulation. The success of such a system is uncertain and silting must have chronically plagued the fishpond owner.

35. Martial 10.30.19. Tibullus (2.3.45) waxes metaphorically when he writes "*claudit et indomitum moles mare lentus ut intra neglegat hibernas piscis adesse minas*" (the mole encloses the wild sea, so that inside the fish take no heed of the stormy threat). For ancient mention of mole construction, see Vitruvius 1.5.12 and Pliny *HN* 16.40, 201.

36. Horace *Odes* 3.1.33: "*contracta pisces aequora sentiunt iactis in altum molibus huc frequens caementa demittit redemptor cum famulis dominusque terrae fastidiosus* (the fishes sense the seas reduced by moles thrown into the deep where many a contractor with his workers and many a master scornful of the land sink their stones).

37. The use of a curving or arching mole can be seen in the plans of the *piscinae* at Fosso Guardiole, Grottacce, Torre Flavia, Palo, Nettuno (Villino Nesi and Castello

del Sangallo), Astura (La Saracca), and the ponds etched on the glass flasks depicting the shoreline of Baia.

38. G. Schmiedt, ed., *Il livello antico del Mar Tirreno. Testimonianze dei resti archeologici* (Florence 1972) 185 – 86. This type of construction is postulated for the ponds at Torre Valdaliga, La Mattonara, and Punta della Vipera.

39. Varro *Rust.* 3.17.2 – 3.

40. Frontinus *De Aquis Urbis Romae* 1.11.22.

41. The *euripus* in the garden of the Praedia Iuliae Felicis and the ponds in the Casa di Gavius Rufus, the Casa di Meleagro, the Casa di Capitelli Colorati, and the house in Regio VIII (VIII 2, 14) were built of concrete with an irregular stone facing. The *piscina* in the località Santa Venera at Paestum was built of ashlar blocks and waterproofed with a pink mortar (*opus signinum*). See J. Higginbotham, in J. G. Pedley and M. Torelli, eds., *The Sanctuary of Santa Venera at Paestum* 1 (Rome 1993) 121 – 47.

42. Curvilinear and rectilinear niches were used also in the design of the ponds located in the Villa dei Papiri at Herculaneum and the Domus Augustana on the Palatine in Rome.

43. McCann et al. (supra n. 27) 115, n. 84. Marshy ground was stabilized in a similar fashion in the ancient port of Marseille (M. Euzennat, "Ancient Marseille in the Light of Recent Excavations," *AJA* 84 [1980] 134, pl. 22, fig. 3).

44. The shift toward freshwater fishponds, observed in the archaeological remains, is subtly implied by the ancient account. In one passage, Columella (*Rust.* 8.16.1 – 3) states that the enthusiasm for fishpond building was keener with his ancestors — those of the Republic — than in his day. In a tone meant to evoke amazement and highlight differences, he tells how these *piscinarii* enclosed the waters of Neptune or salt water. Further, the Elder Pliny (*HN* 9.75 – 76) states that, in the first century A.D., the exotic species of fish popular during the Republic had given way to the eel (*murena*) and the bass (*lupus*). Both the eel and the bass are fish quite at home in fresh or brackish waters and are easy to raise. The preference for fresh water may have been influenced by the wish to raise heartier and more adaptable species of fish.

45. Notable examples include the ponds decorating the Canopus and Poikile in the Villa of Hadrian near Tivoli, the pools in the peristyle gardens at Oplontis and Villa San Marco at Stabiae. The Casa di Pansa (VI 6, 1), the Casa del Citarista (I 4, 5/25), the Casa di D. Octavius Quartio (II 2, 2), and the Casa del Centenario (IX 8, 3/6), all at Pompeii, and the Casa del Rilievo di Telefo (*Insula Orientalis* I 2) at Herculaneum were sites of pools which could have held fish.

46. Columella *Rust.* 8.17.3 – 4.

47. Varro *Rust.* 3.17.3 – 4; Valerius Maximus 9.1.1. Pliny the Elder (*HN* 9.171) tells how Gaius Hirrius devised an enclosure where eels could be kept separate (*privatim*). Pliny (*HN* 9.173) adds that Fulvius Lippinus had ponds (*vivaria coclearum*) which kept different varieties of snails separate. Subdivisions of this type can be seen in the *ostrearium* incised on a series of glass bottles depicting panoramas of the Bay of Naples (G. De Franciscis, "Underwater Discoveries around the Bay of Naples," *Archaeology* 20 [1967] 290 – 96; S. Ostrow, "The Topography of Puteoli and Baiae on Eight Glass Flasks," *Puteoli. Studi di storia antica* 3 [1979] 127 – 30).

48. Slots or runners of this type can be found inside openings or channels in the *piscinae* at Torre Valdaliga, Astura, Ponza, Ventotene, and Circeo.

49. Pliny *HN* 9.185. The author quotes Nigidius, who says that the *lupus* and the *mugil* do get along on occasion; when they do not, though, the *lupus* would eat the *mugil's* tail. Nigidius adds that there is no need for concern because the *mugil* can live without its tail.

50. Columella *Rust.* 8.17.2; Pliny *HN* 9.77.

51. C. Moriarty, *Eels: A Natural and Unnatural History* (New York 1978) 133–35.

52. Loculate fishponds range from the two tanks in the *piscina* at Santa Liberata to over fifty tanks that can be restored within the enclosure at Torre Astura. The only freshwater ponds with more than one tank are the *piscinae* at Grottarossa near Rome and in the so-called Villa of Vopiscus at Tivoli. The addition of more internal walls was a cause for some concern. These structures could absorb heat contributing to the rise in temperature inside the pond and inhibit the flow of water from one tank to another. In cases such as these, more attention to circulation was necessary.

53. R. De Angelis, "Fishing Installations in Brackish Lagoons," *General Fisheries Council for the Mediterranean. Studies and Reviews* 7 (Rome 1959) 14, 16. See Oppian *Hal.* 3.98–116.

54. Gazda and McCann, "Reconstruction and Function: Port, Fishery, and Villa," in McCann et al. (supra n. 27) 148–49.

55. Rock-cut walkways are found in the fishponds at Giglio, Ponza, Ventotene, and the Villa of Agrippa Postumus at Sorrento. Concrete was used to create the walkways at the *piscinae* at Pianosa, Torre Valdaliga, Punta della Vipera, the Domus Tiberiana in Rome, Licenza, Nettuno, Astura, Circeo (Piscina di Lucullo), and Formia (Giardino Publico and the Via Vitruvio).

56. The majority of walkways are found in seaside *piscinae*. Only the inland ponds in the Domus Tiberiana on the Palatine and at the so-called Villa of Horace have broad steps inside their perimeters.

57. R. Del Rosso, *Pesche e peschiere antiche e moderne nell'Etruria marittima* 1 (Florence 1905) 99–123. Del Rosso's plan restores a lozenge-shaped tank inscribed within the concrete perimeter of the fishpond. Scattered hunks of concrete, observed in this area, may be all that remains of this feature.

58. Columella *Rust.* 8.17.2.

59. Ibid.: "*(stagnum) habere debet specus iuxta solum eorumque alios simplices et rectos quo secedant squamosi greges alios in cochleam retortos nec nimis spatiosos in quibus muraenae delitescant*" (a pond ought to have hollows near the bottom, some of these simple and straight where the schools may withdraw, others twisted into a spiral and not too wide in which eels may hide).

60. Columella *Rust.* 8.17.5: "*Multi putant in eiusmodi stagnis longos piscibus recessus et flexuosos in lateribus specus esse fabricandos quo sint opaciores aestuantibus latebrae*" (Many people think that, in ponds of this type, deep recesses and winding hollows should be made in the sides for the fishes where there may be shadier refuges from the heat).

61. Columella *Rust.* 8.17.6: "*Debent tamen similes velut cellae parietibus excavari ut sint quae protegant refugientes ardorem solis et nihilominus facile quam conceperint aquam remittant*" (However, similar recesses, like cells, ought to be excavated in the sides so that they may protect the fish, seeking refuge from the heat of the sun, and let the water, which they have received, flow out easily).

62. Other examples of grotto *piscinae* are found along the sea at Sorrento (Villa of Agrippa Postumus and Villa del Convento dei Cappuccini) and at the inland site of Tivoli (Villa of Manlius Vopiscus).

63. Kostas Davaras ("Rock-Cut Fish Tanks in Eastern Crete," *BSA* 69 [1974] 87–93, pls. 14–17; and "Λαξευτὴ ἰχτηυοδεξαμενὴ στα φὲρμα ῾Ιεραπὲτρας," *ArchDelt* 30 [1974] Α' Μελε'ται 149–54, pls. 59–66) describes two fishponds on the island of Crete, at Ierapetra and Siteia, which were fitted with awnings and roofs.

64. There are remains of a low concrete vault at the seaward end of the Tagliata at Cosa, which may have supported a platform as well as created shade for the water below.

65. The projecting structure in the Piscina di Lucullo near Circeo also is equipped with fifty-one *amphorae* inserted into the fabric of the vaults. Another *piscina*, unearthed in the early part of this century in the Monteverde region of Rome and since destroyed, possessed two projecting structures similar to the arrangement at Tivoli. At Monteverde, huge *dolia* were employed to create the *specus* in contrast to the vaults used at Varus's villa.

66. The arrangement of niches in these ponds is so similar as to suggest a common genesis. All of these inland *piscinae* were built after the earthquake of A.D. 62 and may be the work of a single architect; see L. Richardson, *Pompeii: An Architectural History* (Baltimore 1988) 353.

67. Bridges and low vaults were also employed in the nearby House of D. Octavius Quartio. The gabled *cellae*, which ring the pond in the so-called Villa of Horace near Licenza, are probably examples of the more constricted *specus*.

68. Clay pots were employed by the Romans to function as refuges in other areas of ancient animal husbandry. Individual beehives (*fictilia alv(e)arium*) and dovecotes (*fictilia columbaria*) sometimes were made of *amphorae* or other ceramic vessels. Columella (*Rust.* 9.6.2), echoing Varro (*Rust.* 3.16.15–17), mentions the use of ceramic beehives, though it is the dovecotes that provided the closest analogies to the *amphorae* used in some *piscinae*. Both authors (Varro *Rust.* 3.7.11 and Columella *Rust.* 8.7.3) describe rows of clay dovecotes that were positioned in the walls of aviaries to provide nesting places for pigeons and other birds. The arrangement of pots in the walls of ancient aviaries is remarkably similar to the ceramic *specus* used in Roman fishponds and must have resulted from shared technologies. A close association between bird and fish raising is reflected in the adjacent spaces they occupy in the agricultural treatises of both Varro and Columella.

69. *Amphorae* or other ceramic vessels are found in the remains of fishponds at the Villa of Vopiscus in Tivoli, Monteverde in Rome (destroyed), the Piscina di Lucullo near Circeo, the so-called Villa of Tiberius at Sperlonga, the Piazza Mercato in Santa Maria Cápua Vetere, the Palestra in Herculaneum, the House VIII 2, 14, the House of Gavius Rufus, the House of the Colored Capitals in Pompeii, and the Sanctuary at Santa Venera in Paestum. Outside Italy, in upper Egypt, a fishpond outside the Temple of Amun at Karnak employs a variety of coarseware vessels in the walls of the tank. There are several *piscinae* located on the Abukir peninsula on the Mediterranean coast. One of these was designed with pots in the fabric of its walls (E. Breccia, "Le rovine e i monumenti di Canopo," *Monuments de l'égypte grèco-romaine* [1926] pls. II, IX–XIV).

70. Pliny *HN* 9.171.

71. The fishpond at Santa Venera near Paestum has low freeboard but only two *specus* and no internal subdivisions. Though not equipped as the ponds at Sperlonga or Circeo, the *piscina* at Santa Venera was probably designed for a small population of eels.

72. Varro *Rust.* 3.5.12.

73. I am grateful to Dr. Timothy W. Potter for sending me proofs of the *Excavations at the Mola di Monte Gelato*, which will be published as a joint British School at Rome/British Museum monograph. The rectangular pond at the Mola was equipped with at least four ceramic *tubuli* used for eels. A single eel vertebra was recovered in the lower fill of the pond.

74. Another example of the combination of fishpond with *pergula* from Pompeii is found in the small garden of the House of the Wedding of Alexander (VI Insula occidentalis 42). See W. F. Jashemski, *The Gardens of Pompeii, Herculaneum, and the Villas Destroyed by Vesuvius* 2: *Appendices* (New Rochelle, N.Y. 1993) 166 – 67, figs. 199 – 201, plan 58.

75. Columella *Rust.* 8.16.7 – 10.

76. Ibid.

77. Ibid. The varieties mentioned by Columella include the *murex purpura*, mussel (*concha* and *balanus*), oyster (*ostrea*), spring oyster (*sphondylus*), and sea scallop (*pectunculus*).

78. Isidorus *Orig.* 12.6.23. *Auratae, dentices,* and *umbrae* belong to the family *Sparidae*, which are commonly called porgies and breams. The red fish or *punica* belongs to the family *Sciaenidae*. All are known to inhabit sandy bottoms of shore waters. See E. Migdalski and G. Fichter, *The Fresh and Salt Water Fishes of the World* (New York 1976) 239, 242 – 43.

79. Columella *Rust.* 8.16.8. *Merulae, turdi,* and *melanuri* are members of the family *Labridae* and are commonly called wrasses.

80. Most of the seaside *piscinae* were built on rocky shelves where the fishpond owner would have been able to exploit this type of formation. The ponds, which were sited at the mouths of rivers, such as the *piscinae* at Fosso Guardiole, were located whence sand and silt would accumulate naturally.

81. Of the nine *piscinae* not attached to villas, two were not linked to residential structures. The fishpond in the Palestra at Herculaneum was positioned in a more public place, which may have been used for athletic contests of the town's *iuventus*, and the *piscina* in the località Santa Venera at Paestum decorated an open area attached to a sanctuary of Venus.

82. Pierre Grimal notes that Roman gardens often echoed nature by the use of known toponyms and by the inclusion of real animals (*Les Jardins romains à la fin de la Republique et aux premiers de l'Empire; Essai sur le naturalisme romain* 3rd ed. [Paris 1984] 315 – 18).

83. The location of artificial fishponds in Italy reflects the popularity of real estate with easy access to major political and commercial centers whether by sea or by land. Many fishponds and their associated villas were built close to port facilities or major roads. Harbors are found in conjunction with the sites of Pianosa, Santa Liberata, Cosa, Giglio, La Mattonara, Torre Valdaliga, Fosso Guardiole, Grottacce, Ventotene, Baia, Puteoli, Pausilypon, and Sorrento. In the absence of a proper harbor, boats could be easily landed on the protective moles of many of the seaside fishponds.

Many of these same sites were accessible by roads to major cities. The Via Aurelia linked many of the coastal sites in Etruria to Rome, while the Via Flacca did the same for southern Latium.

84. E. Salza Prina Ricotti, "The Importance of Water in Roman Garden Triclinia," in E. B. MacDougall, ed., *Ancient Roman Villa Gardens* (Washington, D.C. 1987) 135 – 84.

85. At Sperlonga, the small niches built into the terrace, which supports an aestival dining pavilion, were probably used as dovecotes or nesting areas for birds.

86. W. F. Jashemski, *The Gardens of Pompeii, Herculaneum, and the Villas Destroyed by Vesuvius* 1 (New Rochelle, N.Y. 1979).

87. Jashemski (supra n. 74) has compiled an exhaustive inventory of Pompeian gardens and has noted the locations for the majority of the ponds referred to here. See her work for plans and descriptions of specific gardens.

88. *Piscinae* in this type of setting have been noted in at least thirty-four houses at Pompeii. Notable examples include Casa del Citarista (I 4, 5/25), Casa di Paquius Proculus (I 7, 1), Casa del Menandro (I 10, 4/14 – 17), Casa di D. Octavius Quartio (II 2, 2), *Praedia Iuliae Felicis* (II 4), Casa delle Nozze d'Argento (V 2, i), Casa di Polybius (VI Insula occidentalis 23 – 26), Casa di Pansa (VI 6, 1/12), Casa dei Dioscuri (VI 9, 6), the Casa di Meleagro (VI 9, 2), Casa di Gavius Rufus (VII 2, 16), Casa dei Capitelli Colorati (VII 4, 31/51), Casa di Obellius Firmus (IX [14], 4/2), Casa del Centenario (IX 8, 3/6), and the Villa di Diomede.

89. Jashemski (supra n. 74) 78 – 83, figs. 80 – 91.

90. Houses with ponds visible from the *atrium* or its *tablinum* include Casa del Larario (I 6, 4), Casa di A. Trebius Valens (II 2, 1), Casa delle Vestali (VI 1, 7/25), Casa di Pansa (VI 6, 1/12), Casa di Meleagro (VI 9, 2), Casa dei Dioscuri (VI 9, 6), Casa degli Amorini Dorati (VI 16, 7), Casa di Gavius Rufus (VII 2, 16), Casa dei Capitelli Colorati (VII 4, 31/51), Casa della Caccia Antica (VII 4, 48), Casa di A. Umbricius Scaurus (VII Insula occidentalis 12 – 15), Casa di Fabius Rufus (VII Insula occidentalis 16 – 19), Casa di M. Holconius Rufus (VIII 4, 4), Casa di M. Epidius Sabinus (IX 1, 22/29), Casa del Centenario (IX 8, 3/6), and the Casa di Obellius Firmus (IX [14], 4/2).

91. Houses with ponds associated with adjacent dining facilities include Casa di Volusius Faustus (I 2, 10), Casa di Paquius Proculus (I 7, 1), Casa dell'Efebo (I 7, 10 – 12/19), Casa del Menandro (I 10, 4), Casa di Octavius Quartio (II 2, 2), Praedia Iuliae Felicis (II 4), Casa ? (II 9, 6), Casa di Trebius Valens (III 2, 1), Casa delle Nozze d'Argento (V 2, i), Casa ? (V 3, 11), Casa delle Vestali (VI 1, 7/25), Casa delle Nozze di Alessandro (VI Insula occidentalis 42), Casa della Fontana Grande (VI 8, 22/1), Casa delle Pareti Nere (VII 4, 59), Casa del Gallo (VIII 5, 2), Casa di M. Epidius Sabinus (IX 1, 22/29), Casa della Fontana d'Amore (IX 2, 7), Casa di M. Lucretius (IX 3, 5/24), and the Villa di Diomede.

92. Jashemski (supra n. 86) 33 – 34, fig. 53; and (supra n. 74) 137 – 38.

93. Columella *Rust.* 8.17.7: *hac ratione stabulis ordinatis aquatile pecus inducemus.*

94. Martial 3.58.27.

95. Pliny (*HN* 9.59) tells the story of a male *mugil* who was able to lure females of his species into captivity. Oppian (*Hal.* 4.127 – 45) recounts the same tale with a female in the lead. I was told by fishermen on Corcyra that this method is still used on that island. I could find no Italian comparanda, ancient or modern.

96. Pliny (*HN* 9.74) claims that *murenae* can live five or six days out of the water but only if the north wind is blowing.

97. Macrobius *Sat.* 3.16.10.

98. Athenaeus 5.208a. Carbon 14 tests on the Ostia boat provide a date at the beginning of the first century A.D. See V. Santa Maria Scrinari, *Le navi del porto di Claudio* (Rome 1979) 21 – 23, pls. X – XI, fig. 4.

99. Macrobius (*Sat.* 3.15.7) says that fish, after being transported from the open sea, were fattened in ponds before being sent to market.

100. Columella *Rust.* 8.17.12 – 16. Pliny (*HN* 9.92) suggests decaying fish or fish parts. Other items for the fish's diet can be inferred by the various baits suggested for fishing: Oppian *Hal.* 3.177 – 93; 4.336; Martial 5.19.7 – 8; Aelian *NA* 14.22. Where dovecotes and fishponds were in close proximity, bird droppings may have supplied some nutrients to the fish. Niches that may have been nesting sites were positioned just west of the *piscina* at Sperlonga. Modern fisheries in central Africa (Rwanda) place chicken, duck, and even rabbit hutches right over the water of the pond. This arrangement allows droppings to fall directly into the pond and supply the dietary needs of the fish (J. Perlez, "Why Worry about Crops When Fishing's Better!" *New York Times* [December 14, 1989] A4). Interestingly, a former president of Rwanda and many of his ministers possessed elaborate fishponds larger and more complex than those found in the countryside.

101. Plautus (*Rudens* 300 – 305) communicates the need for a reliable source of fish through a fictional fisherman who laments that when the sea is rough it is better to stay in bed than go out to sea (897 – 99).

102. Gazda and McCann in McCann et al. (supra n. 27) 151.

103. Pliny *HN* 9.74 – 75, 132; 21.114. Silius Italicus 5.47.

104. Oppian *Hal.* 3.85, 331 – 56. Sometimes called *naxae* or *nassae* (Plautus *Miles Gloriosus* 2.6.98; Pliny *HN* 9.132), these terms for fish traps are preserved in the modern Italian word *nassari*.

105. Oppian *Hal.* 3.87.

106. Plautus (*Truculentus* 35 – 36) likens the skill of a fisherman to that of a manipulative lover:

> *quasi in piscinam rete qui iaculum parat,*
> *quando abiit rete pessum adducit lineam;*
> *si inierit rete piscis, ne effugiat cavet:*
> *dum huc dum illuc rete circumvortit, impedit*
> *piscis usque adeo donicum eduxit foras*

> just as one who prepares (to throw) his casting net into the fishpond,
> when the net sinks to the bottom, he pulls in the line;
> if a fish enters the net he takes care so that it may not flee:
> while he swirls his net this way and that, he entangles
> the fish continuously until he has taken it out.

107. Oppian *Hal.* 3.79 – 84. Nets were commonly made of hemp, flax, or broom; they were weighted by lead and kept afloat by cork (Oppian *Hal.* 3.103; Aelian *NA* 14.4).

108. Aelian *NA* 15.5; Varro in Nonius 1.244; Philostratus *Imagines* 1.13.

109. Strabo (5.2.6.c223; 5.2.8.c225; 17.3.16.c834) and Oppian (*Hal.* 3.637–38) describe this system in regards to open-sea fishing of tunny and mackerel.

110. Aelian *NA* 15.5; Oppian *Hal.* 3.640–41; D'Arcy Thompson, *A Glossary of Greek Fishes* (London 1947) 86. Operations of the eel ponds at Ioannina were observed by this author on visits during 1988 and 1989.

111. Aelian *NA* 15.5.

112. Oppian *Hal.* 3.72–90.

113. Harpoons and tridents were usually for large fish but could be used inshore for smaller species (Pliny *HN* 9.12, 51). According to Aelian (*NA* 15.5) harpoons were used for fish frequenting coastal waters. A large mosaic in the Bardo Museum in Tunis shows what appears to be a bird's-eye view of a hexagonal pond enclosed by a lattice barrier. The fish, which are depicted as swimming on the inside, are being fished by men in boats.

114. Pliny *HN* 25.98.

115. Oppian *Hal.* 4.647–93. The use of cyclamen was very common, according to Pliny (*HN* 25.116).

116. It is interesting to note that all of these structures were designed with platforms that project from the sides of the enclosures: one attached to each of the short sides of the rectangular *piscinae* at Rome and Tivoli, and a single platform affixed to a side of the circular pond at Circeo. These platforms afforded a place from which the pond could be viewed and created shady places where fish could escape the heat of the day or other predacious fish. The two platforms at Tivoli were supported on a concrete structure pierced by five small intersecting vaults. Three parallel vaults create the shady retreats in the platform at Circeo where *amphorae*, inserted into the walls of the platform, increase the spaces used by the fish for refuge. The two platforms at Monteverde employ large storage jars or *dolia*, which create the vaultlike openings in the projecting structures.

117. Concrete walls faced in *opus quasi-reticulatum* probably date to the first half of the first century B.C. The Little Theater at Pompeii, whose earliest phases are characterized by walls faced in *opus quasi-reticulatum*, is dated on epigraphic grounds to circa 78 B.C. (*CIL* X.844). Similar construction was used in the Forum Baths and the Temple of Jupiter Meilichios and dated to the early years of the colony circa 80 B.C.; see Blake (supra n. 24) 229, pl. 39.3; and Richardson (supra n. 66) 82. For an earlier date for this type of facing, see F. Coarelli, "Public Buildings in Rome between the Second Punic War and Sulla," *PBSR* 45 (1977) 9–19.

118. Concrete faced in *opus reticulatum* was used in the main building phases of the villas at Pianosa, Santa Liberata, Giglio (*quasi-reticulatum*), Torre Valdaliga, La Mattonara, Punta della Vipera, Grottacce, Palo, Astura (La Banca and La Saracca), Torre Astura, Formia (the Villa of Cicero and the Giardino Publico), Ventotene, and Sorrento (Villa of Agrippa Postumus and Villa del Convento dei Cappuccini).

119. Bricks were employed in repairs and additions to preexisting ponds at Punta della Vipera, Circeo (Piscina di Lucullo), and Sorrento (Villa del Convento dei Cappuccini).

120. The fishponds etched on the glass flasks, which depict the shoreline of Baia, suggest that these structures were visible as late as the fourth century A.D. Macrobius (*Saturnalia* 3.15) mentions a fishpond in Rome as late as the fifth century A.D. It is not clear whether the ponds mentioned in later literature were new buildings or restored structures.

243

1. *CIL* III, suppl. 2, 1932 – 34. S. Lauffer, *Diokletians Preisedikt* (Berlin 1971) 5.1 – 12. According to this fourth-century edict, a pound of "roughly scaled" sea fish (*piscis aspratilis marini*) should cost twenty-four *denarii* while the best quality river fish (*piscis fluvialis optimi*) is assigned the price of twelve *denarii* a pound. This edict is discussed by A. C. Andrews, in "The 'Sardinian Fish' of the Greeks and the Romans," *AJP* 70 (1949) 171 – 85, where the author provides a list of the different grades of fish mentioned in the edict of 301. Though this edict reflects pricing two centuries after the heyday of private pisciculture, the values give a sense of the relative worth of various species of fish.

2. Many of the sources important for the connection of ancient terminology with modern species of fish are summarized in the doctoral dissertation of T. H. Corcoran, "The Roman Fishing Industry of the Late Republic and Early Empire" (Ph.D. diss. Northwestern University 1957) 10 – 66. In addition to Corcoran, important secondary sources used for this discussion include H. Blümer, *Die Gewerbliche Thätigkeit der Völker des Klassischen Alterthums* (Leipzig 1869); J. K. Smidth, *Historical Observations on Fishing and Modes of Preserving Fish*, Report of the U.S. Commission for Fish and Fisheries for 1873 – 1875, Part 3 (Washington, D.C. 1876); *DarSag* 4.1 (1877) 409 – 94, s.v. Piscatio (Georges Lafaye); Ludovicus Bunsmann, *De Piscatorum in Graecorum atque Romanorum Litteris Usu* (Monasterii Guestfalorum: Typis Aschendorffii 1910); William Radcliffe, *Fishing from Earliest Times* (London 1921; reprint Chicago 1974); Diedrich Bohlen, *Die Bedeutung der Fischerei für die Antike Wirtschaft. Ein Beitrag zur Geschichte der Antike Fischerei* (Hamburg 1937); J. Cotte, *Poissons et animaux aquatiques au temps de Pline* (Paris 1944); E. De Saint-Denis, *Le Vocabulaire des animaux marins en latin classique* (Paris 1947); E. De Saint-Denis, *Pline l'Ancien Histoire naturelle livre IX* (Paris 1955) 7 – 33, 99 – 152; D'Arcy Thompson, *A Glossary of Greek Fishes* (London 1947); Edward Migdalski and George Fichter, *The Fresh and Salt Water Fishes of the World* (New York 1976).

3. Saint-Denis (supra n. 2); Smidth (supra n. 2).

4. Radcliffe (supra n. 2) 254 – 69 selects nine kinds of fish as being most popular based on the frequency with which they appear in the sources (*mullus, scarus, acipenser, rhombus, lupus, asellus, murena, karpos,* and *solea*). Joachim Marquardt (*Das Privatleben der Romer* [Leipzig 1886] 433 – 35) adds the *aurata* but drops the *solea* and *karpos* from his list of favorites. Corcoran, in his dissertation, selects eighteen varieties as being most valuable as food sources and trade commodities. Seven of these are probably different names for the varieties of tunny known to the Romans. Corcoran's list is the most complete because the tunny (lacking in both Radcliffe's and Marquardt's lists) was one of the most important food fish for the Romans.

5. Information on the appearance, characteristics, and habits of the fish being discussed will be gleaned from a combination of the ancient literary record and secondary sources on fish and fishing. Principal among these are U. D'Ancona, "Fishing and Fish Culture in Brackish-water Lagoons," *FAO Fisheries Bulletin* 7.4 (1954) 1 – 24; R. De Angelis, "Fishing Installations in Brackish Lagoons," *General Fisheries Council for the Mediterranean, Studies and Reviews* 7 (Rome 1959); R. De Angelis, "Mediterranean Brackish Water Lagoons and Their Exploitation," *General Fisheries Council for the Mediterranean, Studies and Reviews* 12 (Rome 1960); Migdalski and Fichter (supra n. 2); V. R. P. Sinha, J. W. Jones, and R. S. Prichett, *The European*

244

Freshwater Eel (Liverpool 1975); F. W. Tesch, *The Eel: Biology and Management of Anguillid Eels*, trans. J. Greenwood (New York 1977); A. Wheeler, *I Pesci. Le Guide Mondadori* (Milan 1978; reprint 1984); C. Moriarty, *Eels: A Natural and Unnatural History* (New York 1978).

6. Corcoran (supra n. 2) 53 – 61.

7. Migdalski and Fichter (supra n. 2) 41 – 42, 99 – 102. There is some confusion due to the use of ancient Latin and Greek names by modern ichthyologists. Early attempts at matching ancient names with modern species were not always precise and can be misleading; for example, the term *murena* is used today to describe the moray eel, which could not have been the exclusive species denoted by the ancient term *murena*. The meat of the moray often contains ciguatoxin, which makes the fish difficult to digest and sometimes poisonous. Edible *murenae* are more likely to be common eels or congers while morays could easily be associated with *murenae* kept as pets. The lamprey (*Petromyzon marinus*), which is sometimes connected with the ancient term *murena*, does not appear to be a fish cultivated to any large extent by the Romans. They are a common fish in the western Mediterranean and good to eat but are difficult to raise.

8. Wheeler (supra n. 5) 54 – 55; Migdalski and Fichter (supra n. 2) 42, 99 – 100; Moriarty (supra n. 5) 28 – 94; A. Usui, *Eel Culture*, trans. I. Hayashi (London 1974) 19 – 28.

9. Plautus *Amphitruo* 319; *Aulularia* 399; *Pseudolus* 382.

10. Columella (*Rust.* 8.16.10) refers to the eel as a "costly fish" (*pretiosus piscis*).

11. Varro *Rust.* 3.3.10; Columella *Rust.* 8.16.5; Macrobius *Sat.* 3.15.2 (after Varro).

12. The large contribution of eels by Hirrius is recorded by the Elder Pliny (*HN* 9.171), and Varro (*Rust.* 3.17.3), who puts the number at two thousand. Cicero (*Paradox* 38) also notes that one Marcus Curius raised large quantities of *murenae*.

13. Pliny *HN* 9.172; Macrobius *Sat.* 3.15.4; Plutarch *De Sollertia Animalium* 976 A.

14. Pliny *HN* 9.172. Congers and common eels have pectoral fins on which earrings (*inaures*) could have been affixed. The moray does not possess the necessary appendages for such decoration (see Pliny *HN* 9.73).

15. Pliny *HN* 9.77; Seneca *De Ira* 3.40; *De Clementia* 1.18; Cassius Dio 54; Tertullian *De Pallio* 5; Tacitus *Annales* 1. Thompson (supra n. 2) 165 suggests that the *murenae* in Pollio's fishpond were voracious lampreys. Lampreys possess no jaw or pectoral fins. Mature they can reach sixty to eighty centimeters in length and weigh about one kilogram. Despite these unimposing statistics, the lamprey is notoriously aggressive and possesses a voracious appetite.

16. Pliny *HN* 9.170 – 71.

17. Moriarty (supra n. 5) 130 – 42.

18. Ten kilograms of elvers constitutes about sixty thousand individuals. Using these data, Elaine Gazda (in A. M. McCann, J. Bourgeois, E. K. Gazda, J. P. Oleson, and E. L. Will, *The Roman Port and Fishery of Cosa* [Princeton 1987] 149) estimates the Roman lagoonal fishery at Cosa could produce forty-eight tons of eels annually.

19. Pliny *HN* 38.75.

20. Ovid *Halieutica* 22, 43; Aelian *De Natura Animalium* 1.33; Oppian *Halieutica* 3.117 – 20; Pliny *HN* 32.12, 14.

21. Athenaeus (*Deipnosophistae* 7.306a – 308) mentions several Greek terms equated with the *mugil*: κεστρεὺς, κέφαλος, μύξων, and χελῶν. Thompson (supra n. 2) 108.

22. Migdalski and Fichter (supra n. 2) 260 – 61; P. Korringa, *Farming Marine Fishes and Shrimps* (Amsterdam 1976) 8 – 9. The gray mullet, particularly *Mugil cephalus* and *Mugil capito*, are very euryhaline and can thrive in a wide range of salinity.

23. De Angelis (1959 supra n. 5) 3 – 4; De Angelis (1960 supra n. 5) 3 – 5; V. Brasola, A. M. Kalfa, and A. Cannas, "Esperienze positive di riproduzione artificiale di *mugil cephalus* effettuate nella Laguna di Orbetello," *Rivista italiana della piscicoltura e ittiologia* 14 (1979) 1 – 6. The *Mugil auratus* migrates, or ascends, into the lagoon in February while the *Mugil cephalus* ascends from October to December.

24. De Angelis (1959 supra n. 5) 14, 16.

25. Athenaeus *Deipnosophistae* 7.306e – 307b.

26. Columella *Rust.* 8.17.8.

27. Pliny *HN* 10.193. This same characteristic of the *mugil* is described by Martial (*Epigrammata* 10.30.23), who witnessed some of these talented fish confined in fishponds located at Formiae.

28. Fishing in the open sea for gray mullet is described by several authors of the early Empire: Pliny *HN* 9.29 – 32, 59; 32.12; Ovid *Halieutica* 3.98 – 116; 4.127 – 46; Oppian *Halieutica* 3.182 – 528; Plutarch *De Sollertia Animalium* 977A. The *mugil* also figures in an unusual form of punishment for adultery (Catullus 15.19; Juvenal 10.317; *CIL* IV.1261).

29. Pliny *HN* 9.61; Martial 13.89; Columella *Rust.* 8.17.8.

30. Athenaeus *Deipnosophistae* 7.319f.

31. Isidorus (*Origines* 12.6.5.) notes that the *lupus* pursues other fish "with relentless voracity" (*improba voracitate*).

32. Migdalski and Fichter (supra n. 2) 210 – 16, 262 – 66.

33. Oppian *Halieutica* 1.115; Columella *Rust.* 8.17.8.

34. Oppian *Halieutica* 1.120; Martial *Epigr.* 10.30.21; 13.89; Pliny *HN* 10.193; Columella *Rust.* 8.17.8.

35. Hicesius (in Athenaeus *Deipnosophistae* 7.310f) calls the λάβραξ superior to all others in wisdom and Aristophanes (in Athenaeus 7.311a) names it the cleverest of all fish. Oppian (*Halieutica* 3.121, 128), Plutarch (*De Sollertia Animalium* 977B, F), Ovid (*Halieutica* 23; 39), and Pliny (*HN* 32.13) relate stories concerning the ability of the *lupus* to evade fishermen.

36. Pliny *HN* 9.169; Macrobius *Sat.* 3.16.14 – 18. Of which two bridges Pliny and Macrobius are speaking is uncertain. De Saint-Denis (1955 supra n. 2) 147 fixes the spot as between the Pons Sublicius and the Pons Cestius. The area between the Sublicius and the Pons Aemilius, which is adjacent to the site of the Forum Piscarum, the fish market, is also possible.

37. Varro *Rust.* 3.3.9: "*Peream ni piscem putavi esse!*" The anecdote is also mentioned by Columella (*Rust.* 8.16.4) and Macrobius (*Sat.* 3.16.11 – 12).

38. Pliny *HN* 9.61; Martial *Epigr.* 13.89.

39. Thompson (supra n. 2) 142 believes the spotted variety (*Labrax punctatus*) to be a younger version of the common *lupus* (*Labrax lupus*), which has an even, unspotted appearance.

40. Ovid *Halieutica* 110; Pliny *HN* 32.153.

41. Migdalski and Fichter (supra n. 2) 288.

42. Columella *Rust.* 8.16.2: ". . . *sed etiam quos rerum natura lacus fecerat convectis marinis seminibus replebant. Inde Velinus inde etiam Sabatinus item Volsiniensis et Ciminius lupos aurotasque procreaverunt ac si qua sunt alia piscium gen-*

era dulcis undae tolerantia" (. . . but also [our ancestors] filled the lakes, which nature had formed, with small fry from the sea. Hence the Veline and Sabatine Lakes, likewise the Volsinian and Ciminian Lakes, produced *lupi* and *auratae* and whatever kinds of fish that can tolerate fresh water).

43. Martial *Epigr.* 13.90; Apicius 151; 437.

44. Pliny *HN* 32.145 and Columella *Rust.* 8.16.1–2. For the association of the *aurata* with Sergius Orata, see Varro *Rust.* 3.3.10; Columella *Rust.* 8.16.5; Macrobius *Sat.* 3.15.2. According to Pliny (*HN* 9.168), the ingenious Sergius Orata is to be credited with the first ponds designed for the raising of oysters as well as the invention of the first *pensiles balneae,* either hypocaust baths or raised tanks. The association of Orata with raised tanks would fit nicely with his eponymous role in Roman pisciculture. I am indebted to Garrett Fagan for his insight into the many talents of Sergius Orata. For more on Orata, see G. Fagan, "What Did C. Sergius Orata Invent near Baiae, c. 100 B.C.," *124th Annual Meeting of the American Philological Association — Abstracts* (New Orleans 1992) 165.

45. Pliny (*HN* 9.66) relates how dying *mulli* exhibit a wide range of color variation when observed in a glass bowl. The bright and changing color of the *mulli* would have added a decorative touch to the fishponds in which they lived.

46. Athenaeus *Deipnosophistae* 7.325d–e.

47. Cotte (supra n. 2) 99; De Saint-Denis (1947 supra n. 2) 68–69; De Saint-Denis (1955 supra n. 2) 118–19; Thompson (supra n. 2) 264–65; Migdalski and Fichter (supra n. 2) 246–47.

48. Pliny (*HN* 9.64–65) is alone in suggesting that there may be more than one variety of *mullus.* According to Pliny, the best kinds are found in open sea, while the less preferred live in coastal waters. Other authors apparently use the term generically for all *mullidae.*

49. Martial *Epigr.* 2.43.2; 2.37.4.

50. Juvenal 11.37; 6.40.

51. Suetonius *Tiberius* 34.

52. Martial *Epigr.* 9.64; 14.97.

53. Horace *Satires* 2.2.33.

54. Seneca *Epistulae Morales* 95.42.

55. Suetonius *Tiberius* 34.

56. Tertullian (*De Pallio* 5) records that during the reign of the emperor Gaius a *mullus* sold for six thousand sesterces. Pliny (*HN* 9.67) tells a similar story where Asinius Celer gave the sum of eight thousand sesterces for a mullet and remarks that the price of the fish was equal to that of nine horses. See Martial *Epigr.* 10.31.

57. Pliny *HN* 9.68. For a discussion of the Roman passion for the *mullus,* consult A. C. Andrews, "The Roman Craze for Surmullets," *CW* 42 (1948–49) 186–88.

58. Macrobius *Sat.* 3.16.9.

59. Pliny *HN* 9.64. Corcoran (supra n. 2) 46–47, n. 2, concludes that Pliny believed that *mulli* could not be raised in ponds. The size of the fish was the topic with which Pliny was dealing when he stated *"nec in vivariis piscinisque crescunt."* *Crescere* conveys the sense of growing rather than living. In addition, tame *mulli* are recorded by Cicero (*Ad Atticum* 2.1.17; *Paradox* 5), and Hortensius is said to have built elaborate fishponds near Bauli for raising this fish (Varro *Rust.* 3.17.6–7).

60. De Saint-Denis (1947 supra n. 2) 68–69; De Saint-Denis (1955 supra n. 2) 118–19; Thompson (supra n. 2) 265; Corcoran (supra n. 2) 47.

61. Migdalski and Fichter (supra n. 2) 289–93.

62. Thompson (supra n. 2) 223.

63. Athenaeus *Deipnosophistae* 8.356b.

64. Pliny *HN* 32.146.

65. Horace *Epodi* 2.50; *Sat.* 1.2.116; 2.2.42, 48, 49, 95; 2.8.30.

66. Martial *Epigr.* 3.60.6; 13.81; Juvenal 4.130; 11.121; Horace *Epodi* 21.50.

67. Columella *Rust.* 8.16.7; Martial *Epigr.* 10.30.21. *Rhombi* imported from Ravenna were quite prized (Horace *Epodi* 2.50; Pliny *HN* 9.169) as were specimens brought in from the Adriatic (Juvenal *Sat.* 4.39; Ovid *Halieutica* 125).

68. Pliny *HN* 32.151. For a discussion of the sources, see Corcoran (supra n. 2) 35 – 41; Radcliffe (supra n. 2) 159.

69. Migdalski and Fichter (supra n. 2) 266 – 67.

70. Pliny *HN* 32.151; 9.62; Horace *Epodi* 2.50; *Sat.* 2.2.22.

71. Macrobius *Sat.* 3.16.10; Pliny (*HN* 9.62) says the parrot wrasse is common in the Carpathian Sea but it never swims south past Cape Lectum in the Troad. Columella (*Rust.* 8.16.9) places the parrot wrasse off the coasts of Asia Minor and Greece and only as far west as Sicily.

72. Pliny *HN* 9.62 – 63; Macrobius *Sat.* 3.16.10.

73. Petronius *Satyricon* 93.2; Suetonius *Vitellius* 13.2.

74. Columella (*Rust.* 8.16.9 – 10) states that once *scari* were transported from their native waters to fishponds they could not be kept for long.

75. Corcoran (supra n. 2) 22 – 25, 34 – 35, 53 – 61, 63 – 65. Horace (*Sat.* 2.5.44) and Pliny (*HN* 9.49, 91; 31.94; 37.66) mention *cetaria* or *cetariae*. These terms refer to salting vats usually located in Spain. It is possible that the term *cetaria* refers to a natural inlet or cove where tunny could be confined and does not necessarily denote an artificial enclosure. For cetariae, see Robert I. Curtis, *Garum and Salsamenta: Production and Commerce in Materia Medica* (Leiden 1991) 53 – 54, n. 43. Tunnies, though important to the Roman fishing industry, may not have been raised with great success in Italian fishponds.

76. Martial (13.79 – 91) selects among others *mulli, murenae, rhombi, scari*, and *lupi* as suitable guest gifts (*xenia*). Shellfish (*ostrea* and *murices*), which were known to be cultivated in ponds, were included in Martial's list.

77. Recent studies of the Pacific or Japanese common eel have confirmed the importance of salinity to the habits of the eel. Whereas North American eels migrate to the Sargasso Sea to spawn, their Pacific cousins make for a spot in the Pacific 1,200 miles east of the Philippines where the salty tropical waters of the South Pacific meet the slightly less salty North Equatorial ocean current. The resulting concentration of salt creates "a particular flavor or odor in the water" attractive to the eels. For preliminary results of Katsumi Tsukamoto research on the Japanese common eel, see R. Mestel, "Quest for Eel Dorado" *Discover* 14.1 (January 1993) 38 – 40.

CHAPTER THREE

1. T. H. Corcoran, "The Roman Fishing Industry of the Late Republic and Early Empire" (Ph.D. diss. Northwestern University 1957); J. H. D'Arms, *Romans on the Bay of Naples: A Social and Cultural Study of Villas and Their Owners from 150 BC to AD 400* (Cambridge, Mass. 1970); J. H. D'Arms, *Commerce and Social Standing in Ancient Rome* (Cambridge, Mass. 1981).

2. Varro (*Rust.* 3.3.1), through the words of Lucius Merula, describes three divisions of animal husbandry typified by the aviary (*ornithon*), the warren (*leporar-*

ium), and the fishpond (*piscina*). He adds that the raising of bees could be included in this group (*Rust.* 3.16.1). For a discussion of Roman specialized farming, see K. D. White, *Roman Farming* (Ithaca, N.Y. 1970) 400 – 401. Columella *Rust.* 8.16.1.

3. Varro *Rust.* 3.17.2.

4. Juvenal (5.92 – 96), railing against gluttony and the excesses of entertaining, remarks with a bit of hyperbole that the seas around Italy have given out and that the provinces now supply fish for Roman tables.

5. For sources relative to the transport of live or fresh fish by the Romans, see Corcoran (supra n. 1) 20 – 65. For a small Roman boat equipped with a live tank unearthed at Ostia, see Otello Testaguzza, *Portus. Illustrazione dei porti di Claudio e Traiano e della città di Porto a Fiumicino* (Rome 1970) 132, 143 – 44.

6. *RE* 8 (1912) 841 – 49, s.v. Garum (R. Zahn); P. Grimal and T. Monod, "Sur le véritable nature du 'garum,'" *REA* 54 (1952) 27 – 38; C. Jardin, "*Garum* et sauces de poisson de l'antiquité," *RStLig* 27 (1961) 70 – 96; T. H. Corcoran, "Roman Fish Sauces," *CJ* 58 (1963) 204 – 10; R. I. Curtis, "In Defense of Garum," *CJ* 78 (1983) 232 – 40; R. I. Curtis, "Salted Fish Products in Ancient Medicine," *Journal of the History of Medicine and Allied Sciences* 39 (1984) 430 – 35; R. I. Curtis, *Garum and Salsamenta: Production and Commerce in Materia Medica* (Leiden 1991) 85 – 96.

7. Pliny the Elder notes the production at Beneventum (*HN* 32.19) and Pompeii (*HN* 31.94) in Campania, and Thurii (*HN* 31.94), which is located on the Gulf on the Taranto. Strabo (6.1.1 c243) records that, due to lack of arable land, Velia undertook the production of processed fish products.

8. Considerable epigraphic evidence from Pompeii indicates that A. Umbricius Scaurus was active in the fish sauce trade during the first century A.D. Yet, no evidence of Scaurus's ponds or processing facilities have been recovered (see R. I. Curtis, "A Personalized Floor Mosaic from Pompeii," *AJA* 88 [1984] 557 – 66; "The Slated Fish Industry of Pompeii," *Archaeology* 37 [1984] 58 – 59, 73 – 75; and "A. Umbricius Scaurus of Pompeii," in *Studia Pompeiana et Classica in Honor of Wilhelmina F. Jashemski* 1 [New Rochelle, N.Y. 1988] 19 – 49). The ethnic "*Puteolanus*" was used by McCann (in A. M. McCann, J. Bourgeois, E. K. Gazda, J. P. Oleson, and E. L. Will, *The Roman Port and Fishery of Cosa* [Princeton 1987] 40) to support the contention that *garum* was produced at or near the port of Puteoli. A recent study of Spanish inscriptions suggests that this ethnic (*Puteolanus*) refers to a Spanish merchant active in the *garum* trade; see E. W. Haley, "The Fish Sauce Trader L. Iunius Puteolanus," *ZPE* 80 (1990) 72 – 78.

9. M. Ponsich and M. Tarradell, *Garum et industries antiques de salaison dans la Méditerranée occidentale* (Paris 1965); O. Da Veiga Ferreira, "Algunas consideracoes sobre as fabricas de conservas de peixeda antiquidade encontradas em Portugal," *Archivo de Beja* 23 – 24 (1966 – 67) 123 – 34; R. Sanquer and P. Galliou, "Garum, sel et salaisons en Armorique gallo-romaine," *Gallia* 30 (1972) 199 – 223.

At Cosa on the western coast of Etruria, excavation of the port and fishery unearthed a considerable quantity of storage *amphorae*, some of which are thought by the investigators to have transported processed fish. The suggestion of Cosa as a center for the production and export of *garum* under the patronage of the Sestii is hypothetical and the assertion that the *amphorae* are indicative of a major manufacturing complex is conjectural. E. L. Will (in McCann et al. [supra n. 8] 201 – 3, 208 – 9, 212 – 15) has identified certain *amphorae* shapes (Will Types 5, 16, 21a, and 24a) as having been used in the transport of *garum* and other processed fish products. The discovery of these shapes in the area of the port and fishery at Cosa has led the investigators to conclude that the Sestii operated a processing installation at this site. However, no remains of the vats or salting facilities were recovered.

10. Curtis (1991 supra n. 6) 152–58.

11. Varro *Rust.* 3.2.16. Both Varro (*Rust.* 3.17.3) and Pliny the Elder (*HN* 9.172) record that the supply of fish in Hirrius's ponds, which made possible a loan to Caesar of several thousand *murenae*, accounted for the high resale value of the villa. See also J. M. Frayn, *Markets and Fairs in Roman Italy* (Oxford 1993) 65–69.

12. Martial (11.21–31), when describing the fishponds at Formiae, notes that they supplied the owner's table with fish and held pet fish, which could be called by name.

13. Most of the evidence for cultic fish kept in ponds is literary. The spring of Arethusa at Syracuse was the site of an enclosure that held a sacred eel (Diodorus Siculus 5.3.5; Silius Italicus 14.53–54; Aelian *NA* 8.4). Lucian (*De Syria Dea* 45–47) describes the sacred lake at Hierapolis in Syria northwest of Aleppo where fish sacred to Atargatis were kept. Aelian (*NA* 12.2) and Pliny the Elder (*HN* 9.55) tell of portents given by these fish at Hierapolis.

14. Varro *Rust.* 3.17.5–9; Pliny *HN* 9.66; 167; 172.

15. Of the nine *piscinae* not attached to villas, two were linked to nonresidential structures. The fishpond in the Palestra at Herculaneum was positioned in a more public place, which may have been used for athletic contests of the town's *iuventus*, and the *piscina* of Santa Venera at Paestum decorated an open area attached to the sanctuary of Venus.

16. Literary associations have led to the naming of some sites with fishponds after well-known personages mentioned in the texts. The so-called villas of Vedius Pollio at Pausilypon and Agrippa Postumus at Surrentum as well as the Piscina di Lucullo at Circeo are linked to these individuals on the basis of ancient literary accounts and circumstantial or geographical evidence.

Direct evidence linking specific ponds to known Romans is very scanty and often circumstantial. The site of Cosa is associated by some with the Domitii Ahenobarbi or the Sestii and probably came into imperial control by at least the reign of Claudius or Nero. This connection is based on the presence of a number of *amphorae* bearing the stamps of the Sestii family at the site and epigraphy from the area which name freedmen belonging to the Domitii and the emperor. D. Manacorda, "Considerazioni sull'epigrafia della regione di Cosa," *Athenaeum* 57 (1979) 80–91, no. 18, fig. B. For evidence of the Sestii at Cosa and the possible acquisition of the site by the Domitii in the late first century B.C., see McCann et al. (supra n. 9) 32–35, 177. The site of Alsium (Palo) was in imperial hands by at least the second century A.D.; see M. Torelli, *Etruria. Guide Archeologiche Laterza* (Rome and Bari 1985) 96; *CIL* XI.3720.

The association with these families to the fishpond at Cosa is not secure. One direct link between pond and owner may be in the *praedia* belonging to Iulia Felix at Pompeii. The complex functioned as a sort of private club and the long pond, or *euripus*, was just one of the more luxurious appointments.

17. Varro *Rust.* 3.17.5; Pliny *HN* 9.172. This villa passed from Hortensius to the wife of the elder Drusus, Antonia, who adorned her *murena* with gold earrings. The earrings probably pierced the lobed pectoral fins of the eel.

18. Varro *Rust.* 3.17.9; Pliny *HN* 9.170; Plutarch *Lucullus* 39.3; J. van Ooteghem, *Lucius Licinius Lucullus* (Brussels 1959) 186–91; D'Arms (1970 supra n. 1) 185–

86. Lucullus's villa at Misenum was built by Marius and sold to Cornelia for 75,000 drachmas and finally was bought by Lucullus for 2.5 million drachmas. According to Varro, upon the death of L. Lucullus his executer, M. Cato Uticensis, sold the fish from his ponds at this villa for 40,000 sesterces (*Rust.* 3.2.17).

19. Hirrius is reported to have supplied 6,000 eels for a banquet celebrating a triumph of Caesar's. This large contribution by Hirrius is recorded by Pliny the Elder (*HN* 9.171), Macrobius (*Sat.* 3.15.10), and Varro (*Rust.* 3.17.3), who puts the number at 2,000.

20. Seneca *Epistulae* 6.55.

21. Varro *Rust.* 3.3.10.

22. According to Varro (*Rust.* 3.17.5) and Pliny (*HN* 9.172), Hortensius is said to have wept on the death of his favorite *murena*. Macrobius (*Sat.* 3.15.4 – 5) attributes this story to L. Licinius Crassus.

23. Varro *Rust.* 3.17.3.

24. This one-upmanship is mentioned by Varro (*Rust.* 1.13.7), who describes the competition between Q. Caecilius Metellus Pius and L. Licinius Lucullus to see who could build the best villa.

25. P. Zanker, *The Power of Images in the Age of Augustus* (Ann Arbor, Mich. 1988) 25.

26. Varro *Rust.* 3.3.10; 3.17.9; Velleius Paterculus 2.33.4; Pliny *HN* 9.170; and Plutarch *Lucullus* 39.3, where the appellation is attributed to Tubero the Stoic.

27. Both Pliny the Younger (*Ep.* 9.7.4) and Martial (19.30.18) describe the leisure practice of fishing from one's bed (*a cubili lectuloque*) just by dropping a line out the bedroom window. The proximity of pavilions, platforms, and living quarters to fishponds at many of the villas in Italy would have made this activity possible.

28. According to the *Digesta Iustiniani* (41.1.14, 30; 43.8.17 trans. A. Watson [Philadelphia 1985] 492, 495, 574), piles built in the sea were *res privatae* as long as they did not obstruct harbors or rivers. Rivers and streams were held to be *res publicae*.

29. Statius *Silvae* 44 – 53.

30. Pliny *HN* 35. 116 – 17. The connection between art and nature and their implication on status in Roman society are discussed by Bettina Bergman in "Painted Perspectives of a Villa Visit: Landscape as Status and Metaphor," in E. K. Gazda, ed., *Roman Art in the Private Sphere: New Perspectives on the Architecture and Decor of the Domus, Villa, and Insula* (Ann Arbor, Mich. 1991) 49 – 70, esp. 50 – 59.

31. D'Arms (1981 supra n. 1) 84 – 85.

32. Géza Alföldy, *The Social History of Rome* (English ed., Baltimore 1988) 42 – 44.

33. Cicero *Ad Atticum* 1.19.6; 1.20.3; 2.9.1; Macrobius *Sat.* 3.15.6. These sources identify the principal *piscinarii* as Lucullus, Hortensius, and Philippus.

34. Typical of this look back at the days when fishponds were popular is the fifth-century author Macrobius (*Sat.* 3.15.2 – 10).

35. For a discussion of this tendency in the villas in Pompeii, see P. Zanker, "Die Villa als Vorbild des späten pompejanischen Wohngeschmacks" *JdI* 94 (1979) 460 – 523. Christine Kondoleon ("Signs of Privilege and Pleasure: Roman Domestic Mosaics," in Gazda [supra n. 30] 106 – 7) argues that artistic representations of fishponds were in part inspired by a desire to be associated with "the tastes and luxuries of the elite class."

36. Martial (13.79 – 91) numbers fish in his poetic list of guest gifts (*xenia*).

37. Martial 7.78.3.

38. Columella *Rust.* 8.16.6: *"maxime laudabilia et honesta."*

39. Columella *Rust.* 8.16.6.

40. Though a somewhat dubious source, the *Scriptores Historiae Augustae* (*Severus Alexander* 26.9 – 10) record the construction of a *"palatium cum stagno"* by the emperor for his mother Mamaea and the building of seawater *stagna* along the coast.

41. Tacitus *Annales* 1.75; 2.47; Suetonius *Tiberius* 47; Seneca *De Beneficiis* 2.7.2; *Epistulae* 122.10; Dio Cassius 57.10.3 – 4. Under Augustus admission into the senatorial order required 1 million sesterces while a position in the *ordo equester* necessitated 400,000 sesterces. For a discussion of the costs and obligations of political status in early imperial Rome, see R. Talbert, *The Senate of Imperial Rome* (Princeton 1984) 48 – 80.

42. Talbert (supra n. 41) 488.

43. See ibid. 54 – 66 for an informed discussion of the financial obligations placed on the imperial Senate. Aulus Gellius (*NA* 2.24.13 – 14) mentions an Augustan *Lex Iulia* which put limits of 200 sesterces on dinner expenditures, 300 sesterces for holidays, and 1,000 sesterces for wedding banquets and feasts.

44. Tacitus *Annales* 3.55.

45. Suppression of this competitive spirit can be seen in literary and artistic areas as well. See Zanker (supra n. 25) 323; and W. Eder, "The Augustan Principate as Binding Link," and M. Toher, "Augustus and Roman Historiography," both in K. Raaflaub and M. Toher, eds., *Between Republic and Empire* (Berkeley, Calif. 1990) 117 – 18 and 150.

46. W. Eck, "Senatorial Self-Representation: Developments in the Augustan Period," in F. Millar and E. Segal, eds., *Caesar Augustus: Seven Aspects* (Oxford 1984) 129 – 67, esp. 141 – 42. Tacitus (*Annales* 3.52 – 54) confirms the extravagant tendencies of Rome's elite, as late as A.D. 22, and Tiberius's reluctance to curtail such behavior.

47. D'Arms (1970 supra n. 1) 77.

48. Suetonius *Augustus* 65; *Tiberius* 53; Tacitus *Annales* 1.53.

49. D'Arms (1970 supra n. 1) 164; R. S. Rogers, "The Roman Emperors as Heirs and Legatees," *TAPA* 78 (1947) 140 – 58. This growing control may be inferred from Juvenal (*Sat.* 4.37 – 52), who describes the excitement in Domitian's court caused by the capture of a large *rhombus* (turbot). The extraordinary size of the fish is so unusual for a catch from the open sea that it is assumed to have escaped from a fishpond, an imperial enclosure (*"vivaria Caesaris"*).

50. F. Millar, *The Emperor in the Roman World* (Ithaca, N.Y. 1977) 16, 24.

51. Cicero *De Legibus* 3.30 – 31.

52. A. Wallace-Hadrill, *Houses and Society in Pompeii and Herculaneum* (Princeton 1994) 29 – 30. Wallace-Hadrill associates the political changes at the beginning of the reign of Augustus with the development of Pompeian Third Style wall decoration, which, he argues, "is the art of private places, private dinner parties for chosen amici" (29).

53. Ibid. 10 – 12.

CONCLUSIONS

1. J. H. D'Arms, *Romans on the Bay of Naples* (Cambridge, Mass. 1970) 77, 164. R. S. Rogers, "The Roman Emperors As Heirs and Legatees," *TAPA* 78 (1947)

140–58. The banishments of Augustus's daughter Julia and Agrippa Postumus suggest imperial ownership of property at Surrentum (Sorrento) and control of the islands of Planasia (Pianosa) and Pandataria (Ventotene). See Suetonius *Augustus* 65; *Tiberius* 53; Tacitus *Annales* 1.53.

2. For the tendency of imperial aristocracy to reside outside Italy, see Pliny *Ep.* 6.19.4 and Scriptores Historiae Augustae *Marcus Antoninus* 11.8.

3. Cassiodorus *Variae* 9.6.

4. Cassiodorus *Institutiones* 1.28–29. See J. J. O'Donnell, *Cassiodorus* (Berkeley, Calif. 1979) 177–222. The site was explored by Pierre Courcelle ("Le site du monastere de Cassiodore," *MélRome* 55 [1938] 259–307) and placed at the site of San Martino di Copanello, which lies south of the river Alessi and the Roman city on the Punta di Staletti. Here three roughly rectangular basins (approximately 12 by 5 meters in plan and between 1.5 and 2.5 meters deep) were connected to the sea and each other by narrow rock-cut channels.

5. Cassiodorus *Institutiones* 1.28.6. For a discussion of the late antique fishponds in the eastern Mediterranean, see J. J. Rossiter, "Roman Villas of the Greek East and the Villa in Gregory of Nyssa Ep. 20," *JRA* 2 (1989) 109–10.

GAZETTEER

1. G. Schmiedt, ed., *Il livello antico del Mar Tirreno. Testimonianze dei resti archeologici* (Florence 1972); E. Pongratz, "Historische Bauwerke als Indikatoren für Küstenmorphologische Veranderungen (Abrasion und Meeresspiegelschwankungen) in Latium," *Münchener Geographische Abhandlungen* 4 (1972) 1–144; B. Frau, "From the Etruscan Ports of Graviscae and Martanum: Elements for a New Methodology in the Field of Maritime Archaeological Research," in A. Raban, ed., "Harbour Archaeology: Proceedings of the First International Workshop on Ancient Mediterranean Harbours, Caesarea Maritima June 24–26, 1983," *BAR* 257 (1985) 93–104.

2. Pliny (*HN* 3.80) locates the island and notes the treacherous sea in the area. Varro (*Rust.* 3.6.2) mentions that the island belongs to Marcus Pupius Piso and is known for raising birds (*pavones*). The exile of Postumus Agrippa by Augustus is recorded in the *Annales* (1.3) of Tacitus. For more references, see *RE* 20 (1950) 2009, s.v. Planasia (R. Hanslik).

3. G. Giuli, "Descrizione di tracce di fabbriche romane in alcune isole tirrene," *Indicatore senese e grossetano* 1 (1833) 10–11; G. Chierici, *Antichi monumenti della Pianosa* (Reggio Emilia 1875).

4. S. Sommier, "L'Isola di Pianosa," *RivGeogrIt* 16 (1909) 441–585; Schmiedt (supra n. 1) 38–48, pls. 37–41.

5. Chierici (supra n. 3) 13; A. Olschki, "Proposta del gruppo richerche scientifiche e tecniche subacquee di Firenze per la costituzione di un parco nazionale insulare all'isola di Pianosa sul mar Tirreno," *Società botanica italiana e di Italia nostra* (Florence 1970) 3 10.

6. Schmiedt (supra n. 1) 47 calculates the sea level to have risen about 90 centimeters since the pond's construction.

7. Ibid. 38; H. Mielsch, *Die römische Villa: Architektur und Lebensform* (Munich 1987) 68.

8. Varro (supra n. 2).

9. Mielsch (supra n. 7) 116.

10. The site has also been variously known as the Santa Reparata or the Grotta nel Villino Staderini.

11. R. Del Rosso, *Pesche e peschiere antiche e moderne nell'Etruria marittima* 1 (Florence 1905) 99 – 123. Del Rosso's plan restores a lozenge-shaped tank inscribed within the concrete perimeter of the fishpond. Scattered hunks of concrete, observed in this area, may be all that remain of this feature.

12. R. C. Bronson and G. Uggeri, "Isola del Giglio, Isola di Giannutri, Monte Argentario, Laguna di Orbetello," *StEtr* 38 (1970) 210, no. 56 and n. 29.

13. Schmiedt (supra n. 1) 22 – 25, pls. 19 – 24. For a recent survey of the coast of the Gulf of Talamone which include the fishpond at Santa Liberata, see V. J. Bruno, E. L. Will, and J. Schwarzer, "Exploring the Gulf of Talamone," *Archaeology* 33 (July – August 1980) 35 – 43.

14. Schmiedt (supra n. 1) 26, pl. 22.

15. Schmiedt (ibid. 25) postulates another fishpond located in the area protected by the westernmost piers. However, I could not verify the existence of this second enclosure.

16. Schmiedt (ibid. 26, pl. 22) noted this line in the concrete along the shore.

17. Ibid. Schmiedt does not carry the channel completely through the eastern wall. I was able to remove some of the debris filling this channel in 1989, thus verifying the position and direction noted by Del Rosso.

18. This date is also easily associated with the activities of the Domitii Ahenobarbi in the region (Caesar *Bellum Civile* 1.34). *Amphorae* fragments found just offshore represent a range of dates from the second century B.C. to the third century A.D. (Bruno et al. [supra n. 13] 42).

19. Strabo 5.2.8; Del Rosso (supra n. 11) 61 – 70 suggests that the tunny watch was located on Monte Argentario.

20. A. M. McCann, J. Bourgeois, E. K. Gazda, J. P. Oleson, and E. L. Will, *The Roman Port and Fishery of Cosa* (Princeton 1987).

21. Gazda, "The Port and Fishery: Description of the Extant Remains and Sequence of Construction," in McCann et al. (supra n. 20) 82 – 97.

22. Gazda and McCann, "Reconstruction and Function: Port, Fishery, and Villa," in McCann et al. (supra n. 20) 141 – 55. For a discussion of the disagreement concerning the date of the second building phase see my note 24.

23. Ibid. 141 – 59 provide a detailed description of the remains, a reconstruction of the fishery, and an explanation of its function.

24. For the Spring House, see Oleson, "The Spring House Complex," in McCann et al. (supra n. 20) 98 – 128. There is some disagreement as to whether the concrete walls of the fishery should be dated as early as the second century B.C. and whether the construction of the pond should be drawn out over an entire century. Fill, used to buttress the exterior of the eastern wall (wall U) of the northern tank, was stabilized by the placement of a layer of wooden logs and planks over a stratum of crushed stone. These layers were topped by a row of *amphorae* (Will Type 4b) laid side by side with their rims positioned toward the wall (at a level 1.5 meters below the top of the wall). It is probable that this unusual fill was laid during the construction of the wall. The date of the *amphorae* (75 B.C. to the end of the century) provides a terminus post quem and suggests that the pond was constructed after the second quarter of the first century B.C.; see McCann et al. (supra n. 20) 115, n. 84.

25. McCann, "The History and Topography," in McCann et al. (supra n. 20) 32 – 33; Will, "The Roman Amphoras," in McCann et al. (supra n. 20) 172 – 77. Will has

linked *amphora* types 5 (125–50 B.C.) and 24a (75–50 B.C.) to the transport of *garum*.

26. Cicero (*Ad Atticum* 16.4.4) remarks that L. Sestius contributed ships to Domitius Ahenobarbus and that P. Sestius possessed a villa at Cosa (*Ad Atticum* 15.27.1). See *RE* 5 (1903) 1315–18, s.v. Domitius (F. Münzer); E. Galli, "Antiche vestigia nel dominio cosano dei Domizi Ahenobarbi," *Historia* 1 (1972) 15–16; P. A. Brunt, "Two Great Roman Landowners," *Latomus* 34 (1975) 619–35.

27. Bronson and Uggeri (supra n. 12) 10–14, nos. 90–95.

28. Bruno et al. (supra n. 13) 32–43. Aerial photographs of the Orbetello lagoon taken by General Schmiedt ([supra n. 1] 19–22, pl. 15–16) show regularly spaced projections from the inner side of the tombolo. These spurs result from the accumulation of sediment against concrete walls.

29. Pomponius Mela 2.7.19; Rutilius Namatianus *De Reditu Suo* 1.305; Del Rosso (supra n. 11) 125–38.

30. *EAA* 3 (1960) 895, s.v. Giglio (G. Maetzke); Schmiedt (supra n. 1) 30–37, pls. 29–36; references in Bronson and Uggeri (supra n. 12) 202–5, n. 22; G. Pellegrini, "Giglio," *NSc* (1901) 5–7; P. Raveggi, "Isola del Giglio—Le rovine romane del 'Castellare' e del 'Bagno del Saraceno,'" *NSc* (1919) 275–79; A. Solari, *Topografia storica dell'Etruria* 2 (1920) 175–77.

31. The level of the sea has risen between 55 and 60 centimeters; see Schmiedt (supra n. 1) 33.

32. Ibid. These cuttings are 50 centimeters deep, 20 centimeters wide, and open above to permit the beams to be placed in position or removed. The two beams that spanned the main opening would have been 11.5 meters long while a beam 3.8 meters long would have been necessary to span the seaward channel.

33. Lead pipes that conveyed fresh water from the hills of the island to the shore were noted early in this century by Del Rosso (supra n. 11) 127, n. 3.

34. Bronson and Uggeri (supra n. 12) 204–5, n. 22; Schmiedt (supra n. 1) 32.

35. Schmiedt (supra n. 1) 31 repeats the assessment of G. Maetzke who notes a mid–first century A.D. phase amplified in the Flavian period.

36. *CIL* XV.367, 853.

37. Caesar *Bellum Civile* 1.34. Del Rosso (supra n. 11) 128 notes a stamped tile found at the site of Castellare on the island that bears the impression of *GN. DOMITI CLEMENTIS* a freedman of the Domitii.

38. G. M. De Rossi, P. G. Di Domenico, and L. Quilici, "La Via Aurelia da Roma a Forum Aureli," *Quaderno dell'Istituto di Topografia Antica della Università di Roma* 4 (1968) 142–43, pls. 324–31; Schmiedt (supra n. 1) 62.

39. De Rossi et al. (supra n. 38) 143, pl. 331.

40. Del Rosso (supra n. 11) 145; De Rossi et al. (supra n. 38) 138–42, pls. 314–23; Schmiedt (supra n. 1) 90–92, pls. 99–102.

41. Schmiedt (supra n. 1) 75, pl. 81, illustrates this type of closure as used by modern fishermen in the ruins of the ancient fishpond at La Mattonara.

42. S. Bastianelli, "Gli antichi avanzi esistenti nel territorio di Civitavecchia— antichità romane," *StEtr* 13 (1939) 398; Schmiedt (supra n. 1) 63–73, pls. 65–68, 71–77; F. Melis and F. R. Serra in De Rossi et al. (supra n. 38) 92–93, pl. 2; *RE* 1.2 (1894) s.v. Algae (C. Hulsen).

43. Channel a is approximately 35 meters long, b is 32.5 meters long, and c is 33.75 meters long.

44. Schmiedt (supra n. 1) 68.

45. Bastianelli (supra n. 42) 398, pl. 23.2, noted pavements made of red-brown *opus signinum* with small regularly spaced *tesserae* of limestone, which he assigned to the villa of the late first century B.C.

46. F. Melis and F. R. Serra in De Rossi et al. (supra n. 38) 92; Schmiedt (supra n. 1) 69, pls. 69, 70, 79, 81; G. Schmiedt, *Atlante aereofotografico delle sedi umane in Italia* (Florence 1970) 146 – 48.

47. Tank 2: west side, 20.4 meters; north side, 14.3 meters; east side, 15.2 meters; south side, 13.9 meters. Tank 3: west side, 5.2 meters; north side, 10.8 meters; east side, 9.5 meters; south side, 13.1 meters.

48. Schmiedt (supra n. 1) 311.

49. Schmiedt (supra n. 1) 62, pl. 63; and (supra n. 46) pl. 139.5.

50. Bastianelli (supra n. 42) 398.

51. Ibid. 399; S. Bastianelli, *Centumcellae — Castrum Novum* (Rome 1954) 31, 46 – 48, 56 – 63; De Rossi et al. (supra n. 38) 70 – 71, pls. 187 – 88; P. A. Gianfrotta, *Castrum Novum — Forma Italiae* 7.3 (Rome 1970) 122 – 33, pls. 261 – 92; Schmiedt (supra n. 46) 144, pl. 139.1; Schmiedt (supra n. 1) 76 – 87, pls. 80, 82 – 92; Pongratz (supra n. 1) 34 – 36.

52. Schmiedt (supra n. 1) 76. Gianfrotta (supra n. 51) 129 and Bastianelli (supra n. 42) 399 publish the mole thickness as being just shy of 3 meters without noting the two-stage construction of the west and south sides.

53. The ponds at Ponza, Torre Astura, and Formia, which employ lozenge-shaped tanks inscribed within a rectilinear enclosure, create a similar configuration of a large central tank with four smaller triangular ones.

54. Gianfrotta (supra n. 51) pls. 282 – 85.

55. Ibid. pls. 280 – 81.

56. Schmiedt (supra n. 1) pls. 82 – 83. The tapered channels would act as "venturis," which increase the rate of flow as the channels constrict.

57. Ibid. 78, pls. 87 – 88.

58. Ibid. 78 – 81. The similarity of the concrete to the natural rock had long obscured this aspect of the pond's design.

59. Gianfrotta (supra n. 51) 132 postulates that these enclosures could have been used to raise eels. However, there are no remarkable design characteristics which support this hypothesis.

60. M. Torelli, *Etruria. Guide Archeologiche Laterza* (Rome and Bari 1985) 110 – 11; "Terza campagna di scavi a Punta della Vipera e scoperti di una laminetta plumbea inscritta," *ArchCl* 18 (1966) 283 – 84; and "Terza campagna di scavi a Punta della Vipera (S. Marinella)," *StEtr* 35 (1967) 347.

61. De Rossi et al. (supra n. 38) 68 – 70, pls. 175, 180 – 84; Gianfrotta (supra n. 51) 98 – 110, pls. 210 – 12; Schmiedt (supra n. 46) 144 – 46, pl. 139.2; Schmiedt (supra n. 1) 88 – 89, pls. 93 – 96; Pongratz (supra n. 1) 32 – 34; Frau (supra n. 1) 97 – 99, fig. 4.

62. E. T. Salmon, "The *Coloniae Maritimae*," *Athenaeum* 41 (1963) 20 – 23; De Rossi et al. (supra n. 38) 66, n. 132; Schmiedt (supra n. 1) 88; Pongratz (supra n. 1) 32 – 34; Frau (supra n. 1) 97 – 98.

63. A stone wedged into these slots appears to be a much later addition and not the original gate as is suggested by Frau (supra n. 1) fig. 4, no. 10.

64. Frau (ibid. fig. 4) interprets these walls as being foundations for the living area of the complex. However, the parallel-walled canals and the position at sea support

an identification as a fishpond. It is entirely possible that these walls could have supported a platform as well, similar to those noted at Torre Valdaliga and La Mattonara.

65. Gianfrotta (supra n. 51) 102 bases his date on the style of construction.

66. Frau (supra n. 1) 98, calculating the change in sea level as a function of time, asserts that the magnitude of the change (65 centimeters above the ancient level) would indicate a date in the late second or early first century B.C. for the construction of the rectangular fishpond. This reasoning is flawed on two counts: the rate of change over time is not constant and, as Giulio Schmiedt's study (supra n. 1) has shown, the magnitude of change can vary between two locations on the same coast.

67. The remains of a villa located in the garden of the Castello Odescalchi were uncovered during the first half of the nineteenth century (E. Braun, *BdI* [1838] 1–4; G. Abeken, *BdI* [1839] 85) and excavated by Luigi Borsari (*NSc* [1895] 195–201) later in the century. Excavation of this site is sometimes confused with the villa at Grottacce (cf. A. Del Bufalo in De Rossi et al. [supra n. 38] 57). The Castello Odescalchi is associated with the *statio* of Punicum and the villa there with that of Cn. Domitius Annius Ulpianus. Excavations around the villa uncovered remains of a small private port and a fishpond, as well as lead pipes bearing the name of Ulpianus (*CIL* XI.3587).

68. A. Del Bufalo in De Rossi et al. (supra n. 38) 57–64, pls. 150–69; Gianfrotta (supra n. 51) 40–47, pls. 56–79; Schmiedt (supra n. 46) 143, pl. 141.3; Schmiedt (supra n. 1) 89–90, pls. 97–98.

69. [CN(EI).DO]MITI [GEMI]NI. Gianfrotta (supra n. 51) 46, pl. 73.

70. Ibid. 46.

71. Schmiedt (supra n. 46) pl. 131.4; Schmiedt (supra n. 1) 62, n. 4, pl. 64.

72. J. P. Oleson, "Underwater Survey and Excavation in the Port of Pyrgi (Santa Severa), 1974," *JFA* 4 (1977) 302–8, fig. 4.

73. De Rossi et al. (supra n. 38) 54–55, pls. 142–44; Schmiedt (supra n. 1) 92.

74. De Rossi et al. (supra n. 38) 50–52, pls. 123–28. Given the general rise in sea level since antiquity, the position of the *euripus* would have been more than the present 20 meters from the shore.

75. The long wall of the pond's north side is preserved for a distance of 35.6 meters while the south wall is 37.4 meters long.

76. Strabo 5.2.8; Pliny *HN* 3.51; Rutilius Namatianus *De Reditu Suo* 1.223–24; De Rossi et al. (supra n. 38) 45–50, pls. 113–20; Salmon (supra n. 62) 24–25.

77. R. Lanciani, *Codex Vaticanus Latinus* 13045 f.337r; De Rossi et al. (supra n. 38) pl. 119.

78. De Rossi et al. (supra n. 38) 49, n. 103.

79. Many villas in this locale are attested in the ancient literary record. Cicero places villas belonging to Pompey, Caesar, and others in the vicinity of Alsium (*Pro Milone* 20.54; *Ad Atticum* 13.50; *Ad Familiares* 9.6.1). Valerius Maximus (8.1.7) records that M. Aemilius Porcina was accused by the Censor L. Crassus (124 B.C.) of having built his villa too high.

80. *CIL* XI.3720.

81. T. Ashby and M. A. Fell, "The Via Flaminia," *JRS* 11 (1921) 140–41.

82. M. L. Bruto, C. Vannicola, and G. Messineo, "Monumenti sepolcrali della Via Flaminia ed altre recenti scoperte nel settore nord del suburbio di Roma," *Archeologia Laziale* 4 (1981) 158. The first walls of one of the fishponds were partially un-

covered in 1980 and not identified as such. The rest of the complex was excavated by 1988 but I have yet to see any published report.

83. Another more remote possibility is that the circular tank of this pond is, in fact, the ruined core of a *tumulus*. Tombs of this sort are commonly constructed of concrete faced with *opus quadratum* with interior arrangements reminiscent of this pond's donut shape.

84. The island channel is 40 centimeters wide, 40 centimeters high, and sits 50 centimeters above the floor of the pond. Water was probably supplied to the island by means of a wooded trough, which could span the 3.5 meters between the central tanks and the perimeter of the pond.

85. For the remains of villas in this area, see Ashby and Fell (supra n. 81) 125 – 90; E. Stefani, "Grottarossa. Ruderi di una villa repubblicana," *NSc* (1944 – 45) 52 – 72.

86. G. Mancini, "Roma. Recenti trovamenti di antichità nella città e nel suburbio," *NSc* 21 (1924) 55 – 61. The pond was destroyed during the construction of the hospital.

87. Mancini (supra n. 86) 58 notes that almost all of the *dolia* bore identical fabricant stamps ([*caduceus*] M.CAILIVS.M.L.EVCR) on their rims.

88. The circular wall and the four buttresses were built at the same time and share the same concrete core. Tufa quoins were used to face the angles between these features and the reticulate pyramids of the facing were arranged in an irregular pattern.

89. Mancini (supra n. 86) 56; E. B. Van Deman, *The Building of the Roman Aqueducts* (Washington, D.C. 1934) 180, 184 – 85.

90. Frontinus *De Aquis Urbis Romae* 1.11.

91. P. Rosa, "Scavi del Palatino," *AnnInst* (1865) 346, 365 – 67; P. Rosa, *Plan des fouilles du Palais des Césars* (Rome 1870); R. Lanciani, *The Ruins and Excavations of Ancient Rome* (London 1897) 150 – 57, fig. 54; P. Romanelli, *Il Palatino* (Rome 1976) fig. 53. Lanciani expresses some reservations about the antiquity of the oval tank and suggests that it may be a Renaissance limekiln (155).

92. M. E. Blake, *Roman Construction in Italy from Tiberius through the Flavians* (Washington, D.C. 1959) 16, n. 90. Although Blake includes the fishpond in the discussion of the Tiberian Palace, she does suggest that it may be a later addition.

93. The oval plan is best compared with the fountains flanking the large *triclinium* in the Flavian palace.

94. C. F. Giuliani, "Note sull'architettura delle residenze imperiale dal I al III secolo d.Cr.," *ANRW* 2.12.1 (1982) 231 – 58.

95. A. Bartoli, "Scavi del Palatino (Domus Augustana) 1926 – 28," *NSc* 5 (1929) 17 – 21, figs. 5 – 6; A. Bartoli, *Domus Augustana* (Rome 1939); G. Lugli, *Roma antica. Il centro monumentale* (Rome 1946) 486 – 92, 509 – 16; G. Carettoni, "Excavations and Discoveries in the Roman Forum and on the Palatine during the Last Fifty Years," *JRS* 50 (1960) 197 – 203; G. Wataghin Cantino, *La Domus Augustana* (Turin 1966); H. Finsen, "La résidence de Domitien sur le Palatin," *AnalRom* 5 suppl. (1969).

96. Martial *Epigr.* 7.56.2; 8.36 – 39; Statius *Silvae* 4.2; Suetonius *Domitianus* 14.

97. Bartoli (1929 supra n. 95) 20 – 21, fig. 6. The end of the bridge, which joins with the side of the pond, is obscured by the roots of a large tree. It is possible to restore two arches under the tree, which, when added to the five that are visible, total seven.

98. The stamp (*CIL* XV.1628) is dated to between A.D. 292 – 305.

99. G. M. Zappi (d. 1596) in *Annali e memorie di Tivoli di Giovanni Maria Zappi*, ed. V. Pacifici (Tivoli 1920) fols. 79 – 80. This interpretation was reiterated by Filippo Sebastiani in the nineteenth century in *Viaggio a Tivoli. Antichissima città latino-sabina fatto nel 1825* (Foligno 1828) 90. For an account of the early exploration of the site, see T. Ashby, "Classical Topography of the Roman Campagna, II," *PBSR* 3 (1906) 154 – 61; C. F. Giuliani, *Tibur — Forma Italiae* 1.7 pars prima (Florence 1970) 329 – 35.

100. Aside from Hadrian's villa, the villa of Quintilius Varus is the largest ancient villa in the territory of Tivoli.

101. This pond has been referred to as a reflecting pool and even a swimming pool; cf. N. Neuerburg, "The Other Villas of Tivoli," *Archaeology* 21 (1968) 290; and Mielsch (supra n. 7) 43. Zappi (supra n. 99) records the existence of a second fishpond in this villa equipped with recesses for fish ("un altra Bellissima Peschiera con diversi ricettacoli di Accqua per i Pesci"). No physical evidence of this pond remains.

102. Mosaics depicting animals and fish were removed from the villa during excavation in the sixteenth century (P. Ligorio *Codex Vaticanus Latinus* 5295 fol. 4; Ashby [supra n. 99] 156). The fishpond would have provided more animated decoration along the same theme.

103. Lanciani (supra n. 77) 13047 fol. 257v; Ashby (supra n. 99) 160; Giuliani (supra n. 99) 331.

104. Giuliani (supra n. 99) 324.

105. Ibid. 320 – 21.

106. Ibid. 331; F. Coarelli, *Lazio. Guide Archeologiche Laterza* (Rome and Bari 1984) 103 – 4.

107. Giuliani (supra n. 99) 334. The toponym of *Fundus Quintiliolus*, known since the tenth century, is reflected in the name of the chiesetta near the site — Madonna di Quintiliolo.

108. Horace *Odes* 1.18; 1.24; *Ars Poetica* 438 – 42.

109. For a discussion of the connection between the Vari and this villa, see R. G. M. Nisbet and M. Hubbard, *A Commentary on Horace: Book I* (Oxford 1970) 227, 279.

110. Giuliani (supra n. 99) 268 – 87.

111. Ibid. 270 – 73.

112. The accumulation of soil in these rooms has raised the floor level and I was unable to determine the actual level. All measurements reflect distances from this packed earth floor and it must be assumed that all of these are underestimates.

113. The walls can be measured to a height of 3 meters but must have risen higher. The level of water inside these tanks was just over 3 meters and the front walls had to be high enough to contain it.

114. The front walls, which close off these rooms, do not bond with the side walls of the vaults. It is apparent that the half walls in the front were added shortly after the construction of the vaults (the concrete and the facing are identical). This building sequence probably resulted from the need to have the vault open in order to facilitate construction.

115. Statius *Silvae* 1.3.1 – 110. For a discussion of the search for the villa of Vopiscus, see Giuliani (supra n. 99) 274 – 87.

116. Sebastiani (supra n. 99) 79.

117. R. Del Re, *La villa tiburtina di Manlio Vopisco* (Tivoli 1899).

118. Coarelli (supra n. 106) 112. The earliest studies were carried out in the eighteenth century. See D. de Sanctis, *Dissertazione sopra la villa di Orazio Flacco dell'abbate Domenico de Sanctis fra gli arcadi Falcisco Caristio* (Rome 1761); B. Capmartin de Chaupy, *Decouverte de la maison de campagne d'Horace* (Rome 1767 – 69).

119. Lugli took over on the death of Pasqui and published the initial results in "La villa sabina di Orazio," *MonAnt* 31 (1926) cols. 457 – 598. Thomas Price accompanied Lugli back to the field in 1930 to clarify some architectural questions; see T. Price, "A Restoration of 'Horace's Sabine Villa,'" *MAAR* 10 (1932) 135 – 42. Some excavation was carried out by the soprintendenza in 1957 but I have seen no published reports of this campaign.

120. Lugli (supra n. 119) col. 553.

121. Columella (*Rust.* 8.17.5 – 6) mentions this problem saying that the recesses should be designed so that water could freely circulate.

122. This aperture lies at the same level and supplemented the function of the triangular drain but was closed at some date after construction.

123. The large pool (Fig. 46:P), located in the lower quadriporticus, may have functioned as the villa's first fishpond. Lugli (supra n. 119) col. 544; Price (supra n. 119) 140 – 41.

124. Horace *Epist.* 1.14.2 – 3.

125. M. E. Blake, *Ancient Roman Construction in Italy from the Prehistoric Period to Augustus* (Washington, D.C. 1947) 242 – 43.

260

126. Lugli (supra n. 119) cols. 557 – 58 suggests that the fishpond was a fountain or nymphaeum in its original guise and later adapted to the raising of fish. I could not identify the two phases mentioned by Lugli. The gabled niches, which are crucial for the identification of the fishpond, appear to be part of the original construction. The pond could have functioned easily as both a fishpond and a fountain. The suggestion of glass windows through which the fish could be viewed seems most improbable.

127. L. Jacono, "Nettuno—*Piscinae in litorae constructae*," *NSc* 21 (1924) 333 – 40, pl. 16. No date for the construction of these fishponds was offered by Jacono, and the remains are too scanty today to offer any specific estimate.

128. Ibid. 334 – 35, fig. 1. Jacono does not describe the architecture used in the construction of the ancient villa.

129. Ibid. 335 – 37, fig. 2.

130. Ibid. 337, fig. 3.

131. Moving from north to south the tanks measure in meters: 5.5 by 5.5, 6.7 by 5.5, and 5.5 by 5.5 in the northern row; 5.5 by 8.7, 6.7 by 8.7, and 5.5 by 8.7 in the middle row; 5.5 by 3.2, 6.7 by 3.2, and 5.5 by 3.2 in the southern row.

132. Cicero *Ad Atticum* 12.9; 12.19.1; 12.40.2 – 3; 12.45.2; 13.21.3; 13.26.2; 13.34; 13.38.2; 14.2.4; 14.5.3; 14.11.1; 14.15.3; 14.19.5; 15.12.1 – 2; *Epist.* 6.19; Livy 8.13.5; Strabo 5.3.232; Suetonius *Augustus* 97; *Tiberius* 72; Pliny *HN* 3.57; 3.81; 32.4; Plutarch *Cicero* 47; Festus 317.

133. R. Lanciani identified twelve villas between Anzio and Astura (*manoscritto* 86/2 of the Collezione Lanciani in the Biblioteca di Archeologia e Storia dell'Arte [Palazzo Venezia, Roma] fol. 152). The ruins of the villas at La Saracca, La Banca, and Torre Astura are the most visible structures along this stretch of beach. Certainly there are others buried in the dunes that line this coast.

134. A. Monaci, "Regesto di San Alessio all'Aventino," *ArchSocRomSt* 27 (1904) 368, document of A.D. 987. For a discussion of the early history, see F. Piccarreta, *Astura — Forma Italiae* 1.13 (Florence 1977) 10 – 12.

135. P. Cluverius, *Italia Antiqua II* (Lugduni Batavorum 1674) 990; G. R. Volpi, *Vetus Latium Profanum et Sacrum IV* (Padova 1726) 199; A. Nibby, *Analisi storico-topografico-antiquaria della Carta de' dintorni di Roma I* (Rome 1837) 275.

136. L. Jacono, "Note di archeologia marittima," *Neapolis* 1 (1913) 357 – 65; F. Castagnoli, "Astura," *StRom* 11 (1963) 637 – 44, pls. 97 – 104; Schmiedt (supra n. 46) 132 – 35, 144, pl. 134; Schmiedt (supra n. 1) 108 – 20; L. Quilici, "Il problema di Torre Astura," *Italia Nostra* 75 – 76 (1970) 18 – 21; Piccarreta (supra n. 134).

137. Volpi (supra n. 135) pl. 20; Nibby (supra n. 135) 276; Castagnoli (supra n. 136) 642; Schmiedt (supra n. 1) 114 – 20, pls. 121 – 27; Piccarreta (supra n. 134) 68 – 74, figs. 122 – 24.

138. Nibby (supra n. 135) 277; Castagnoli (supra n. 136) 642; Piccarreta (supra n. 134) 67 – 68, pls. 119 – 20.

139. This pier is now badly weathered and preserved in two large sections. It is possible that the center of this pier was pierced by an opening to allow the circulation of seawater.

140. Cluverius (supra n. 135) 990.

141. Cicero (supra n. 132). The connection of the ruins at Torre Astura with the villa of Cicero was maintained by scholars well into this century; see T. Ashby, *The Roman Campagna* (London 1927) 13. Recent studies (beginning with Castagnoli [supra n. 136] 641 – 42) have cast serious doubt on this connection.

142. Piccarreta (supra n. 134) 21 – 66. For earlier discussions, see Castagnoli (supra n. 136) 637 – 44; Schmiedt (supra n. 1) 108 – 13; Quilici (supra n. 136) 18 – 21. The breathtaking view from and substantial ruins of Torre Astura prompted the selection of the site for maritime sets of the 1963 film *Cleopatra*.

143. Piccarreta (supra n. 134) 55. The differing axes of the walls may be indicative of the difficulties inherent in open-sea concrete construction where the walls' orientation was dependent on the location of seabeds stable enough for the placement of their foundation.

144. The eastern tanks are virtually covered by subsequent architecture and sand while the tanks to the west are completely exposed. If symmetry is assumed in the design of the area, it is possible to reconstruct the plan of one from the other.

145. One major conduit, located on the pond's east side, carried fresh water to the perimeter channel. Others distributed fresh water into the tanks of the inner enclosure that fronts the terrace. The great number of gates in these channels and in the walls of the tanks suggests a rather complex system of regulating water flow and salinity.

146. Piccarreta (supra n. 134) 62 suggests that Astura benefited from the attention paid by the emperor Claudius to improving the anchorages along this coast (i.e., Ostia, Antium, and Terracina).

147. Writing in the first century B.C., the geographer Strabo (5.3.5), while listing the anchorages along this coast, does not mention a harbor at Astura. In the following century, Pliny (*HN* 3.57; 3.81) mentions the island and river at Astura but neglects to note a harbor, though he does not mention the harbor at Ostia either.

148. Pliny *HN* 3.57; 3.81.

149. Cicero *Ad Atticum* 12.19.1: "*est hic quidem locus amoenus et in mari ipso qui et Antio et Circeiis aspici possit.*"

150. Piccarreta (supra n. 134) 23. Castagnoli (supra n. 136) 641–42 uses building style to date the original phase to the reign of Augustus or his immediate successors.

151. G. Lugli, *Ager Pomptinus. Circeii — Forma Italiae* 1.1 pars secunda (Rome 1928) cols. 48–50, figs. a, 4. Thomas Ashby ("Monte Circeo," *MEFRA* 25 [1905] 194) did not believe the remains to be ancient.

152. V. Ginetta Chiappella, "Esplorazione della cosiddetta 'Piscina di Lucullo' sul lago di Paola," *NSc* suppl. (1965) 146–60.

153. The walls that enclose the terrace emerged only 10 centimeters above the level of the ground and thus constituted only an ornamental barrier.

154. The vaults of this platform were added to the already completed perimeter of the pond. As a result the southern ends of the lateral vaults, following the curve of the pond, measure between 6.4 and 6.9 meters long.

155. Three small access ports (measuring 20 centimeters square) were positioned in the floor of the platform one above each vault. The ports were fashioned of stone and possess a recessed ledge that would allow the placement of a cover flush with the floor. The function of these ports is open to conjecture.

156. Chiappella (supra n. 152) 159 notes that tepid sulfurous springs, like the one issuing from the bottom of the Piscina di Lucullo, are conducive to the raising of fish and mollusks, especially in winter.

157. Stone blocks fitted into the walls of the canal were equipped with vertical runners for the precise placement of the gate.

158. Coarelli (supra n. 106) 305.

159. Chiappella (supra n. 152) 157 would place the platform and the trapezoidal tanks in some later imperial construction phase based on the use of brick. However, the brick-faced concrete appears to have been employed as repairs to these elements and should not date their original construction.

160. Suetonius *Augustus* 16.4. Walls faced in *opus reticulatum* could date from Augustan activity.

161. The canal, initiated by Nero, which would have linked the Lacus Avernus with the mouth of the Tiber, might have included work in the area of Circeo (Tacitus *Annales* 15.42).

162. G. Jacopi, "Scavi nella villa di Domiziano in località 'Palazzo' sul lago di Paola," *NSc* (1936) 21–50; R. Righi, "La villa di Domiziano in località Palazzo sul lago di Sabaudia: pavimenti in *opus sectile* dell'edificio balneare ad esedre," *Archeologia Laziale* 3 (1980) 97–110.

163. *CIL* X.6428:

L.FABERIUS C.F.POM.MURENA
AUGUR.IIII.VIR.AED.
AQUA(M) QUAE FLUEBAT EX LACU CONLEGIT ET SALIENTEM IN LACU(M)
REDEGIT
D(E) S(UA) P(ECUNIA) F(ACIUNDUM) C(URAVIT)

Lucius Faberius Murena, son of Gaius,
Augur, Quattuorvir, and Aedile,
channeled the water which flows from the lake and restored the spring
flowing into the lake.
He saw to it with his own funds.

Another lead pipe found in the vicinity of the Torre di Paola and inscribed as belonging to the people of Circeii (REI.P.CIRCEIENS *CIL* X.6431) may also be connected with the activities already documented.

164. G. Lugli (supra n. 151) cols. 13–14, fig. f. I was unable to distinguish any submerged walls below Torre del Fico. Construction along this shore in the past half century has probably covered or destroyed many of the ancient coastal remains. P. Mingazzini and F. Pfister (*Surrentum — Forma Italiae* 1.2 [Florence 1946] 43) expressed some doubt about the existence of the fishpond at Torre del Fico.

165. X. Lafon, "La voie littorale Sperlonga-Gaeta-Formia," *MEFRA* 91 (1979) 399–429, fig. 2, no. 32; H. Broise and X. Lafon, "Les villas littorales de la zone de Sperlonga," *Archeologia Laziale* 3 (1980) 111–12, pl. 25.2.

166. Broise and Lafon (supra n. 165) 111; F. Fasolo, "Architetture classiche a mare. II: Altre antichità del litorale di Sperlonga," *Quaderni dell'Istituto di Storia dell'Architettura* 20–21 (1957) 13–18.

167. Coarelli (supra n. 106) 342.

168. Tacitus *Annales* 4.59; Suetonius *Tiberius* 39. The grotto is the probable site where the emperor was saved from a falling boulder by Sejanus in A.D. 25.

169. B. Conticello and B. Andreae, "Die Skulpturen von Sperlonga," *Antike Plastik* 14 (1974) 13–29.

170. G. Jacopi, *L'antro di Tiberio a Sperlonga* (Rome 1963). For a preliminary discussion of the grotto, see Fasolo (supra n. 166) 19–22, figs. 16, 18–26. Subsequent discussions include E. Ricotti, "Il gruppo di Polifemo a Sperlonga," *RendPontAcc* 42 (1969–70) 117–34; F. Coarelli, "Sperlonga e Tiberio," *Dialoghi di archeologia* 7 (1973) 97–122; Conticello and Andreae (supra n. 169).

171. The openings were closed at some later date by mortar and rubble.

172. Inside the island tanks the *amphorae* were arranged in three rows around the interior of these enclosures. The other vessels are located on the exterior of the island (at least 24), the north wall of the rectangular pond (38), and the two projecting walls (4), which are positioned between the circular (A) and rectangular (B) ponds. At least 120 *amphorae* were used in this design and many more probably existed in the damaged walls of the pond's island.

173. This rock-cut ship was once covered with mosaics which included glass *tesserae*. A section of this mosaic bearing the name *NAVIS ARGO* (Jason's ship) was recovered in the little grotto and is now on display in the museum at Sperlonga (G. Jacopi, *L'antro di Tiberio ed il Museo Archeologico* [Rome 1965] 6–7, 19, pl. 40).

174. Blake (supra n. 125) 229–30, pls. 39.3 and 40.4. *Opus quasi-reticulatum* was used in the construction of the covered theater (*theatrum tectum*) at Pompeii which is dated by an inscription (*CIL* X.844) to shortly after 80 B.C. (L. Richardson, *Pompeii: An Architectural History* [Baltimore 1988] 131). For an earlier date for *opus quasi-reticulatum*, see F. Coarelli, "Public Building in Rome between the Second Punic War and Sulla," *PBSR* 45 (1977) 9–19.

175. The Scylla group was situated on the pedestal in the center of the grotto while the Polyphemus group was placed in an alcove at the back of the cave.

176. Cicero (*Ad Atticum* 2.4; 2.12) owned a villa at Formiae and it was here that the orator was murdered (Plutarch *Cicero* 47–49). L. Munatius Plancus, who proposed to the Senate that Octavian's name be changed to Augustus, was buried on a hill overlooking Gaeta. Mamurra, the *praefectus fabrum* under Caesar and much de-

rided by Catullus (29, 41, 43, and 51), was closely linked to Formiae and the site was known as *mamurrarum urbs* (Horace *Sat.* 1.5.37).

177. Martial 10.30; 11.17–31.

178. L. Jacono (supra n. 136) 360–63. See also S. Aurigemma and A. De Santis, *Gaeta-Formia-Minturno* (Rome 1979) 29–31, figs. 3–4.

179. C. F. Giuliani and M. Guaitoli, "Il ninfeo minore della villa detta di Cicerone a Formia," *RM* 72 (1972) 191–219; Coarelli (supra n. 106) 365–66.

180. The positions of the nymphaea in the villa above align with the location of the pond and attest to the presence of ample freshwater supplies.

181. Jacono (supra n. 136) 360–61, fig. 2; Aurigemma and De Santis (supra n. 178) 29–31, pl. 16; Schmiedt (supra n. 1) 139–42, pls. 154–55.

182. Coarelli (supra n. 106) 366.

183. Jacono (supra n. 136) 360.

184. Schmiedt (supra n. 1) 141, pl. 154.

185. Jacono (supra n. 136) 361–62, fig. 3.

186. Three walls connecting the perimeter to the small tanks were seen on the pond's east and west sides. These walls probably supported walkways leading to the central tanks.

187. Aurigemma and De Santis (supra n. 178) 60–61, pl. 36; Schmiedt (supra n. 1) 142–45, pls. 156–58.

188. Livy 9.28.7.

189. J. H. D'Arms, *Romans on the Bay of Naples* (Cambridge, Mass. 1970) 77–78.

190. According to Suetonius (*Tiberius* 54.2), Nero, the brother of Caligula, was sent here by Tiberius and died in exile in A.D. 31. Caligula, upon becoming emperor, went to the Pontine islands to retrieve the ashes of his brother and his mother who had died on nearby Pandataria (Suetonius *Gaius Caligula* 15.1). Caligula made use of the island himself when he exiled his wife Livia Orestilla and his sisters Julia and Agrippina to Pontia (Cassius Dio 59.22.8; Suetonius *Gaius Caligula* 25.1).

191. Commonly called the "Grotte di Pilato" (Caves of Pontius Pilate), these rock-cut chambers probably were cut from preexisting caves and fissures common to this island. The island is made of volcanic trachyte, a soft stone that is easily worked.

192. The ponds were first studied in 1912 by Jacono and published many years later; see L. Jacono, "Una singolare piscina marittima in Ponza," *Campania Romana* 1 (1938) 145–62. For an early survey of the remains on the island, see A. Maiuri, "Ricognizione archeologica nell'isola di Ponza," *BdA* 6 (1926–27) 224–32.

193. The soft volcanic stone would not have withstood the constant abrasion caused by raising and lowering the gate. Hard basalt was better suited to retain the runners for the movable gates.

194. Jacono (supra n. 192) 155–57 suggested that these tanks, along with the tank in the large niche, were intended to hold sacred fish. Another possibility is that the circular tanks held different types or ages of marine life (young fry, shellfish, crustaceans) from those confined in the main pond; compare Mielsch (supra n. 7) 27.

195. Paired circular cuttings at this end of the corridor may have held the vertical elements of a platform on which to store equipment (nets, tackle, etc.) to be used in the fishponds; see Schmiedt (supra n. 1) 166, pl. 178.

196. Twelve steps were noted by Jacono (supra n. 192) 151, though now the stairway appears as a ramp with no recognizable steps.

197. Jacono (ibid. 152) noted evidence for a gate in one of these channels though no traces can be found today (nor were they visible during Schmiedt's study [supra n. 1] 156, n. 1).

198. Channel 4, as noted already, is connected to the east side of pond A (Fig. 74:4).

199. Schmiedt (supra n. 1) pl. 170.

200. Jacono (supra n. 192) 152.

201. Jacono (ibid. 146) noted that these stairs were destroyed during a violent storm (*mareggiata*) in 1912.

202. Ibid. 154–55.

203. Maiuri (supra n. 192) 226–27 discusses the remains of cisterns and aqueducts on Ponza.

204. During an examination of the interior of the large grotto (A) in 1988, I observed scores of eels. Local fisherman claim that these grottoes and other natural fissures around the island are preferred fishing spots.

205. L. Jacono, "Solarium di una villa romana nell'isola di Ponza," *NSc* (1926) 219–32; (supra n. 192) 146–47.

206. Supra n. 190

207. C. Bon, R. Buitoni, G. M. De Rossi, and M. Liverani, *Le isole pontine I. Ventotene. Immagini di un'isola* (Rome 1984) 34, 36, fig. 4.

208. D'Arms (supra n. 189) 108.

209. Schmiedt (supra n. 1) 181–97, pls. 189–202. Subsequent work includes M. Cancellieri, "Le isole pontine," *Mondo archeologico* 47 (1980) 11–17; G. M. De Rossi, *Lazio meridionale* (Rome 1980) 309–44; G. M. De Rossi, "Note archeologiche sull'archipelago pontino," *Lunario Romano* (1983) 581–92; and Bon et al. (supra n. 207) 9, 17–32.

210. Portions of channel c, which ran under the back walkway of grotto A, collapsed and were repaired with concrete during ancient operations.

211. The northern gate was fixed by runners cut into blocks of basalt, which were inserted in the sides of the opening.

212. Traces of concrete in tank C may indicate that this tank was subdivided in a fashion similar to the arrangement in tank D.

213. Julia, the daughter of Augustus, was exiled to Pandataria by the emperor in A.D. 2 (Velleius Paterculus 2.100.3; Tacitus *Annales* 1.53; Suetonius *Augustus* 63.1). Agrippina, the wife of Germanicus, was imprisoned on the island by Tiberius in A.D. 29 and subsequently died on Pandataria (Suetonius *Tiberius* 53). Later exiles included Octavia, the wife of Nero (Tacitus *Annales* 14.63–64), and Flavia Domitilla, the daughter of the emperor Titus. The connection of this island with prisons continued into this century as is attested by the remains of the Carcere di S. Stefano, which lies just off the east end of the Ventotene.

214. The villa, which covers over 30,000 square meters, was built of concrete faced in *opus reticulatum* and decorated with frescoes of the Pompeian Third Style (Augustan). See L. Jacono, "Un porto duo millenario," *Atti del III Congresso Nazionale di Studi Romani* 1 (1933) 318–24, pl. 46.

215. D'Arms (supra n. 189) 78, 108.

216. Schmiedt (supra n. 1) 220.

217. For sources and further discussion, see Chapter 3, nn. 17–22.

218. Jacono (supra n. 136) 366 notes the remains of fishponds west of the Castel dell'Ovo in Naples. These ponds were designed with channels that had closable

gates; see G. M. Fusco, *Giunta al commento critico-archeologico sul frammento di Fabio Giordano* (Naples 1842) 93.

219. I. Sgobbo, "I nuclei monumentali delle terme romane di Baia per la prima volta riconosciuti," *Atti del III Congresso di Studi Romani* (1934) 249. Identification of the ruins as baths persisted during the early years of study; see A. Maiuri, *I campi flegrei* (Rome 1958) 65 – 86; "Le terme di Baia e il loro problema geofisico," *Atti-PontAcc* 7 (1957 – 58) 267; and *EAA* 1 (1958) 960, s.v. Baia (M. Napoli).

220. A. De Franciscis, "Underwater Discoveries around the Bay of Naples," *Archaeology* 20 (1967) 212 – 15; M. Borriello and A. D'Ambrosio, *Baiae-Misenum — Forma Italiae* 1.14 (Florence 1979) 63 – 69; G. De Angelis D'Ossat, "Note sull'architettura nei Campi Flegrei," *Puteoli. Studi di storia antica* 4 – 5 (1980 – 81) 365 – 75.

221. G. De Angelis D'Ossat, "L'Architettura delle 'terme' di Baia in i Campi Flegrei nell'archeologia a nella storia," *Atti dei Convegni Lincei* 33 (1977) 227 – 74. The circular pond was positioned so that it could be viewed easily from the hemicycle terrace above; see A. G. McKay, "Pleasure Domes at Baiae," *Studia Pompeiana et Classica in Honor of Wilhelmina F. Jashemski* 2 (New Rochelle, N.Y. 1989) 160 – 61.

222. Maiuri (1958 supra n. 219) 74 identified the large open area below this terrace as a *piscina* on no compelling evidence. This area appears to have been a garden or grove enclosed by a portico (cf. De Angelis D'Ossat [supra n. 220] 374). McKay (supra n. 221) 160 – 61 repeats Maiuri's misidentification of the lower terrace as a large pool. D'Ossat (241 – 43) relates the hemicycle terrace to a similar design in the Neronian villa at Antium (Anzio) and suggests that both were constructed during the rule of Nero.

223. The Warsaw flask is sometimes referred to as the Rome flask.

224. Some recent studies: J. H. D'Arms, "Puteoli in the Second Century of the Roman Empire," *JRS* 64 (1974); K. S. Painter, "Roman Flasks with Scenes of Baiae and Puteoli," *Journal of Glass Studies* 17 (1975) 54 – 67; J. Kolendo, "Parcs a huîtres et viviers à Baiae sur un flacon en verre du Musée National de Varsovie," *Puteoli. Studi di storia antica* 1 (1977) 108 – 27; S. Ostrow, "The Topography of Puteoli and Baiae on the Eight Glass Flasks," *Puteoli. Studi di storia antica* 3 (1979) 77 – 140.

225. The Ampurias flask depicts the right pond with a triangular section and the left semicircular.

226. Varro *Rust.* 3.17.4; Valerius Maximus 9.1.1.

227. C. Picard ("Pouzzoles et le paysage portuaire," *Latomus* 18 [1959] 30, 37), while accepting the elevated perspective of the oyster bed, insists on seeing the flanking structures straight on and thus identifies them as building fronts.

228. The Populonia bottle is labeled *STAGNU* while the Ampurias and the Warsaw flasks are labeled *STAGNU NERONIS*.

229. De Franciscis (supra n. 220) 212 identifies the *palatium* with the so-called Terme di Baia, which would put the ponds to the north beyond the Punta del Fortino Vecchio.

230. P. Mingazzini, "Le terme di Baia," *Puteoli. Studi di storia antica* 4 – 5 (1980 – 81) 275. Examination of aerial photographs has led some to postulate that the fishponds and oyster beds at Baiae were located in the Lacus Baianus, which is placed in the water just south of the Punta Epitaffio; see G. Di Fraia, N. Lombardo, and E. Scognamiglio, "Contributi alla topografia di Baia sommersa," *Puteoli. Studi di storia antica* 9 – 10 (1985 – 86) 258 – 62, fig. 21.

231. The enclosure is noted on the Carta di Mario Cartaro, which dates to the beginning of the seventeenth century (M. Borriello and A. D'Ambrosio, *Baiae-Misenum — Forma Italiae* 1.14 [Florence 1979] 12 – 13, fig. 5).

232. C. Du Bois, "Pouzzoles antique," *BEFAR* 98 (1907) 261 – 63; P. Sommella, "Forma e urbanistica di Pozzuoli romana," *Puteoli. Studi di storia antica* 2 (1978) 74, no. 56, fig. 167.

233. Kolendo (supra n. 224) 120 – 21, fig. 8.

234. R. T. Gunther, *Pausilypon: The Imperial Villa near Naples* (Oxford 1913).

235. R. T. Gunther, *Contributions to the Study of Earth-Movements in the Bay of Naples* (Oxford 1903). Gunther calculates the change in sea level to be between 3 and 4 meters. Jacono (supra n. 136) 358 estimates that the rise in sea level since the first century B.C. was approximately 1 meter.

236. Jacono (supra n. 136) 365 –71; G. Della Valle, "La villa sillana e augustea Pausilypon," *Campania Romana* 1 (1938) 205 – 67; *RE* 18 (1949) 2420, s.v. Pausily-pon (Scherling); M. Pagano, "Gli impianti marittimi della villa 'Pausilypon,'" *Puteoli. Studi di storia antica* 4 – 5 (1980 – 81) 245 – 55.

237. Gunther (supra n. 235) 149 – 62 describes the ruins around the islands but does not identify the remains as being fishponds. He locates the fishponds of Pollio in the ruins around the promontory near the village of Marechiano (177 –79).

238. Pagano (supra n. 236) 252 notes that grooves in the concrete lining may have carried conduits or plumbing, which further supports the notion of freshwater circulation.

239. Gunther (supra n. 235) 161 noted the presence of these fish during his study of the villa.

240. Ibid.

241. Pliny *HN* 9.77; Seneca *De Ira* 3.40; *De Clementia* 1.18; Cassius Dio 54.23.1 – 6; Tertullian *De Pallio* 5; Tacitus *Annales* 1. R. Syme, "Who Was Vedius Pollio?," *JRS* 51 (1961) 23 – 30.

242. Cassius Dio 54.23.1.

243. D'Arms (supra n. 189) 111 – 12, 229 – 30. Blake (supra n. 125) 245 associates the irregular (wavy) *opus reticulatum* with an early Augustan date while the regular *opus reticulatum* is thought by her to be late Augustan or Tiberian.

244. Rectangular pools can be found in the Casa dello Scheletro (III 3), Casa dell'Atrio a Mosaico (IV 1–2), Casa del Rilievo di Telefo (Insula orientalis I 2 –3), and in a small peristyle adjacent to the Great Palestra (Insula orientalis II). A cruciform tank was unearthed inside a small peristyle in the Casa di Galba (VIII 2). In addition, excavation has uncovered the eastern rounded end of a long *euripus* in Casa detta del Genio (II 3).

245. C. Weber, *Pianta della Villa Ercolanese* (Museo Nazionale di Napoli 1750–54).

246. D. Comparetti and G. de Pietra, *La Villa Ercolanese dei Pisoni* (Turin 1883); D. Mustilli, "La villa pseudourbana ercolanese," *RendNap* 31 (1956) 77 – 97; A. Maiuri, *Herculaneum und the Villa of the Papyri* (Novara 1963); J. J. Deiss, *Herculaneum: Italy's Buried Treasure* (New York 1966) 45 – 57; W. F. Jashemski, *The Gardens of Pompeii, Herculaneum, and the Villas Destroyed by Vesuvius* 1 (New Rochelle, N.Y. 1979) 322, 326 – 28; W. F. Jashemski, *The Gardens of Pompeii, Herculaneum, and the Villas Destroyed by Vesuvius* 2: *Appendices* (New Rochelle, N.Y. 1993) 302 – 3; M. R. Wojcik, *La Villa dei Papiri ad Ercolano* (Rome 1986).

267

247. Cicero *De Finibus* 2.35.119; *In Pisonem* 29.68. See H. Bloch, "L. Calpurnius Piso Caesoninus in Samothrace and Herculaneum," *AJA* 44 (1940) 490 – 93; D'Arms (supra n. 189) 173 – 74. The absence of epigraphic corroboration has led Wojcik (supra n. 246) to suggest that the villa could belong to any of a number of Roman philhellenes. He proposed that the Villa dei Papiri was owned by Appius Claudius Pulcher (cos. 54 B.C.), who donated the Lesser Propylaea at Eleusis.

248. A. Maiuri, *Ercolano: I nuovi scavi (1927–1958)* 1 (Rome 1958) 113 – 43. The grounds of the palestra were excavated in a systematic fashion beginning in the 1920s and continued to 1952.

249. Ibid. 136 – 37; Jashemski (1979 supra n. 246) 162 – 63; Jashemski (1993 supra n. 246) 275 – 76, fig. 308.

250. A large bronze fountain (2.42 meters high), which was cast in the form of a five-headed snake (hydra), was found inside the pool. See A. Maiuri, "Fontana monumentale in bronzo nei nuovi scavi di Ercolano," *BdA* 3 (1954) 193.

251. The north side of the pond was equipped with sixteen *amphorae*, the south side with fifteen (one of which is missing), and the short east and west sides held two vessels each.

252. Jashemski (1979 supra n. 246) 163 suggests that the smaller pond was used for swimming as well, but she does not explain the presence of the *amphorae* or the lack of steps in this deeper pool.

253. Maiuri (1958 supra n. 248) 136, 143 suggested that the large cruciform pool, with its easy access and ornamental fountains, served as a decorative wading pool or *frigida lavatio*.

254. I. Sgobbo, "Serino—L'Acquedotto romano della Campania: *Fontis Augustei Aqueductus*," *NSc* (1938) 75 – 97; D'Arms (supra n. 189) 79 – 80. Jashemski (1979 supra n. 246) 32 – 33.

255. H. Myging, "Die Wasserversorgung Pompejis," *Janus* 22 (1917) 294 – 351; A. Maiuri, "Pozzi e condutture d'acqua nell'antica Pompei," *NSc* (1931) 546 – 76.

256. A house, in which fish sauces were produced, was located within the city (I 12, 8). Various vessels, some of which were labeled as to their contents, were excavated from this house. It is possible that this private industry was supplied with fish, in part, from ponds within the city. See Jashemski (1979 supra n. 246) 195 – 96; A. Maiuri, "La bottega del salsamentario," in A. Maiuri, *Mestiere d'archeologia* (Milan 1978) 635 – 36; R. Curtis, "The Garum Shop of Pompeii, I xii 8," *Cronache pompeiane* 5 (1979) 5 – 23.

257. Examples include pools within the Casa di L. Volusius Faustus (I 2, 10), the Casa del Citarista (I 4, 5/25), the Casa del Larario (I 6, 4), the Casa di P. Paquius Proculus (I 7, 1), the Casa del Menandro (I 10, 4/14 – 17), the Casa di A. Trebius Valens (III 2, 1), the Casa delle Nozze d'Argento (V 2, i), the Casa delle Vestali (VI 1, 7/25), the Casa di Pansa (VI 6, 1), the Casa dei Vasi d'Argento (VI 7, 20), the Casa di Apollo (VI 7, 23), the Casa della Fontana Grande (VI 8, 22/1), the Casa della Fontana Piccola (VI 8, 23), the Casa di Castore e Polluce (VI 9, 6/7), the Casa degli Amorini Dorati (VI 16, 7/38), the Casa di Polibio (VI Ins. Occ. 23 – 26), the Casa delle Nozze d'Alessandro (VI Ins. Occ. 42), the Casa di C. Vibius (VII 2, 18), the Casa della Caccia Antica (VII 4, 48), the Casa del Gran Duca di Toscana (VII 4, 56), the Casa delle Pareti Nere (VII 4, 59), the Casa di Trittolemo (VII 7, 5/14), Casa della Caccia Nuova (VII 10, 3/14), the Casa di A. Umbricius Scaurus (VII Ins. Occ. 12 – 15), the Casa di Fabius Rufus (VII Ins. Occ. 16 – 19), the Casa di M. Holconius Rufus (VIII 4,

4), the Casa di T. Mescinius Gelo (VIII 4, 9), the Casa del Gallo (VIII 5, 2), the Casa di M. Epidius Sabinus (IX 1, 22/29), the Casa della Fontana d'Amore (IX 2, 7), the Casa di Marcus Lucretius (IX 3, 5/24), the Casa di Iasone (IX 5, 18 – 21), the Casa del Centenario (IX 8, 3/6), and the Casa di Obellius Firmus (IX [14] 4/2).

258. Aquatic scenes with fish and plants on blue background are recorded in the garden ponds of the Casa di Pansa (VI 6, 1/12), the Casa della Fontana Grande (VI 8, 22/1), the Casa di M. Epidius Sabinus (IX 1 22/29), and the Casa del Centenario (IX 8, 3/6). For short descriptions and bibliography on these ponds, see Jashemski (1993 supra n. 246) 127, 135, 226 – 27, 244 – 45.

259. Ibid. 244. Various fish bones and scales were recovered from a single garden pool in the Casa del Centenario (IX 8, 3/6) but, subsequently, these were lost and never identified as to species.

260. F. Noack and K. Lehmann-Hartleben, *Baugeschichtliche Untersuchungen am Stadtrand von Pompeji* (Berlin 1936); A. de Vos and M. de Vos, *Pompei, Ercolano, Stabia. Guide Archeologiche Laterza* (Bari 1982) 57 – 58.

261. Jashemski (1979 supra n. 246) 110, fig. 178, n. 94, illustrates the east end of the pond but identifies it as the west. Her illustration (fig. 178) shows the side of the pond closest to the portico (east side) with a row of six vessels over five. This side is described (n. 94) as a single row of eight. Apparently the lower row was obscured by debris when Jashemski made her count (see Figs. 90, 91), while the photo published by her shows this side when it was first excavated (free of debris).

262. De Vos and de Vos (supra n. 260) 57.

263. G. Fiorelli, ed., *Pompeianarum Antiquitatum Historia* (Naples 1860 – 64) 2:264 – 88; J.-P. Descoeudres, "A Pompeian House Revisited—VII 4,31/51," *Australian Natural History* 20.4 (1980) 117 – 22; L. Richardson, *Pompeii: An Architectural History* (Baltimore 1989) 120 – 24; Jashemski (1993 supra n. 246) 179.

264. De Vos and de Vos (supra n. 260) 167.

265. Richardson (supra n. 263) 122. The column was built of brick and may have been merely a statue base. I could observe no evidence of the piping associated with a fountain jet.

266. Jashemski (1993 supra n. 246) 173, fig. 208. Richardson (supra n. 263) 310 – 11 classifies this residence as a "peristyle town house" which possesses a large peristyle garden directly accessible from the *atrium* with no intervening *tablinum*. The attribution of the house to Gavius Rufus is not secure.

267. De Vos and de Vos (supra n. 260) 193. Most of the frescoes are housed in the Museo Nazionale di Napoli.

268. Fiorelli (supra n. 263) 2:224 – 40. Subsequent studies include J. Overbeck and A. Mau, *Pompeji in seinen Gebauden, Altertümern und Kunstwerken* (4th ed., Leipzig 1884) 307 – 14; M. Della Corte, *Case ed abitanti di Pompei* (3rd ed., Naples 1965) 47 – 48, nos. 38 – 39, who suggests that the house originally belonged to L. Cornelius Primogenes; Jashemski (1979 supra n. 246) 33 – 34; Richardson (supra n. 268) 318 – 22.

269. Jashemski (1993 supra n. 246) 137 – 38 also suggests that this small tank could have served as a cooler for drinks.

270. De Vos and de Vos (supra n. 260) 186; Richardson (supra n. 263) 320.

271. De Vos and de Vos (supra n. 260) 243 – 44. For a record of the excavation and discoveries, see Fiorelli (supra n. 263) 1.1:249 – 80, 1.2:156 – 60.

272. Jashemski (1993 supra n. 246) 280, fig. 312.

273. Studies of the villa include A. Mau, *Pompei: Its Life and Art* (2nd ed., New York 1907) 355 – 60; Overbeck and Mau (supra n. 268) 369 – 71; A. Maiuri and R. Pane, *La Casa di Loreio Tiburtino e la Villa di Diomede in Pompei* (Rome 1947) 10 – 17, pls. 9 – 16; Jashemski (1979 supra n. 246) 315 – 17, and (1993 supra n. 246) 281; Richardson (supra n. 263) 348 – 55.

274. Fiorelli (supra n. 263) 1.1:257. A marble disk was recovered, pierced through the center to accommodate the pipe of the water jet.

275. Amedeo Maiuri (*L'ultima fase edilizia di Pompei* [Rome 1942] 157 – 58) identified three periods of construction with the republican villa followed by Augustan and postearthquake phases. Cf. P. Mingazzini, "Un criterio di datazione della Villa di Diomede a Pompei," *ArchCl* 1 (1949) 202 – 3.

276. Richardson (supra n. 263) 354.

277. Fiorelli (supra n. 263) 1.1:12 – 41; A. Maiuri, "I giardini di Pompei," *La Vie d'Italia* 9 (1961) 1139; de Vos and de Vos (supra n. 265) 141 – 45; Richardson (supra n. 263) 292.

278. Recent discussions include Jashemski (1979 supra n. 246) 48 – 49; H. B. Van der Poel, L. Garcia y Garcia, and J. McConnell, *Corpus Topographicum Pompeianum: The Insulae of Regions I–IV* (Rome 1986) 46 – 47; Richardson (supra n. 263) 292 – 98; C. Parslow, "The Praedia Iuliae Felicis in Pompeii" (Ph.D. diss. Duke University 1989).

279. The connection of this *praedia* with Iulia Felix was preserved in a painted text (*CIL* IV.1136), which notes the bath, the shops with lofts, and the apartments belonging to the villa.

280. Fiorelli (supra n. 263) 1.2:98, nos. 46, 51, 54, 57, 58, 59, 61.

281. F. Rakob, "Ein Grottentriklinium in Pompeji," *RM* 71 (1964) 182 – 94.

282. Jashemski (1979 supra n. 246) 48; de Vos and de Vos (supra n. 260) 142; Richardson (supra n. 263) 290.

283. Maiuri and Pane (supra n. 273) 2 – 9, pls. 1 – 8; V. Spinazzola, *Pompeii alla luce degli scavi nuovi di Via dell'Abbondanza (anni 1910 – 1923)*, I–III, ed. S. Aurigemma (Rome 1953) 367 – 421, 971 – 1008; de Vos and de Vos (supra n. 260) 138 – 41; Jashemski (1979 supra n. 246) 45 – 46, figs. 76 – 80; Richardson (supra n. 263) 337 – 43.

284. The aedicula niche is not equipped with pipes and does not appear to have functioned as a fountain or *nymphaeum*. See E. Salza Prina Ricotti, "Forme speciali di triclini" *CronPomp* 5 (1979) 106 – 30.

285. Jashemski (1993 supra n. 246) 79 – 82, figs. 81 – 86.

286. Ibid. figs. 87 – 88.

287. Spinazzola (supra n. 283) 407 – 18.

288. P. Mingazzini and F. Pfister, *Surrentum — Forma Italiae* 1.2 (Florence 1946) 102 – 4, fig. 14.

289. Columella *Rust.* 8.16.8.

290. The section of concrete walkway, which spanned the fissure, has fallen away but may have been fitted with a slot for the placement of a gate like those employed in the ponds on Ponza and Ventotene.

291. Mingazzini and Pfister (supra n. 288) 94.

292. Ibid. 107 – 19.

293. A set of stairs (c) built into the wall of the channel, which connected both ponds, may have led to the villa above the shore. The exact destination of these stairs is uncertain.

294. A much smaller niche, which was cut into wall of the grotto just inside the entrance, probably held a lamp.

295. The walkways are covered today by 30 to 40 centimeters of water. It is probable that these walkways were designed to emerge slightly from the level of water inside the pond. Therefore, the depth of the pond, as measured from the top of the walkways to the bottom, was approximately 90 centimeters.

296. Rock-cut features, such as these lightwells, are impossible to date with precision and may have been later additions to this room. However, it is likely that there would have been some provision for light and air in the original design of the pond.

297. Mingazzini and Pfister (supra n. 288) 118.

298. Suetonius (*Augustus* 65.1) records that Postumus was first sent to Surrentum and later exiled to the island of Planasia. Postumus's stay in the villa at Surrentum is dated to between A.D. 5 and 7. D'Arms (supra n. 189) 75.

299. Dio Cassius 54.28.

300. Dio Cassius (55.32) tells of the youth's penchant for fish and fishing and how this obsession contributed to his exile from Rome.

301. Mingazzini and Pfister (supra n. 288) 119; D'Arms (supra n. 189) 214.

302. Mingazzini and Pfister (supra n. 288) 117.

303. J. G. Pedley, *Paestum — Greeks and Romans in Southern Italy* (London 1990) 157 – 62, figs. 116 – 21.

304. The *Piscina* was excavated between 1982 and 1985 with field reports by W. Johannowsky, J. G. Pedley, and M. Torelli, "Excavations at Paestum 1982," *AJA* 87 (1983) 293 – 303; J. G. Pedley and M. Torelli, "Excavations at Paestum 1983," *AJA* 88 (1984) 367 –77; J. G. Pedley, "Excavations at Paestum 1984," *AJA* 89 (1985) 58 –59. Most recent discussions include Pedley (1990 supra n. 303) 152 – 57, figs 110 – 14; J. Higginbotham, in J. G. Pedley and M. Torelli, eds., *The Sanctuary of Santa Venera at Paestum* 1 (Rome 1993) 121 – 47.

305. The long eastern and western walls of the pond do not form perfect right angles with the northern wall and thus form a trapezoidal plan. The length of the northern wall was 3 meters; the western wall, 6 meters; the eastern wall, 5.9 meters; and the southern wall, 2.9 meters.

306. This was discovered after chipping away layers (2 to 10 centimeters thick) of calcium carbonate that had accumulated on the inside of the pond. The water from the Capodifiume (River Salso) is supercharged with calcium carbonate ions and any surface that comes in prolonged contact with the water becomes coated with this mineral.

307. This complex was excavated but never published. During the 1983 excavation season, after the basin attached to the *piscina* at Santa Venera was discovered, the structure in the Hera sanctuary was studied and a measured drawing made.

308. The lack of space around the pond and the intrusive presence of architecture in the western end of the enclosure casts some doubt on the use of this structure in a gymnasium complex. The cult of Venus Verticordia/Fortuna Virilis involved the washing of the cult statue and the ritual bathing of cult followers. See E. Greco and D. Theodorescu, *Poseidonia-Paestum* 3 (Rome 1985) fig. 71; Pedley (1990 supra n. 303) 121 – 23.

309. Recent clearing (summer of 1993) of the area east of the Temple of Hera II has uncovered the ruins of a small *piscina* built of faced concrete with pots incorporated into the fabric of the walls. This pond awaits further study.

SELECTED BIBLIOGRAPHY

André, Jacques. *L'Alimentation et la cuisine à Rome* 2nd ed. (Paris 1981).

Ashby, Thomas. "Monte Circeo." *Mélanges de l'école française de Rome, Antiquité* 25 (1905) 157–209.

Bartoli, Alfonso. "Scavi del Palatino (Domus Augustana) 1926–28." *Notizie degli scavi Antichità* 5 (1929) 3–29.

Bennett, George W. *Management of Artificial Lakes and Ponds* (New York 1962).

Benoit, Fernand. "L'archéologie sousmarine en Provence, VI. Industrie de pêcherie et de salaison." *Rivista di studi liguri* 18 (1952) 237–307.

Blake, Marion Elizabeth. *Ancient Roman Construction from the Prehistoric Period to Augustus* (Washington, D.C. 1947).

———. *Roman Construction in Italy from Nerva through the Antonines* (Philadelphia 1973).

———. *Roman Construction in Italy from Tiberius through the Flavians* (Washington, D.C. 1959).

Bloch, Herbert. "L. Calpurnius Piso Caesoninus in Samothrace and Herculaneum." *American Journal of Archaeology* 44 (1940) 485–93.

Blümer, Hugo. *Die Gewerbliche Thätigkeit der Völker des Klassischen Alterthums* (Leipzig 1869).

Bohlen, Diedrich. *Die Bedeutung der Fischerei für die Antike Wirtschaft. Ein Beitrag zur Geschichte der Antike Fischerei* (Hamburg 1937).

Bon, Caterina, Raimondo Buitoni, Giovanni Maria De Rossi, and Mariella Liverani. *Le isole pontine I. Ventotene. Immagini di un'isola* (Rome 1984).

Brasola, V., A. M. Kalfa, and A. Cannas. "Esperienze positive di riproduzione artificiale di *mugil cephalus* effettuate nella Laguna di Orbetello." *Rivista italiana della piscicoltura e ittiologia* 14 (1979) 1–6.

Bronson, Richard C., and Giovanni Uggeri. "Isola del Giglio, Isola di Giannutri, Monte Argentario, Laguna di Orbetello." *Studi etruschi* 38 (1970) 201–14.

Brunt, Peter A. "Two Great Roman Landowners." *Latomus* 34 (1975) 619–35.

Bunsmann, Ludovicus. *De Piscatorum in Graecorum atque Romanorum Litteris Usu* (Monasterii Guestfalorum: Typis Aschendorffii 1910).

Castagnoli, Ferdinando. "Astura." *Studi Romani* 11 (1963) 637–44.

Chiappella, V. Ginetta. "Esplorazione della cosidetto 'Piscina di Lucullo' sul lago di Paola." *Notizie degli scavi* suppl. (1965) 146–60.

Coarelli, Filippo. "Public Building in Rome between the Second Punic War and Sulla." *Papers of the British School of Archaeology at Rome* 45 (1977) 1–23.

———. *Lazio. Guide archeologiche Laterza* (Rome and Bari 1984).

———. *Roma. Guide archeologiche Laterza* (Rome and Bari 1981).

Corcoran, Thomas H. "The Roman Fishing Industry of the Late Republic and Early Empire" (Ph.D. diss. Northwestern University 1957).

———. "Roman Fishponds." *Classical Bulletin* 35 (1959) 37–43.

———. "Roman Fish Sauces." *Classical Journal* 58 (1963) 204–10.

Coull, James R. *The Fisheries of Europe: An Economic Geography* (London 1972).

Courcelle, Pierre. "Le site du monastere de Cassiodore." *Mélanges de l'école française de Rome, Antiquité* 55 (1938) 259–307.

Cumont, R. "Ichthys." In A. Pauly and G. Wissowa, *Real-Encyclopädie der klassischen Altertumswissenschaft* 9 (1914) 844–50.

Curtis, Robert I. *Garum and Salsamenta: Production and Commerce in Materia Medica* (Leiden 1991).

———. "In Defense of Garum." *Classical Journal* 78 (1983) 232–40.

———. "A Personalized Floor Mosaic from Pompeii." *American Journal of Archaeology* 88 (1984) 557–66.

———. "The Production and Commerce of Fishsauce in the Western Roman Empire: A Social and Economic Study" (Ph.D. diss. University of Maryland 1978).

———. "The Salted Fish Industry of Pompeii." *Archaeology* 37 (1984) 58–59, 73–75.

———. "Salted Fish Products in Ancient Medicine." *Journal of the History of Medicine and Allied Sciences* 39 (1984) 430–35.

———. "A. Umbricius Scaurus of Pompeii." *Studia Pompeiana et Classica in Honor of Wilhelmina F. Jashemski* 1 (New Rochelle, N.Y. 1988) 19–49.

D'Ancona, U. "Fishing and Fish Culture in Brackish-Water Lagoons." *FAO Fisheries Bulletin* 7.4 (1954) 1–24.

D'Arms, John H. *Commerce and Social Standing in Ancient Rome* (Cambridge, Mass. 1981).

———. *Romans on the Bay of Naples: A Social and Cultural Study of Villas and Their Owners from 150 BC to AD 400* (Cambridge, Mass. 1970).

De Angelis, R. "Fishing Installations in Brackish Lagoons." *General Fisheries Council for the Mediterranean. Studies and Reviews* 7 (Rome 1959).

———. "Mediterranean Brackish-Water Lagoons and Their Exploitation." *General Fisheries Council for the Mediterranean. Studies and Reviews* 12 (Rome 1960).

De Caro, Stefano, and Angela Greco. *Campania. Guide archeologiche Laterza* (Rome and Bari 1981).

De Franciscis, Alfonso. "Underwater Discoveries around the Bay of Naples." *Archaeology* 20 (1967) 209 – 16.

Del Rosso, Raffaele. *Pesche e peschiere antiche e moderne nell'Etruria marittima* 1 (Florence 1905).

De Rossi, Giovanni M., Pier Giorgio Di Domenico, and Lorenzo Quilici. "La Via Aurelia da Roma a Forum Aureli." *Quaderno dell'Istituto di Topographia Antica della Università di Roma* 4 (1968).

De Saint-Denis, E. *Le Vocabulaire des animaux marins en latin classique* (Paris 1947).

De Vos, Arnold, and Mariette de Vos. *Pompeii, Ercolano, Stabia. Guide archeologiche Laterza* (Rome and Bari 1982).

Flinder, Alexander. "A Piscina at Caesarea — a Preliminary Survey." *Israel Exploration Journal* 26 (1976) 77 – 80.

———. "The Piscinas at Caesarea and Lapithos." *British Archaeological Reports* (1985) 173 – 78.

Gazda, Elaine K., ed. *Roman Art in the Private Sphere: New Perspectives on the Architecture and Decor of the Domus, Villa, and Insula* (Ann Arbor, Mich. 1991).

Gerking, Shelby D., ed. *Ecology of Freshwater Fish Production* (Oxford 1978).

Gianfrotta, Piero Alfredo. *Castrum Novum — Forma Italiae* 7.3 (Rome 1970).

Giuliani, Cairoli F. *Tibur — Forma Italiae* 1.7 pars prima (Florence 1970).

Grimal, Pierre. *Les Jardins romains à la fin de la Republique et aux premiers de l'Empire; Essai sur le naturalisme romain* 3rd ed. (Paris 1984).

Higginbotham, James. "The Piscina." In John G. Pedley and Mario Torelli, eds., *The Sanctuary of Santa Venera at Paestum* 1 (Rome 1993) 121 – 47.

Hohlfelder, Robert L. "The Ports of Roman Baetica: A Preliminary Reconnaissance." *Journal of Field Archaeology* 3 (1976) 465.

Huet, Marcel. *Textbook of Fish Culture: Breeding and Cultivation of Fish*, trans. H. Kahn (London 1970).

Jacono, Luigi. "Nettuno—*Piscinae in litore constructae*." *Notizie degli scavi Antichità* 21 (1924) 333 – 40, pl. 16.

———. "Note di archeologia marittima." *Neapolis* 1 (1913) 353 – 71.

———. "Una singolare piscina marittima in Ponza." *Campania Romana* 1 (1938) 145 – 62, pls. 18 – 21.

———. "Solarium di una villa romana nell'isola di Ponza." *Notizie degli scavi Antichità* (1926) 219 – 32.

Jacopi, Giulio. *L'antro di Tiberio a Sperlonga* (Rome 1963).

Jashemski, Wilhelmina F. *The Gardens of Pompeii: Herculaneum and the Villas Destroyed by Vesuvius* 1 (New Rochelle, N.Y. 1979).

———. *The Gardens of Pompeii: Herculaneum and the Villas Destroyed by Vesuvius* 2: *Appendices* (New Rochelle, N.Y. 1993).

Johannowsky, Werner, John Griffiths Pedley, and Mario Torelli. "Excavations at Paestum 1982." *American Journal of Archaeology* 87 (1983) 293 – 303.

Kolendo, Jerzy. "Parcs a huîtres et viviers à Baiae sur un flacon en verre du Musée National de Varsovie." *Puteoli. Studi di storia antica* 1 (1977) 108 – 12.

Korringa, Pieter. *Farming Marine Fishes and Shrimps* (Amsterdam 1976).

LaFaye, Georges. "Vivarium." In Charles Daremberg and Edmond Saglio, *Dictionnaire des antiquités grecques et romaines d'après les textes et les monuments* 5 (1919) 959 – 62.

Lugli, Giuseppe. *Ager Pomptinus. Circeii — Forma Italiae* 1.1 pars secunda (Rome 1928).

―――. *Roma antica. Il centro monumentale* (Rome 1946).

―――. *La technica edilizia romana con particulare riguardo a Roma e Lazio* (Rome 1957).

MacDougall, Elizabeth B., ed. *Ancient Roman Villa Gardens* (Washington, D.C. 1987).

McCann, Anna Marguerite, and John Peter Oleson. "Le ricerche della missione italo-americano (1974) nell'antico porto di Populonia (Golfo di Baratti) e nelle acque di Pirgi." *Atti del V Congresso Internazionale di Archeologia Sottomarina* (Lipari 1976).

―――. "Underwater Excavations at the Etruscan Ports of Populonia and Pyrgi." *Journal of Field Archaeology* 1 (1974) 398 – 402.

McCann, Anna Marguerite, Joanne Bourgeois, Elaine K. Gazda, John Peter Oleson, and Elizabeth Lyding Will. *The Roman Port and Fishery of Cosa* (Princeton 1987).

Mielsch, Harald. *Die römische Villa: Architektur und Lebensform* (Munich 1987).

Migdalski, Edward, and George Fichter. *The Fresh and Salt Water Fishes of the World.* (New York 1976).

Mingazzini, Paolino, and Friedrich Pfister. *Surrentum — Forma Italiae* 1.2 (Florence 1946).

Oleson, John Peter. "Underwater Survey and Excavation in the Port of Pyrgi (Santa Severa), 1974." *Journal of Field Archaeology* 4 (1977) 297 – 308.

Ooteghem, Jules van. "Piscinarii." *Les études classique* 36 (1968) 41 – 46.

Ostrow, Steven E. "The Topography of Puteoli and Baiae on Eight Glass Flasks." *Puteoli. Studi di storia antica* 3 (1979) 77 – 140.

Palombi, Arturo. "La fauna marina nei mosaici e nei dipinti pompeiani." *Pompeiana* (Naples 1950) 425 – 55.

Parslow, Christopher. "The Praedia Iuliae Felicis in Pompeii" (Ph.D. diss. Duke University 1989).

Pedley, John Griffiths. "Excavations at Paestum 1984." *American Journal of Archaeology* 89 (1985) 53 – 60.

―――. *Paestum — Greeks and Romans in Southern Italy* (London 1990).

Pedley, John Griffiths, and Mario Torelli. "Excavations at Paestum 1983." *American Journal of Archaeology* 88 (1984) 367 – 77.

Piccarreta, Fabio. *Astura — Forma Italiae* 1.13 (Florence 1977).

Ponsich, Michel, and Miguel Tarradell. *Garum et industries antiques de salaison dans la Méditerranée occidentale* (Paris 1965).

Purpura, Gianfranco. "Pesce e stabilimenti antichi per la lavorazione delle pesce in Sicilia, 1. S. Vito (Trapani), Cala Minnola (Levanzo)." *Sicilia archeologica* 48 (1982) 45 – 60.

―――. "Pesce e stabilimenti antichi per la lavorazione delle pesce in Sicilia, 2. Isola delle Femine (Palermo), Punta Molinazzo (Punta Rais), Tonnara del Cofano (Trapani), S. Nicola (Favignana)." *Sicilia archeologica* 57 – 58 (1985) 59 – 86.

Ravagnan, G. *Elementi di Vallicoltura Moderna-Proposte operative per la ristrutturazione e lo sviluppo della itticoltura salmastra italiana* (Bologna 1978).

Richardson, Lawrence. *Pompeii: An Architectural History* (Baltimore 1988).

Schmiedt, Giulio. "Contributo della foto-interpretazione alla ricostruzione della situazione geografica-topografica degli insediamenti antichi scomparsi in Italia." *Universo* 6 (1964) 955 – 96.

―――, ed. *Atlante aereofotografico delle sedi umane in Italia* (Florence 1970).

————, ed. *Il livello antico del Mar Tirreno. Testimonianze dei resti archeologici* (Florence 1972).

Schneider, K. "Piscina." In A. Pauly and G. Wissowa, *Real-Encyclopädie der klassischen Altertumswissenschaft* 20 (1950) 1783 – 85.

Sebastiani, Di Filippo Alessandro. *Viaggio a Tivoli. Antichissima città latinosabina fatto nel 1825* (Foligno 1828) 89 – 99.

Syme, Sir Ronald. "Who Was Vedius Pollio?" *Journal of Roman Studies* 51 (1961) 23 – 30.

Talbert, Richard. *The Senate of Imperial Rome* (Princeton 1984).

Thompson, D'Arcy. *A Glossary of Greek Fishes* (London 1947).

Toynbee, Joceyln M. C. *Animals in Roman Life and Art* (London 1973).

Torelli, Mario. *Etruria. Guide Archeologiche Laterza* (Rome and Bari 1985).

————. "Terza campagna di scavi a Punta della Vipera e scoperti di una laminetta plumbea inscritta." *Archeologia classica* 18 (1966) 283 – 91.

————. "Terza campagna di scavi a Punta della Vipera (S. Marinella)." *Studi etruschi* 35 (1967) 331 – 52.

Wallace-Hadrill, Andrew. *Houses and Society in Pompeii and Herculaneum* (Princeton 1994).

White, K. D. *Roman Farming* (Ithaca, N.Y. 1970).

Yorke, R. A., and M. F. Dallas. "Underwater Surveys of North Africa, Jugoslavia, and Italy." *Underwater Association Report* (1968) 21 – 34.

Zanker, Paul. "Die Villa als Vorbild des späten pompejanischen Wohngeschmacks." *Jahrbuch des Deutschen Archäologischen Instituts* 94 (1979) 460 – 523.

INDEX

Spain, 2, 7, 56, 57
Sparidae. See Fish: *auratae*
Specus, 10, 25, 26, 27, 116, 128, 129–
    31, 154–56, 162–63, 185, 187, 196,
    198–200, 201, 205, 207, 212, 221
Sperlonga, 11, 16, 27, 31, 39, 159–63
Spigola. *See* Fish: *lupi*
Springs, 16, 80–81, 82, 84, 131, 163,
    166. *See also* Water
Stagnum, 7, 188
Strabo, 80
Sturgeon, 52

Tablina, 33, 64, 241 (n. 90)
Tacitus, Cornelius, 62
Tanks: circular, 24, 74, 87, 99–100,
    107, 116, 132–33, 157, 182, 186–87;
    lozenge-shaped, 24–25, 36, 76, 150,
    164, 165, 167, 177–78; live, 34, 52
Thunnus (*thynnus*), 43, 52
Thurii, 56
Tiberius, the Emperor, 49, 63, 159, 179,
    197
Tidal basins, 7, 17, 90
Tides, 15, 24, 82, 151
Tivoli (Tibur), 128; Villa of Manlius
    Vopiscus, 125–28; Villa of Quintilius
    Varus, 2, 20, 26, 31, 39, 122–25
Torre Astura. *See* Astura: Torre Astura
Torre del Fico. *See* Circeo: Torre del
    Fico
Torre Flavia, 22, 24, 39, 72, 107–8
Torre Valdaliga, 10, 11, 17, 31, 34, 39,
    90–93, 96
Towers, 10, 37, 96
Traps, 10, 34, 35–36, 90, 140, 182
Triclinia. See Dining rooms: *triclinia*
Tunnels, 26
Tunny, 43, 52
Turbot. *See* Fish: *rhombi*
Tusculum, 63

Umbrina, 29

Varro, M. Terentius, 4, 5, 61; fishpond
    costs, 56; fishpond design, 22–23;
    fishpond operation, 58–59; species
    of fish, 42; ignorance of freshwater
    hydraulics, 14; social status, 20, 21,

58; villa at Casinum, 27, 48; Pianosa,
    75; water circulation, 12; water
    sources, 11–12
Varus, Quintilius, 122, 125
Velia, 56
Ventotene (Pandataria), 11, 20, 24, 25,
    39, 63, 179–85
Vesuvius, eruption of, 40, 194, 196,
    197, 219, 222
Villae maritimae. See Villas: seaside
Villa of Agrippa Postumus. *See* Sor-
    rento: Villa of Agrippa Postumus
Villa of Horace. *See* Licenza: Villa of
    Horace
Villa of Manlius Vopiscus. *See* Tivoli:
    Villa of Manlius Vopiscus
Villa of Quintilius Varus. *See* Tivoli:
    Villa of Quintilius Varus
Villas: rural, 20, 21, 27, 31, 115, 122–31
    passim; seaside, 3, 17, 24–25, 30–32,
    39, 58, 61, 72, 75, 79–80, 85–96
    passim, 101, 104, 105, 109–10, 135,
    140, 142, 144, 151, 158, 164, 168,
    179, 184, 191, 213; urban, 1, 24, 25,
    26, 118, 120–21, 125, 126, 191–94,
    204
Vitruvius, Pollio, 14, 22
Vivarium, 7
Vivarium (Squillace), 67
Volcanic ash, 18
Vopiscus, Manlius. *See* Tivoli: Villa of
    Manlius Vopiscus

Walkways, 24, 37, 90, 99, 135, 149, 150,
    152, 165–81 passim, 191, 212, 213,
    214, 215, 216, 217
Water: brackish, 11, 15–18, 27, 34,
    44, 46, 80–81, 101, 104, 138, 140,
    151, 166, 218, 234–35 (n. 22); circu-
    lation of, 11, 12–15, 17, 26, 32, 75,
    77–78, 82, 85, 86, 94, 96, 100–101,
    104, 115, 133, 139, 142–43, 144, 150,
    152, 165–76 passim, 177, 181–85,
    193, 207–10, 215, 217–18, 221–22;
    salinity, 1, 10, 11, 12, 15, 41, 46, 92,
    101, 139, 165; stagnate, 12, 17; tem-
    perature, 12, 13, 16, 46, 92
Weels. *See* Traps
Wrasse. *See* Fish: *lupi*

284